Mary Jones, Diane Fellowes-Freeman and David Sang

Cambridge Checkpoint **Science**

Coursebook

9

CAMBRIDGE
UNIVERSITY PRESS

University Printing House, Cambridge CB2 8BS, United Kingdom

One Liberty Plaza, 20th Floor, New York, NY 10006, USA

477 Williamstown Road, Port Melbourne, VIC 3207, Australia

4843/24, 2nd Floor, Ansari Road, Daryaganj, Delhi – 110002, India

79 Anson Road, #06–04/06, Singapore 079906

Cambridge University Press is part of the University of Cambridge.

It furthers the University's mission by disseminating knowledge in the pursuit of education, learning and research at the highest international levels of excellence.

Information on this title: education.cambridge.org

First published 2013
20 19 18 17

Printed in Dubai by Oriental Press

A catalogue record for this publication is available from the British Library

ISBN 978-1-107-62606-5 Paperback

NOTICE TO TEACHERS

References to Activities contained in these resources are provided 'as is' and information provided is on the understanding that teachers and technicians shall undertake a thorough and appropriate risk assessment before undertaking any of the Activities listed. Cambridge University Press makes no warranties, representations or claims of any kind concerning the Activities. To the extent permitted by law, Cambridge University Press will not be liable for any loss, injury, claim, liability or damage of any kind resulting from the use of the Activities.

Welcome to the third stage of your Cambridge Secondary 1 Science course!

This book covers the third year, Stage 9, of the Cambridge Secondary 1 Science curriculum. At the end of the year, your teacher may ask you to take a test called a Progression Test. You may also take a test called Checkpoint. This book will help you to learn how to be a good scientist, and to do well in the tests.

The main areas of science

The book is divided into three main sections, each one dealing with one of three main areas of science. These are:

Biology – the study of living organisms

Chemistry – the study of the substances from which the Earth and the rest of the Universe are made

Physics – the study of the nature and properties of matter, energy and forces.

There are no sharp dividing lines between these three branches of science. You will find many overlaps between them.

Learning to be a scientist

During your course so far, you have learnt a lot of facts and information. You have also been learning to think like a scientist. You have learnt how to observe carefully, and how to do experiments to try to find out answers to questions. You have learnt how to record results, and how to use them to make a conclusion.

This book will help you to continue to improve these skills. When you see this symbol SE, it means that the task will help you to develop your scientific enquiry skills.

Using your knowledge

It's important to learn facts and scientific ideas as you go through your science course. But it is just as important to be able to **use** these facts and ideas.

When you see this symbol A+I, it means that you are being asked to use your knowledge to work out an answer. You will have to think hard to find the answer for yourself, using the science that you have learnt. (A+I stands for Applications and Implications.)

Contents

Physics

Unit 9 Forces in action

Unit 10 Electricity

Unit 11 Energy

Reference

1.1 Photosynthesis

Photosynthesis is the way that plants make food. They use carbon dioxide and water to make glucose and oxygen.

Photosynthesis is a chemical reaction. We can summarise it using a word equation:

carbon dioxide + water → glucose + oxygen

Energy transfer

The photosynthesis reaction needs a supply of energy to make it happen. This energy comes from light. During photosynthesis, the plant's leaves absorb the energy of light. The energy is stored in the glucose that is made. The glucose is a store of chemical potential energy.

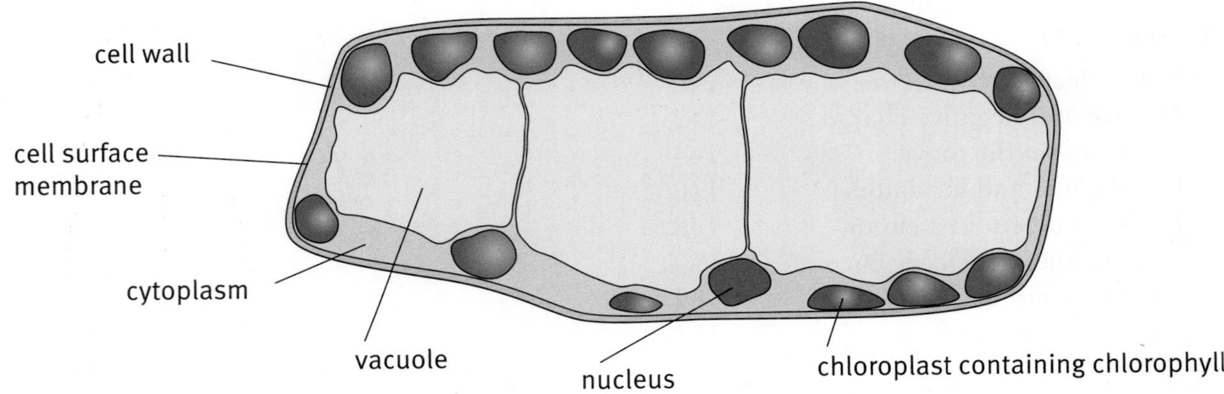

Photosynthesis happens inside the chloroplasts in a palisade cell like this one.

Questions

1 Think back to (remember) what you have already learnt about photosynthesis.
  a Where do plants get carbon dioxide from?
  b Where do plants get water from?

2 Explain why photosynthesis only takes place inside chloroplasts.

Storing carbohydrates

Glucose is a sugar. Sugars belong to a group of chemicals called **carbohydrates**.

Plants usually make much more glucose than they need to use immediately. They store some of it to use later. But they do not store it as glucose. Glucose is soluble in water, which makes it difficult to store inside a cell.

Instead, the plant changes some of the glucose into a different kind of carbohydrate – **starch**. A starch molecule is made of thousands of glucose molecules linked together in a long chain. Starch molecules are too big to dissolve in water. They stay as insoluble grains, inside the chloroplasts in the plant cell.

Activity 1.1
Testing a leaf for starch

You will remember that we can test for starch using iodine solution. But just adding iodine solution to a leaf won't work, because the starch is inside the leaf cells. Iodine solution can't get through the cell membranes of the leaf cells.

1 Boil some water in a beaker. Add a leaf to the boiling water. This will break down the cell membranes around the leaf cells.
2 Turn off your Bunsen burner or spirit burner. This is important because you are going to use ethanol in the next step, and ethanol is very flammable. Using forceps (tweezers), remove the leaf from the water. Be gentle – it will be very soft and easily torn.
3 Collect some ethanol in a test tube. Stand the test tube in the beaker of very hot water. Put the leaf into the ethanol. You will see the green colour (chlorophyll) coming out of the leaf, into the ethanol.
4 When you think most of the colour has come out, take the leaf out of the ethanol and dip it into the water to soften it. Spread the leaf out on a tile.
5 Now you can add iodine solution to the leaf. If the leaf contains any starch, it will turn blue-black.

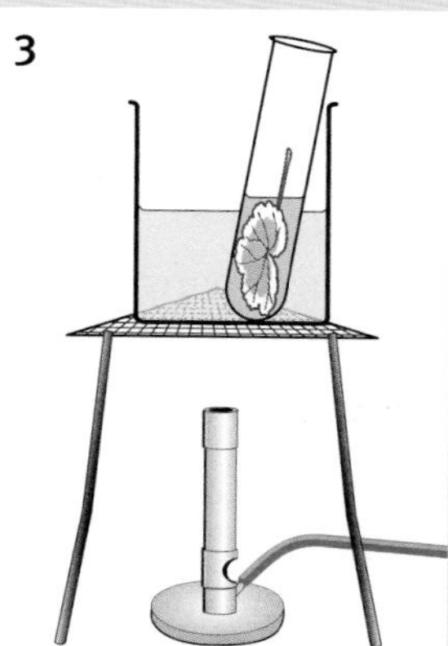

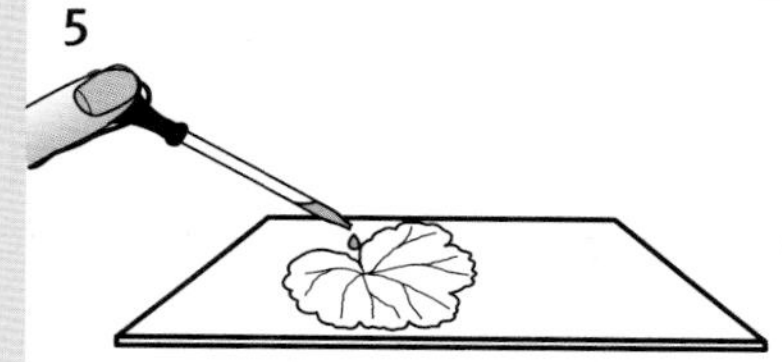

Questions

A1 Explain why the leaf needed to be boiled before testing with iodine solution.
A2 Suggest why it was useful to remove the green colour from the leaf, before testing it with iodine solution.
A3 Describe **two** things that you did in step 2 to reduce the risk of anyone being hurt.
A4 Explain why leaves often contain starch.

Summary

- Photosynthesis is the production of glucose and oxygen, by reacting water and carbon dioxide, using energy from light.
- Plants often change some of the glucose into starch, for storage.
- Before testing a leaf for starch, you need to boil it to break down the cell membranes.

1.2 Mineral salts for plants

Farmers and gardeners often add **fertilisers** to the soil where their crops are growing. The fertilisers provide mineral salts, which make the plants grow larger and healthier. Although fertilisers are expensive, the cost to farmers is outweighed by the extra money they can get for their crop.

This farmer in Indonesia is giving fertiliser to his growing rice plants.

What are fertilisers?

Fertilisers contain **mineral salts**. These are substances that plants normally get from the soil. But often the soil does not contain enough of some kinds of mineral salts, which stops the plants growing as large and strong as they could.

Plants need many different kinds of mineral salts. Two of the most important ones are nitrate and magnesium.

Nitrate is needed so that the plant can make proteins. You'll remember that proteins are nutrients that living organisms need for making new cells. A plant that has not got enough nitrate can't make enough proteins, so it cannot make enough new cells to grow well.

Nitrate is also needed to make chlorophyll. If a plant does not have enough nitrate, it will become yellow instead of green.

Plants that are short of nitrate are stunted (small) and yellow.

Magnesium is also needed for making chlorophyll. So a shortage of magnesium makes plant leaves go yellow.

This tomato leaf is showing symptoms of magnesium deficiency.

Questions

A+I

1 Give **two** examples of mineral salts that are needed by plants.
2 Explain why a plant that does not have enough magnesium will not grow well.
3 Think about what you know about plant roots. How do plants absorb mineral salts from the soil?

Activity 1.2

Investigating the effect of fertilisers on plant growth

Duckweed is a tiny plant that grows on the surface of ponds and lakes. Each plant is made up of a leaf-like structure, often with tiny roots hanging down into the water.

A frog surrounded by duckweed plants.

If you add a single duckweed plant to some water, it will produce new plants as it grows. You can measure how fast the duckweed grows by counting how many plants there are after a certain period of time.

Plan an investigation to find out how fertiliser affects the rate of growth of duckweed. Your teacher will show you the plants and the fertiliser that you can use.

Think about these questions:

- What you will change in your experiment?
- How will you change this?
- What variables will you keep the same?
- What will you measure?
- When you will measure this?
- Will you do repeats in your experiment? If so, how many?

When your teacher has checked your plan, you can set up your experiment. You will have to be patient, as it may take several weeks before you have your results.

Record your results clearly. You may be able to draw a graph to display them.

Summary

- **Plants need nitrate to make proteins, which are needed to make new cells for growth.**
- **Plants need magnesium to make chlorophyll.**

1.3 Plants and water

Everyone knows that plants need water. If you grow plants in pots, you need to water them regularly.

Water for support

The photograph shows one reason why plants need water – it helps them to stand upright.

Plant cells contain a lot of water, especially inside their vacuoles. A plant cell that has plenty of water is strong and firm. When all the cells in a plant are like this, they press out against each other and make the whole plant firm and well-supported.

When a plant cell doesn't contain enough water, it becomes soft and floppy. When all the cells in a plant are like this, the plant collapses. We say that it has wilted.

Water for transport

You may remember that plants contain long tubes, called xylem, which transport water from the roots up to the leaves. There are mineral salts dissolved in the water, and this is how they are transported around the plant.

Water for cooling

When the water in the xylem gets into the leaves, it spreads out through each leaf. Some of it evaporates into the air spaces inside the leaf.

When water evaporates, it absorbs heat energy. This cools down the surroundings. The water evaporating inside a plant leaf helps to keep the plant cool. This is really important for plants that live in very hot environments.

The plant on the left has not been watered for three days. The photograph on the right shows the same plant a few hours after it was watered.

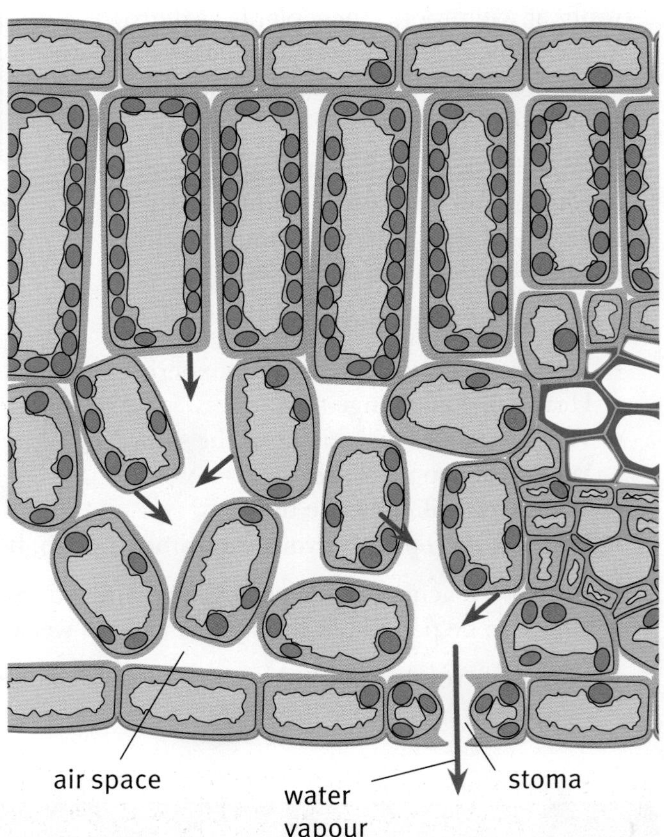

Most of the water that is taken up by a plant's roots is eventually lost from its leaves in the form of water vapour.

Water for photosynthesis

Water is one of the reactants in photosynthesis. Water combines with carbon dioxide, inside chloroplasts, to make glucose and oxygen.

In fact, only a very small proportion of the water taken up by a plant's roots is used in photosynthesis.

Water vapour diffusing out of plant leaves helps to keep the air moist.

Questions

1. Explain why a plant wilts if it is short of (lacks) water.
2. How does water help a plant to keep cool?
3. Water from the soil is absorbed by a plant. Eventually, it ends up in the air as water vapour. List the parts of the plant that it passes through on this journey.

Activity 1.3

Water loss from plants

1. Collect two very similar potted plants. Make sure both of them have moist soil. Cover the two pots with plastic bags as shown in the diagrams.
2. Measure the mass of each plant in its pot, using a top pan balance. Record this mass.
3. Each day for the next week, measure the mass of each plant in its pot again. Try to do this at about the same time each day. Record all of your readings in a results table.
4. When you have finished all your measurements, look carefully at the inside of the plastic bag covering the plant. You may find little droplets of liquid. To check if these are water, touch one of them with some blue cobalt chloride paper. If the liquid is water, the paper will go pink.
5. Draw a line graph to display your results. You could draw two lines on the same graph – one for each plant.

Questions

A1 What was the variable that you changed in this experiment?
A2 What variables did you keep the same?
A3 Compare the change in the mass in the two plants in their pots.
A4 Explain why the droplets of water formed on the inside of the plastic bag.
A5 Explain the reasons for the differences between the results for the two plants.

Summary

- **Plants need water for support, cooling, transport and photosynthesis.**
- **Most of the water taken up by the roots eventually diffuses out of the plant's leaves, as water vapour.**

1.4 Flowers

The photograph shows wild flowers growing. Many flowers are brightly coloured like this. Why are flowers so colourful?

Flowers are brightly coloured to attract insects and birds. They do this because the insects and birds help plants to reproduce. Flowers are the reproductive organs of plants.

Brightly coloured wild flowers.

The parts of a flower

Flowers come in all sorts of different shapes and sizes. But you can usually find the same parts in most flowers that you look at.

The **petals** are usually the most colourful part of the flower. They attract insects or birds to the flower. Some flowers produce scents (smells), which also help to attract insects.

The insects or birds feed on sweet, sugary **nectar** produced at the base of the petals. They may also eat some of the **pollen**, produced in the **anthers**. The pollen contains the male gametes of the flower.

The female gametes are inside the **ovules**, which are inside the **ovaries**.

Unlike animals, many plants produce both male gametes and female gametes.

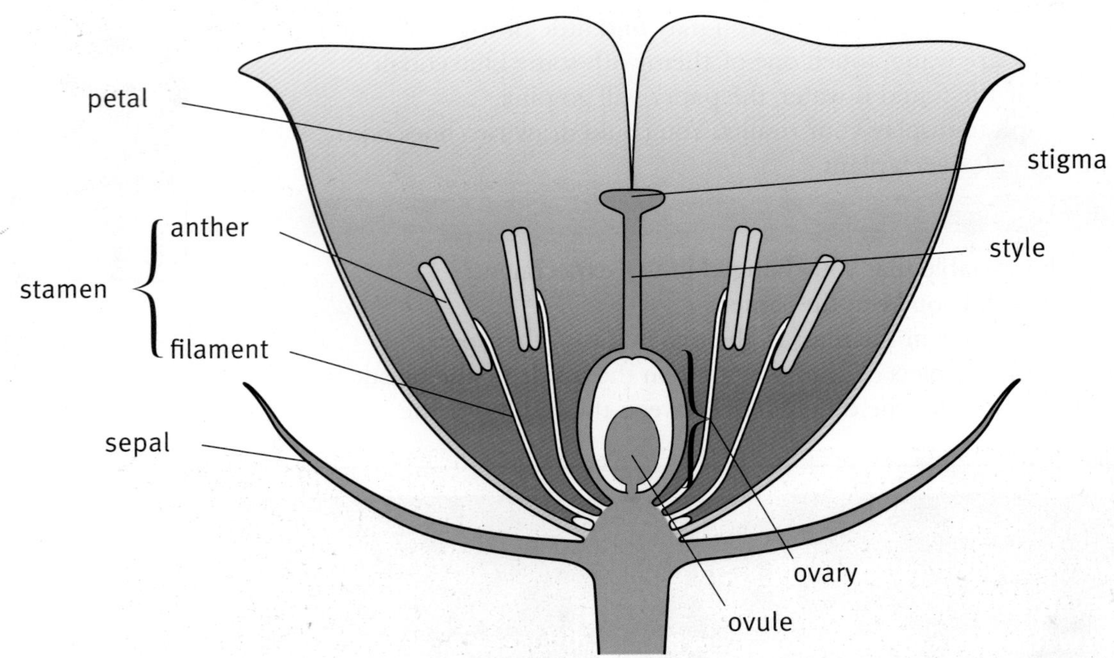

The structure of a flower.

Questions

1 Many people use the word 'flower' when they really mean 'plant'. Explain the difference between a plant and a flower.

A+I 2 Insects can often smell flowers from hundreds of metres away. Suggest how the scent from the flowers spreads out into the air around them.

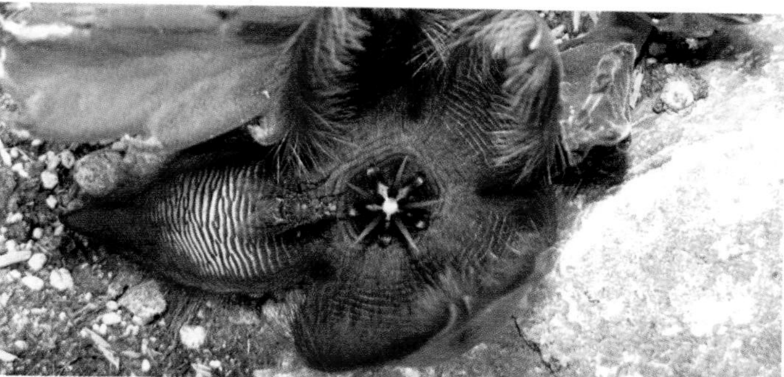

Not all flowers produce smells that we like. This flower is a stapelia. It has a scent like rotting meat, and attracts flies.

Activity 1.4

Investigating flower structure

You are going to take a flower apart and stick the various parts into your notebook.

1 Look carefully at your flower.
- How many sepals does it have?
- Carefully remove each of the sepals, and stick them in a neat row in your book. Write a label to remind you what they are.
- How many petals does your flower have? What colour are they?
- Some petals have guidelines, to direct insects to where they can find nectar at the base of the petals. Does your flower have guidelines?
- Carefully remove each of the petals, and stick them into your book.

3 Now look at the stamens. These are the male parts of the flower.
- How many stamens does your flower have? Can you see any pollen at the top of them?
- Remove them carefully and stick them into your book. On one of them, label the anther and filament.

4 Now you should only have the stigmas, styles and ovaries left. These are the female parts of the flower.
- How many does your flower have?
- Carefully cut an ovary open. What can you see inside it?
- Stick the stigmas, styles and ovaries into your book, and label them.

Summary
- Flowers are the reproductive organs of plants.
- The male parts of a flower are the stamens. Pollen contains the male gametes.
- The female parts of a flower are the ovaries, style and stigma. Ovules contain the female gametes.
- Petals have bright colours and strong scents to attract insects and birds.

1.5 Pollination

Flowers are organs where sexual reproduction takes place. You will remember that sexual reproduction involves gametes (sex cells).

In humans, the male gametes are the sperm cells. They can swim to find an egg.

Flowers do not have swimming sperm cells. Their male gametes are simply nuclei inside their pollen grains. They cannot swim.

So flowers have to use another method of getting their male gametes to their female gametes. Many of them use insects or birds. Some use the wind.

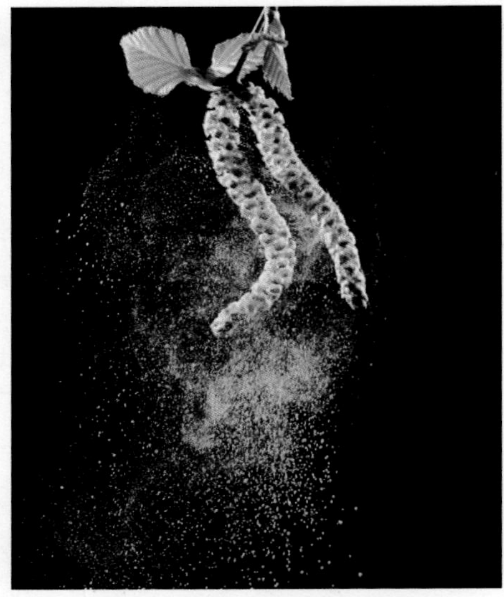

The yellow powder falling from these catkins contains thousands of lightweight pollen grains. Catkins are made of lots of tiny flowers.

Pollen grains

Pollen grains are made in the anthers of flowers. Pollen grains contain the male gametes.

These spiky pollen grains are from a ragweed plant. Their spikes help them to stick to insects' bodies (magnification ×1600).

Activity 1.5
Looking at pollen grains

1. Collect a microscope and set it up with the low power objective lens over the stage.
2. Collect a clean microscope slide. Carefully tap a little pollen from a flower onto the centre of the slide.
3. Place the slide on the stage of the microscope. Focus on the pollen. Make a drawing of one or two pollen grains.
4. Repeat steps **2** and **3** using pollen from a different kind of flower.
5. Describe any differences that you can see between the two types of pollen.

Transferring pollen grains

To help the male gametes get close to the female gametes, pollen grains must be carried from the anthers (where they are made) to the **stigma** of a flower.

Insects often help with this. When the insect comes to a flower to collect nectar, pollen gets stuck onto its body. When the insect goes to another flower, some of the pollen rubs off onto the stigma.

The transfer of pollen from an anther to a stigma is called **pollination**.

Many flowers are pollinated by insects or birds. Some, for example grasses, are pollinated by the wind. The wind blows pollen off the anthers. Just by luck, some of the pollen may land on the stigmas of other flowers.

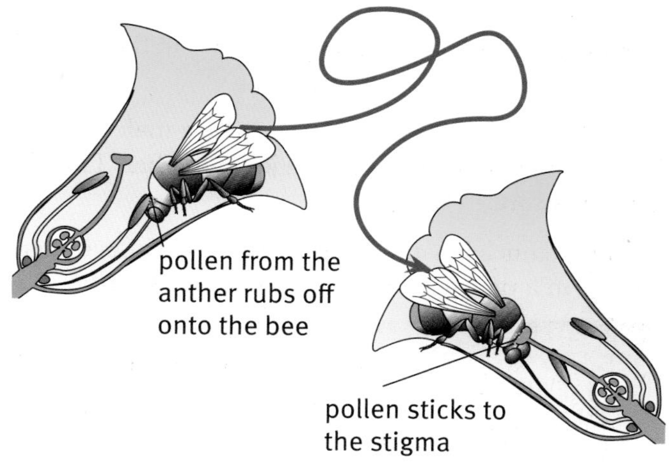
pollen from the anther rubs off onto the bee
pollen sticks to the stigma

Insects can transfer pollen from an anther to a stigma.

This Cape sugarbird is collecting nectar. When it flies to another flower, it may carry pollen with it on its feathers.

Questions

1. Where are the female gametes found in a flower?
2. Where are the male gametes found in a flower?
3. Explain why plants need help to get their male gametes to their female gametes.

4. The table shows two differences between insect-pollinated and wind-pollinated flowers. Suggest reasons for these differences.

Insect-pollinated flowers	Wind-pollinated flowers
brightly coloured	not brightly coloured
have spiky or sticky pollen	have smooth pollen

Summary

- The male gametes of a flower are inside the pollen grains. The female gametes are inside the ovules.
- The male gametes cannot move by themselves, so flowers make use of insects, birds or the wind to move their pollen grains.
- The transfer of pollen from an anther to a stigma is called pollination.

1.6 Fertilisation

The kind of reproduction that happens in flowers is sexual reproduction.

In sexual reproduction, the nucleus of a male gamete and the nucleus of a female gamete join together. This is called **fertilisation**.

When the nuclei of the two gametes have joined together, they form a new cell. This cell is called a **zygote**.

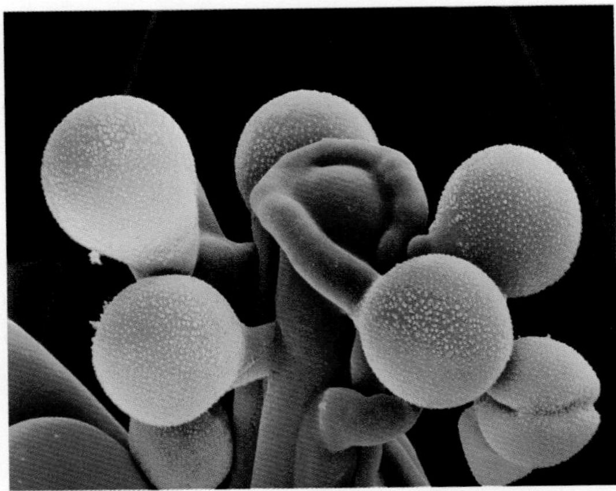

The yellow spheres are pollen grains of a poppy. The orange-red structure is a stigma on a poppy flower. You can see tubes starting to grow from the pollen grains (magnified ×3600).

Questions

Think about what you have learnt about sexual reproduction in humans.

1 What is the name of the male gamete in humans?
2 What is the name of the female gamete in humans?
3 Where does fertilisation happen in humans?

Fertilisation in a flower

In flowers, the male gamete is a nucleus inside a pollen grain. The female gamete is a nucleus inside an ovule.

When a flower has been pollinated, there are pollen grains on its stigma.

The diagram shows how a male nucleus gets from a stigma to a female gamete.

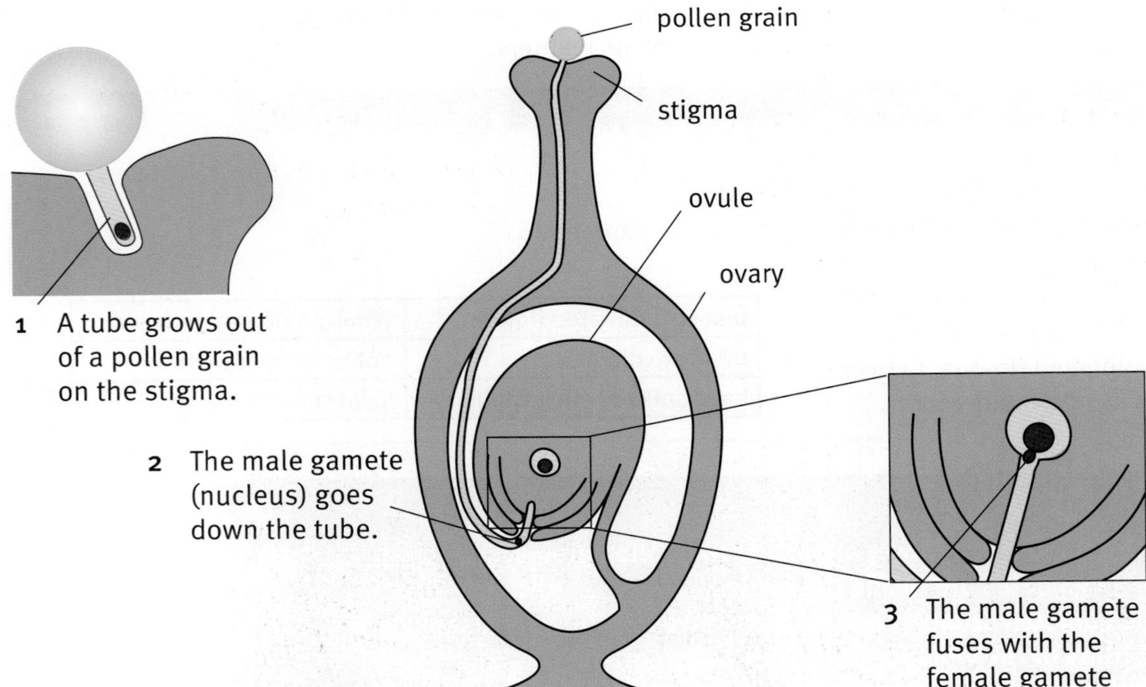
pollen grain
stigma
ovule
ovary
1 A tube grows out of a pollen grain on the stigma.
2 The male gamete (nucleus) goes down the tube.
3 The male gamete fuses with the female gamete inside an ovule.

Fertilisation in a flower.

Seed formation

When the male nucleus fuses with the female nucleus inside an ovule, it produces a zygote.

The zygote starts to divide. It produces a little group of cells called an **embryo**. This embryo will eventually grow into a new plant.

The ovule also begins to change. It gradually grows into a **seed**.

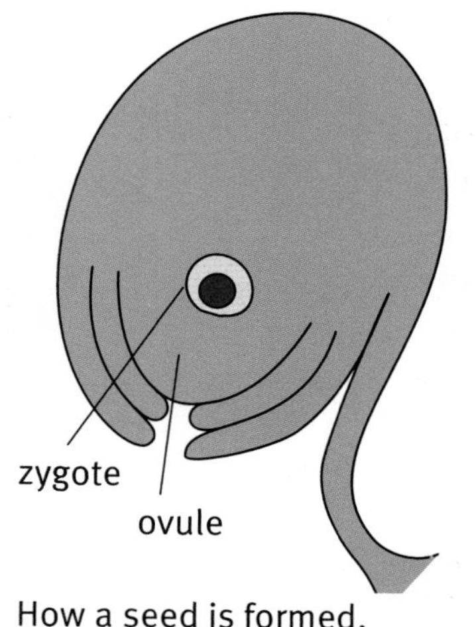

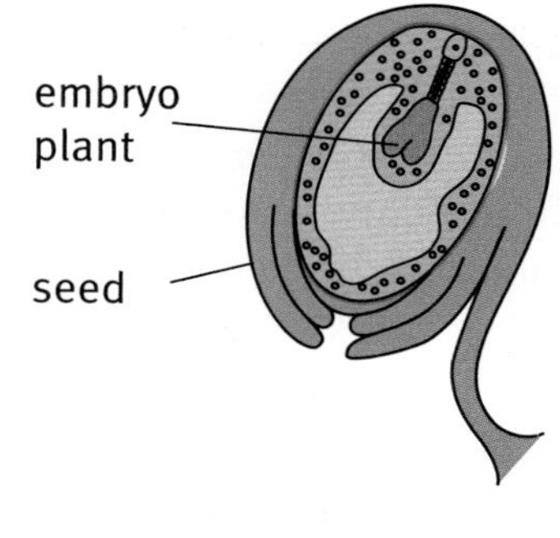

How a seed is formed.

Activity 1.6

Investigating seed structure

Beans are seeds. You are going to look carefully at the structure of a bean seed. It is easier to do this if the bean has been soaked in water for a few hours first, to soften it.

1. Look carefully at the bean seed. Find the structures shown on the diagram. The **testa** is the tough outer coat of the seed. The **micropyle** is a tiny hole where the pollen tube grew into the ovule. (Remember – the seed began as an ovule.)
2. Peel the testa away from the seed. Inside, you should find two creamy-coloured structures. These are called **cotyledons**. They contain food stores for the embryo to use when it starts to grow.
3. Gently pull the cotyledons apart. You will find the embryo plant in between them.

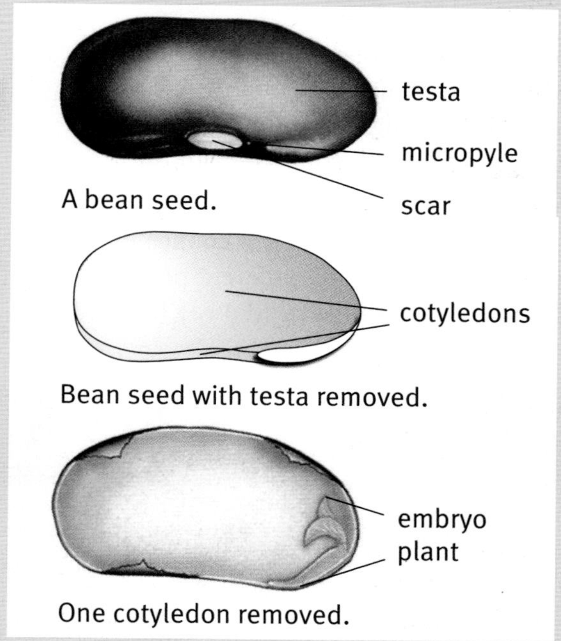

A bean seed.

Bean seed with testa removed.

One cotyledon removed.

Summary

- When a pollen grain has landed on a stigma, it grows a tube down to an ovule.
- The male gamete (nucleus) goes down the tube. It fuses with the female nucleus inside an ovule, producing a zygote.
- The zygote divides over and over again, and produces an embryo plant.
- The ovule becomes a seed, with the embryo plant inside it.

1.7 Fruits

Look at the diagram on page **16**. You will see that the ovule is inside an ovary.

When an ovule develops into a seed, it is still inside the ovary. While the ovule is developing into a seed, the ovary is changing too. The ovary changes into a **fruit**. This means that fruits contain seeds.

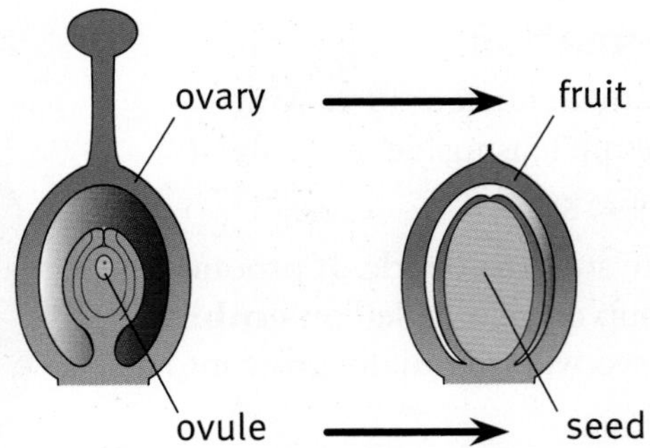

After fertilisation, the ovary develops into a fruit with one or more seeds inside it.

Dispersal

Seeds contain embryo plants. When they start to grow, each plant will need a little space of its own. Each plant will need water, light and mineral salts in order to grow well.

If all the seeds just fell off the plant onto the ground, they would all be trying to grow in the same place. The new little plants would all have to compete with each other for water, light and mineral salts. They would have to compete with the parent plant, too.

The new plants have a better chance of growing if they are in a different place. They need to be **dispersed** away from the parent plant.

If seedlings (young plants) grow next to the parent plant, they may not get enough water, light or mineral salts to grow well.

Seedlings have a better chance of survival if they grow away from their parent and from each other.

Activity 1.7A
Adaptations of fruits

Your teacher will give you several different fruits. You may be surprised that some of them are fruits! Remember that in science a fruit is something that contains seeds.

1 Look at each fruit carefully. Think about how this fruit might help the seeds inside it to be spread away from the parent plant. Some possibilities are:
- Does the fruit have adaptations that would encourage animals to carry it away?
- Does the fruit have adaptations that help it to be blown away by the wind?
- Does the fruit have adaptations that help it to float away on water?

2 Make a large, labelled diagram of at least two of the fruits. Label your diagrams to explain how each fruit is adapted to help to disperse the seeds inside it.

This fruit is shaped like a parachute. It carries the seed away on the wind.

The hooks of this fruit catch in the fur of animals and the seeds are carried off.

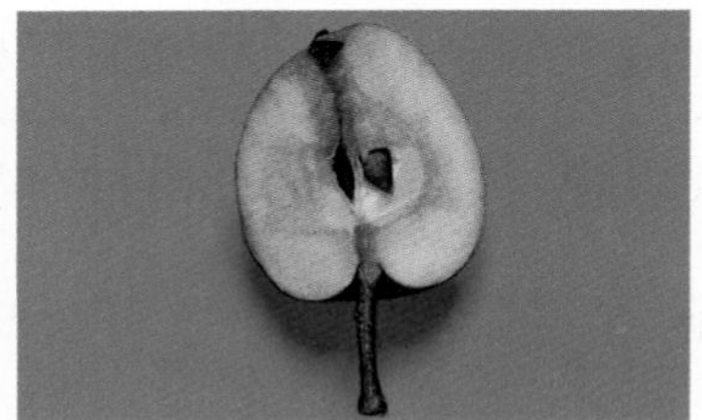

The flesh of the apple fruit attracts birds that carry the seeds away by accident.

Activity 1.7B

What affects the time it takes for a fruit to fall to the ground?

Some fruits have wings. These help them to stay in the air, and perhaps be blown far away from the parent plant.

You can make model fruits using paper. You can use paper clips to represent a heavy seed.

Plan an investigation to find out how one feature of a winged fruit affects the time taken for it to fall to the ground.

You could think about your work on the effect of gravity on objects, to help you to come up with ideas. Make a prediction about what you think you will find out.

When you have written your plan, check it with your teacher before doing your experiment.

Record your results clearly, and write down your conclusions.

Evaluate your experiment and suggest how you could improve it if you were able to do it again.

Questions

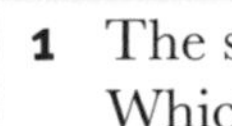

1 The scientific meaning of the word 'fruit' is a structure that contains seeds. Which of these are fruits?

orange   mango   tomato   bean pod   potato

2 **a** Explain what is meant by 'seed dispersal'.

b Explain why seed dispersal is important for plants.

c List **three** ways in which fruits can help with seed dispersal.

Summary

- Ovaries develop into fruits after fertilisation.
- Fruits contain seeds.
- Fruits have adaptations to help the seeds inside them disperse to new places.
- Seed dispersal helps to avoid competition with the parent plant.

Unit 1 End of unit questions

1.1 **a** Copy and complete the word equation for photosynthesis.
carbon dioxide + ... → .... + ... [3]
b Explain how chlorophyll helps this reaction to happen. [2]

1.2 Carri tested a leaf for starch. The list of steps shows what she did, but they are in the wrong order.

A Put iodine solution onto the leaf.
B Put the leaf into hot ethanol.
C Dip the leaf into water to soften it.
D Put the leaf into boiling water for five minutes.

a List the steps in the correct sequence. [1]
b Explain why Carri carried out step **D**. [2]
c Explain why Carri carried out step **B**. [2]

1.3 Yousef did an experiment to find out how giving plants different amounts of water affected their growth.

Yousef sowed (planted) nine seeds, each in separate pots. He poured 20 cm^3 of water into each pot, to encourage the seeds to germinate. He left all the pots in the same place in the lab.

When all the seeds had germinated, Yousef separated the pots into three groups, with three pots in each group. Each day, for seven days, he added a measured volume of water to each pot.

Yousef measured the height of each seedling on day **1** and day **7**. These are his results.

Group	Seedling	Height of seedling / mm		Increase in height / mm
		Day 1	Day 7	
A no water	1	6.0	6.5	0.5
	2	5.5	6.0	0.5
	3	5.5	6.0	0.5
B 2 cm^3 water	4	5.5	7.5	2.0
	5	6.0	8.0	2.0
	6	6.0	8.5	2.5
C 5 cm^3 water	7	6.0	9.5	
	8	5.5	9.5	
	9	6.0	10.0	

a Calculate the increase in height for each of the seedlings 7, 8 and 9. [1]
b Calculate the mean increase in height for each group of seedlings. [2]
c On graph paper, draw a bar chart to show Yousef's results. Put volume of water on the x-axis, and mean increase in height on the y-axis. [4]
d Write a conclusion that Yousef could make from his results. [1]

1.4 The diagram shows a flower.

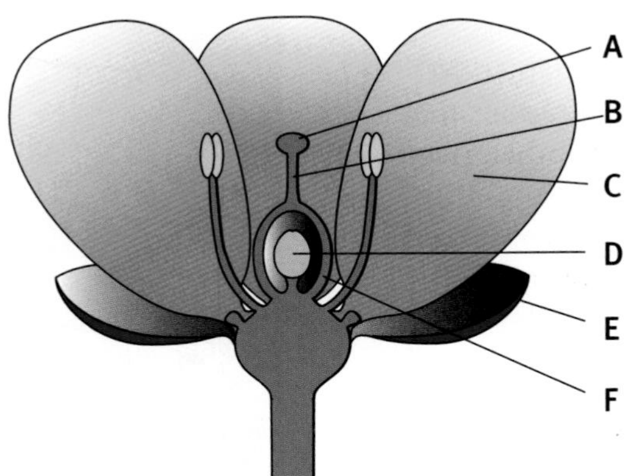

a Name the parts labelled **A** and **B**. [2]
b Give the letter of the part that attracts insects to the flower. [1]
c Explain why it is useful to the plant to attract insects to its flowers. [5]
d Give the letter of the part of the flower that will develop into a seed. [1]

1.5 The photograph shows a fruit which has been cut in half.

a Explain how you can tell that this is a fruit. [1]
b Name the part of a flower from which a fruit develops. [1]
c Suggest how this fruit helps the seeds to be dispersed. Explain your answer. [3]
d Explain why it is important for seeds to be dispersed. [3]

2.1 Plant adaptations

In Stage **7**, you learnt about some of the ways in which organisms are adapted to live in their habitats. A **habitat** is a place where an organism lives.

Question

1 Can you remember how a cactus is adapted to live in the desert? Describe **two** adaptations that help it to do this. (If you cannot remember, page **39** in the Stage **7** book will help you.)

Here are some ways in which plants are adapted to live in three very different environments.

Spruce trees in the Arctic

Siberian spruce trees live in the huge forests that grow north of the Arctic circle. In summer, the days are long and warm. In winter, the days are very short, it is always very cold and there is a lot of snow. Spruce trees are conifers. Their leaves are thin, strong needles. The needles have a thick, waxy covering layer. This prevents them from losing too much water in winter, when the roots cannot take up water from the ground because it is all frozen solid.

Siberian spruce trees have a tall, narrow shape, with downward sloping branches. The heavy snow can lie on the needles and branches without breaking them. If even more snow falls, it will slide off.

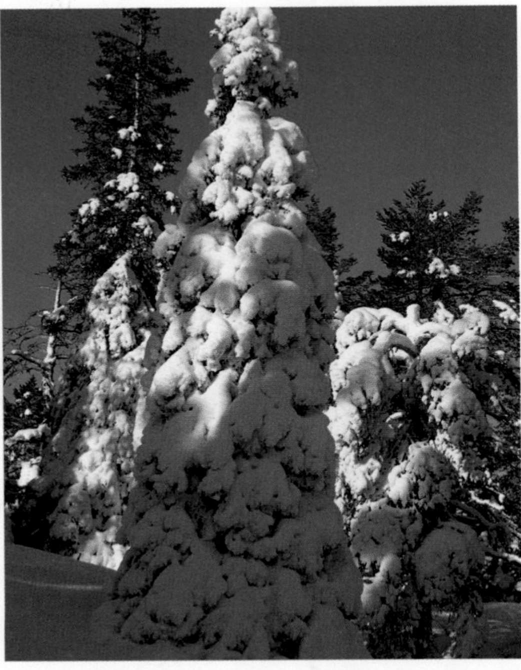

A spruce tree in northern Finland, in winter.

Strangler figs in a rainforest

Rainforests are good places for a plant to live. It is warm, there is a lot of sunlight, and there is always plenty of water. However, there are so many plants living in these ideal conditions that the taller ones block the light from plants growing close to the ground.

Strangler figs are adapted to live in these conditions. Instead of germinating on the dark forest floor, their seeds germinate in a crack high up in a mature tree, where the tiny seedlings can get light. The seedling's roots grow downwards and coil around the tree trunk. As the fig gets older, its roots and stems get thicker and more woody. Sometimes, the fig gets so big that it kills the tree that it has grown around. But this doesn't matter to the fig tree, because its stems and roots are now strong enough to hold it up on their own.

A young strangler fig, growing around a forest tree in Peru.

Weeds in a crop

A weed is a plant that grows where people do not want it to grow, for example in amongst a farmer's crops, or in a pavement. They may have to compete with crop plants for light, water and mineral salts.

Many weeds are **annual plants**. This means that they germinate, grow, produce seeds and die in less than one year. Some weeds can do this in just a few weeks, before people can kill them. Their seeds can survive for long periods of time in difficult conditions – for example during a very dry summer, or a very cold winter. Other plants without these features would not survive.

Hoeing weeds in a cassava crop in Rwanda.

Questions

A+I **2** Siberian spruce trees do all of their growing during the summer, not during the winter. Suggest at least **two** explanations for this.

A+I **3** Strangler figs produce sweet, juicy fruits. Suggest how this helps their seeds to be dispersed to a suitable place for germination.

A+I **4** Suggest how being an annual plant helps a weed to live in its habitat.

Activity 2.1
Adaptations for living in water

Organisms that live in water are said to be **aquatic**.

Choose an aquatic plant that grows in your country. Possibilities include:

- duckweed (which you may have used in Activity **1.2**)
- water hyacinth
- lotus.

Find out how your plant is adapted to live in water. You can use the internet and books, but if possible you should also study specimens of the plant itself.

Make a large diagram of your plant. Label it to explain how it is adapted to live in its habitat.

A lotus plant growing in a lake in Thailand.

Summary

- Plants are adapted to live in their habitats.
- Plant adaptations often help them to get light for photosynthesis.
- Annual plants grow, produce seeds and die in less than one year.

2.2 Animal adaptations

Arabian oryx in the desert

A desert is a place that gets very little rainfall each year. Some deserts are cold, and others are hot.

Deserts in Arabia are hot deserts. The Arabian oryx is adapted to live there. They are adapted to survive with very little water. Arabian oryx will drink if they can, and herds travel long distances to follow any rainfall. However, they can go for months without drinking, getting all the water that they need from the plants that they eat.

Oryx feed mostly at night, when it is cooler, so they do not lose too much water from their bodies by evaporation. During the day, they usually rest in the shade. They make a small depression (dent) in the sand to lie in, so that their body heat is conducted into the cooler ground. They have hooves with a large area, which helps to stop them from sinking into soft sand. (You can find out how this works, in terms of pressure, on page **126**.) Their light coloured coats reflect much of the radiation from the Sun, helping to keep them cool.

An Arabian oryx in Sir Bani Yas Island Wildlife Reserve, Abu Dhabi.

Sealions in the sea

Sealions are mammals that are adapted to hunt their prey in sea water, but they also spend time on land.

Sealions have smooth, streamlined bodies that help them to move easily through water by reducing friction. Their front and hind legs have become flippers, which have a large surface area to push against the water to propel them forward. They can turn their hind flippers to face forwards, which helps them to push off the ground and shuffle around when they are on land.

When a sealion dives, its nostrils close to stop water getting into its lungs. Sealions can hold their breath for over an hour. They are carnivores, and have sharp teeth to help them to capture and kill their prey.

Australian sealions.

Earthworms in the soil

Earthworms belong to the group of invertebrates called annelids. They spend most of their time underground, in burrows that they make by eating soil.

Earthworms have long, slim, smooth bodies that slide easily through their burrows. They have tiny bristles on their undersides, called chaetae, which can grip the sides of the burrow. This is particularly useful if a predator tries to pull them out.

The little bristles on an earthworm's body help it to hold on tight to the sides of its burrow.

Activity 2.2
Behavioural adaptations of woodlice

Most kinds of woodlice live in dark, moist places. This helps them to avoid predators, and to make sure that they do not lose too much water by evaporation.

You are going to plan and carry out an experiment to investigate how the behaviour of woodlice helps them to survive.

You will need a piece of apparatus called a **choice chamber**. The diagram shows a choice chamber. If you do not have one, you can make a simple one out of a Petri dish and a lid.

You can set up the choice chamber so that the conditions are different on each side of it – for example, damp on one side and dry on the other, or light and dark. Then put the animals into it and count how many end up on each side.

Once you have decided what to investigate you will need to think carefully about which variables you are changing, and how you will keep all the other variables constant. Record your results carefully and write your conclusion.

Compare your results with others in your class. Do they all agree with each other? If not, can you suggest why not?

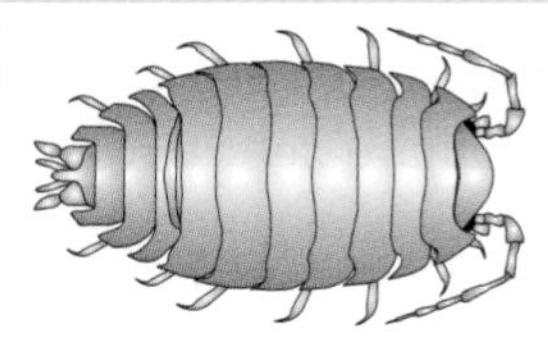

A woodlouse.

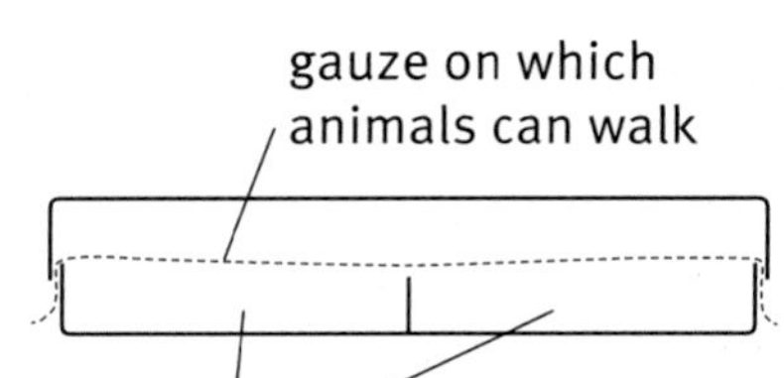

A choice chamber. Small animals can move freely inside it.

Questions

1 Using examples described on these two pages, describe:
   a **one** structural adaptation that helps an animal to survive,
   b **one** behavioural adaptation that helps an animal to survive.

A+I
2 Use particle theory to explain why oryx lose less water by evaporation at night, when it is cooler.

A+I
3 It is thought that the first humans lived on the open, grassy savannahs of Africa. Suggest how the structure of our bodies, and our behaviour, might be adapted to help us to survive in that habitat.

Summary

- Animals may have structural and behavioural adaptations that help them to survive in their habitats.

2.3 Ecology

Ecologists are scientists who study organisms in their environment. This study is called **ecology**. Like other scientists, ecologists ask questions and then do experiments to try to find answers.

Investigating camel grazing in Dubai

Large areas of Dubai are desert. Many kinds of plants are adapted to live in the desert. But, in many places, the number of small plants is gradually decreasing.

Some ecologists wanted to find out if grazing (feeding) by camels was causing this decrease. They chose an area in the Dubai Desert Conservation Reserve where there is a fence several kilometres long. On one side of the fence, camels are allowed to graze. On the other side of the fence, only oryx and gazelles graze.

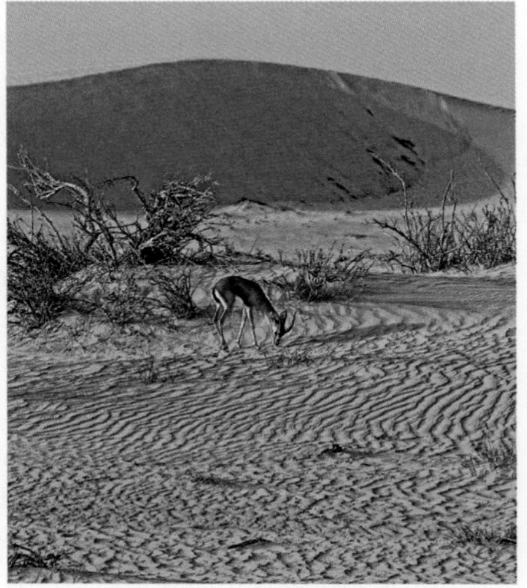

A gazelle grazing in the Dubai Desert Conservation Reserve.

The ecologists marked out 43 pairs of plots. In each pair, one plot was on the camel side of the fence, and the other plot was on the oryx side, just opposite the first one. Each plot was the same size.

Then the ecologists counted the number of plants in each plot and the number of plant species per plot. They calculated the mean numbers per plot. Their results are shown in the table.

	Grazed by camels	Grazed by oryx and gazelles
Mean number of plants per plot	64	87
Mean number of plant species per plot	4	5

Questions

SE 1 What was the independent variable in the ecologists' investigation?

SE 2 What were the **two** dependent variables?

SE 3 State **two** variables that the ecologists kept constant in their investigation.

SE 4 Write down any conclusions the ecologists can make from their results.

SE 5 Suggest how the ecologists could improve their experiment.

Sampling

In the camel grazing experiment, the ecologists did not count all of the plants in the whole area on each side of the fence. It would have taken too long. Instead, they counted the plants in 43 pairs of plots. This is called **sampling**.

When ecologists use sampling techniques, they must be careful to:

- use a fairly large sample
- place their samples randomly.

If they only used 10 pairs of plots, then their results might not show the true pattern for the whole area. If they chose the parts of the area where the vegetation looked most interesting, then once again their results might not show the true overall pattern.

This student is sampling the invertebrates that live in a river.

Questions

SE 6 Suggest how the students in the photographs could use the net to sample the invertebrates in the river.

SE 7 Suggest how the students could find out if there is a correlation between the number of invertebrates and the concentration of dissolved oxygen.

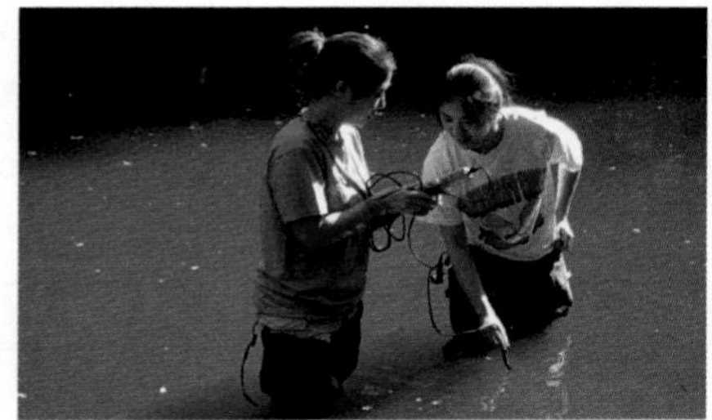
The students use an oxygen meter to measure the concentration of dissolved oxygen in the water.

Activity 2.3
An ecology investigation

SE

You are going to plan an experiment to find out the answer to a question about ecology. You could do your experiment in the school grounds.

Go for a walk around the school grounds, looking closely at the organisms that you find. Think about a question that you could investigate. Questions about plants are usually easier to try to answer than questions about animals. For example:

- Are there more daisy plants in sunny places than in shady places?
- Does grass grow faster where people don't walk on it?

Now plan your investigation. You will probably want to use a sampling technique. Ecologists often mark out little square plots with sides 0.5 m long. A quick way of doing this is to make a frame exactly that shape and size, which you can put down onto the ground. This frame is called a **quadrat**.

Once you have chosen the two areas you are going to sample, you need to try to place your quadrats randomly inside them. One way of doing this is to stand with your back to the area and throw your quadrat behind you – but do make sure there is no-one standing nearby! Your teacher may be able to suggest other ways of doing this.

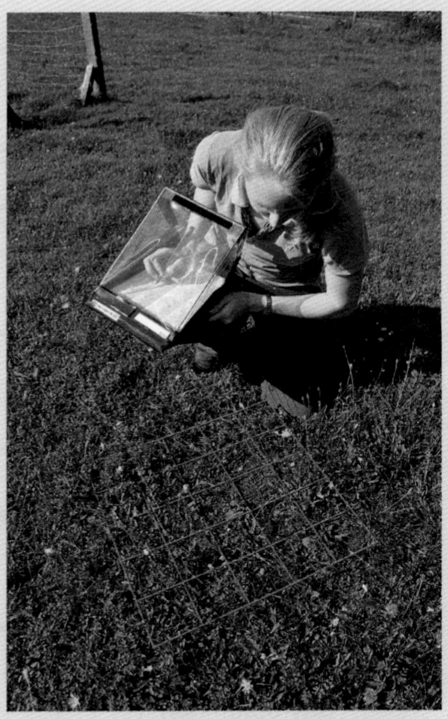
This ecologist is using a quadrat marked out in smaller squares, to make it easier for her to count the plants inside it.

Summary

- **Ecologists study organisms in their environment.**
- **Ecologists often use sampling techniques. Sampling involves finding results for a small, representative part of the area you are studying.**

2.4 Food webs and energy flow

You probably remember from Stage **7** that a food chain shows how energy is transferred from one organism to another. The arrows show the direction of energy transfer.

Here are two food chains. **Phytoplankton** are microscopic plants that float in the water. **Zooplankton** are microscopic, floating animals.

phytoplankton → krill → fish → leopard seal

phytoplankton → zooplankton → squid → leopard seal

Two food chains in the Southern Ocean (Antarctic Ocean).

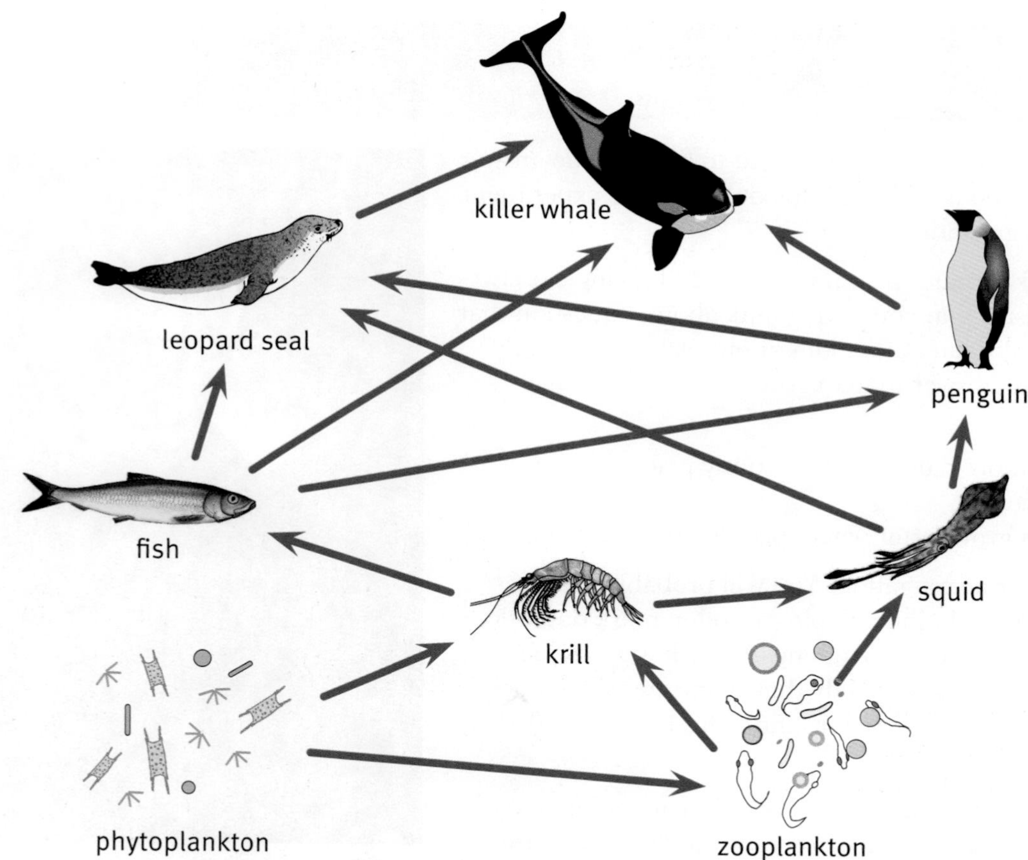

A food web in the Southern Ocean (Antarctic Ocean).

Questions

These questions are about the Southern Ocean food web. To answer them, you will need to remember what you have learnt about food chains.

1. Name the producer in the Southern Ocean food web.
2. Name **three** consumers in the food web.
3. Find a food chain with six organisms in it. (Start with the producer, and follow the arrows.) Draw your food chain.

Activity 2.4
Researching a food web

SE

You are going to find information that will help you to construct a food web for a habitat in your country.

Your teacher will help you to choose a suitable habitat to work on.

Here are some points to think about:

- How will you find out the information that you need? Will you do this by observing the organisms in their habitat? By using reference books or the internet? Or both of these?
- If you are able to visit the habitat, what observations will you try to make?
- If you are able to visit the habitat, how will you keep safe while you are collecting information?

You will not be able to include every single species in your food web. A good number to aim for is between 8 and 12. Make sure there is at least one plant in your food web, at least one **herbivore** and at least one **carnivore**. (A herbivore is an animal that eats plants. A carnivore is an animal that eats other animals.)

If two or more groups work on the same habitat, you may be able to pool your results to construct a more complete food web.

Questions

Look at the photograph of the students studying organisms from a river.

4 What are they doing to keep safe? What else should they do?

5 Suggest how they will be able to identify the small organisms that they find.

6 If the students want to construct a food web for the river, what else will they need to find out?

Summary

- A food web shows how energy is transferred between organisms.
- A food web is made up of many interconnecting food chains.

2.5 Decomposers

The food chains and food webs that we have looked at so far are made up of living organisms. But what happens to dead organisms, and the waste material that they produce? What happens to parts of an organism that don't get eaten – such as that apple core you throw away, or those left-over fries that you put into the waste bin?

All of these substances contain **organic matter**. And, as you may remember from Stage **7**, many micro-organisms can break down (decompose) organic matter. This is where they get their energy.

Organisms that get their energy by breaking down dead bodies and waste from animals and plants are called **decomposers**. Earthworms, fungi, some insect larvae and bacteria are decomposers.

These earthworms have been decomposing dead leaves and food waste. They are turning it into compost that can be used to help new plants grow.

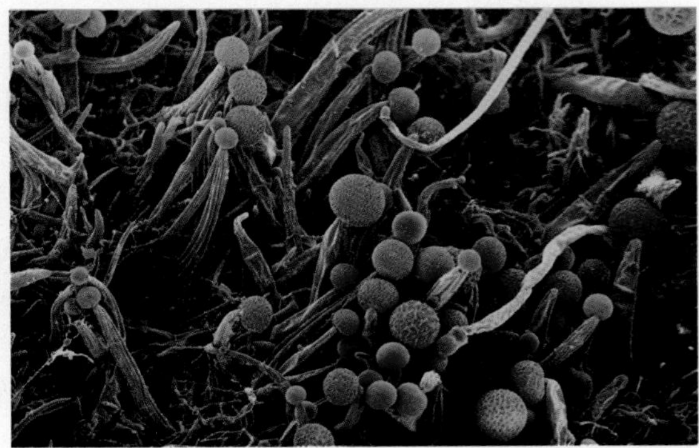

Mouldy bread seen through a microscope.

How do decomposers feed?

Inside your digestive system, you produce **enzymes** that break down large molecules – such as starch and protein – in your food into small ones. The small molecules can then be absorbed through the walls of your digestive system, and get into your blood.

Decomposers also produce enzymes. But many decomposers do not have digestive systems.

The diagram shows how a fungus breaks down bread. The fungus is made of many tiny thread-like structures, called **hyphae**. The hyphae produce enzymes that digest the starch and protein in the bread around them. The small molecules that are produced can then diffuse into the hyphae. The fungus can use them for energy, or for making new cells for growth.

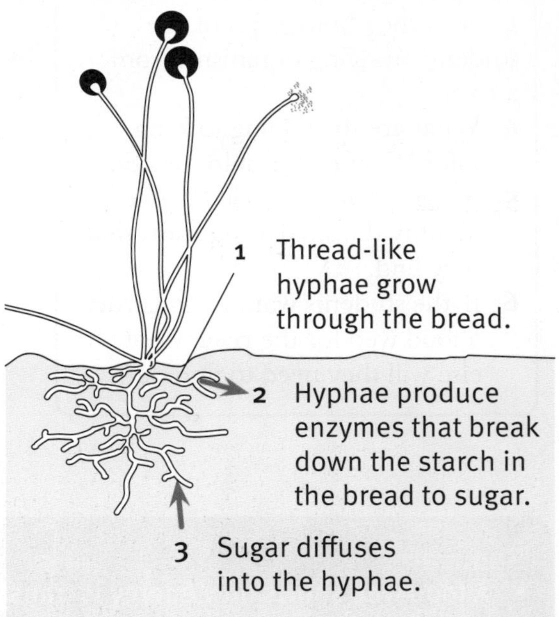

1 Thread-like hyphae grow through the bread.
2 Hyphae produce enzymes that break down the starch in the bread to sugar.
3 Sugar diffuses into the hyphae.

How a fungus digests bread.

Questions

1. Draw a food chain that ends with a fungus.
2. Give **two** similarities between the way that a fungus feeds, and the way that you feed.
3. Describe the differences between the way that a fungus feeds, and the way that you feed.

The importance of decomposers

Many people feel a little bit sick when they see decomposers feeding. Have you ever seen maggots (fly larvae) on a piece of rotten meat? It's good to feel repulsed by them, because it stops us eating something that could make us ill.

But decomposers are really important. Imagine what would happen if there were none. All the dead bodies and waste material – including animal faeces – would just pile up on the Earth. They would never disappear.

When decomposers break down dead bodies and waste, they make it possible for the atoms in them to be reused by other organisms. For example, the worms in a compost heap break down dead leaves. Molecules and atoms released from the dead leaves can be used by new plants growing in the compost. The worms themselves get energy from the dead leaves. Birds or other animals can eat the worms, and get energy themselves, as part of a food chain. So nothing is wasted.

Activity 2.5
Decomposing fruit

Put a piece of fruit, such as an apple, orange, or half a mango, on a plate or dish. Label it with your name and the date. Do not cover it. Leave it in the laboratory or another warm place.

Look at your fruit every two or three days. Note any changes that you can see. You could make labelled drawings on some days, or take digital photographs. If you position the camera in exactly the same place each day, you might be able to make a very short time-lapse sequence to show how the fruit changes over time.

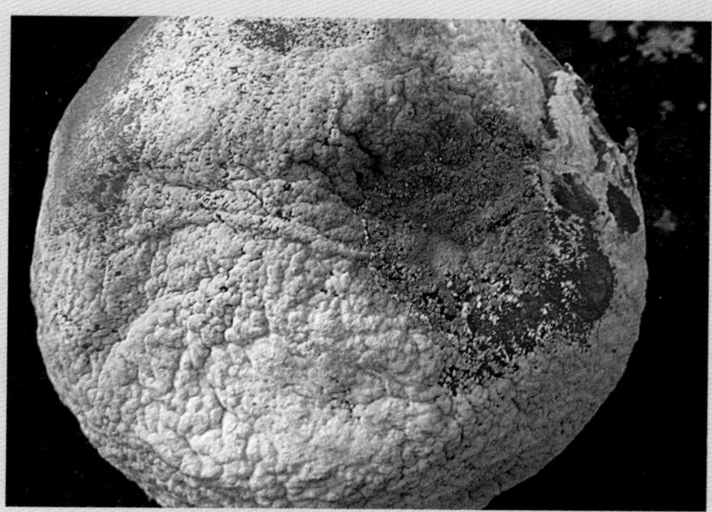

What sort of decomposers are growing on this orange?

Summary

- Decomposers are organisms that get their energy from dead organisms or their waste products.
- Decomposers help to recycle substances from dead organisms and waste, so that other living organisms can use them.

2.6 Populations

You have probably heard that the human population is growing fast. The United Nations estimated there were more than 7 billion people on Earth in early 2012. Some scientists think that our population will reach 10 billion by 2050. (10 billion is 10 000 000 000.)

How will we cope when there are an extra 3 billion people on Earth?

No-one can be sure what will happen to our population in the future. The size of a population increases when the number of births per year is greater than the number of deaths per year. In many countries, better health care, and better supplies of food and water, are reducing the number of deaths per year. To keep the population steady, the number of births must also decrease.

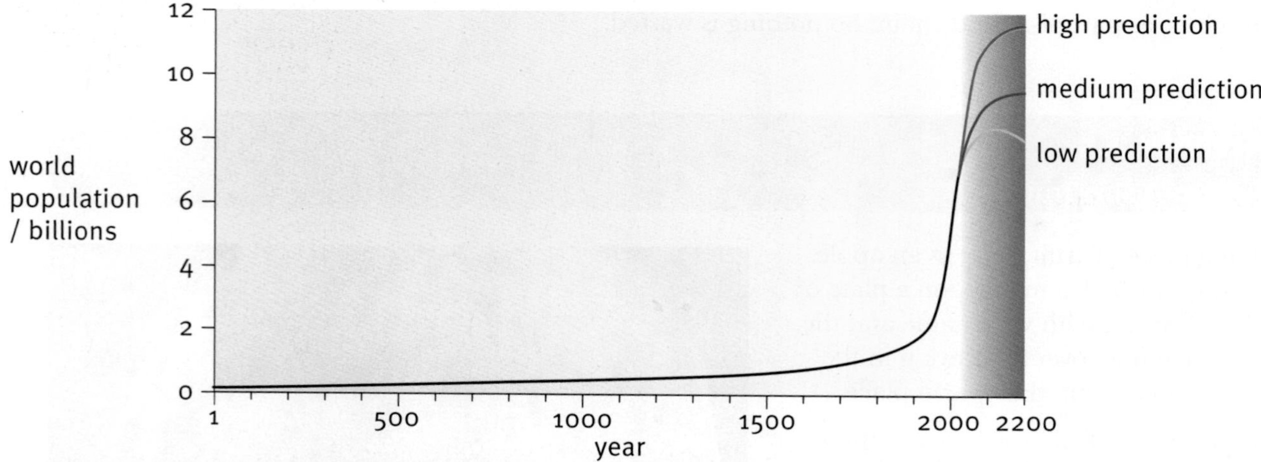

This graph shows how the human population has changed in the last 2000 years (yellow background), and how it is predicted to change by 2200 (purple background).

Questions

A+I **1** Look at the graph. What can you conclude about the number of births and deaths per year between the year 1 and the year 1000?

A+I **2** Suggest reasons for the shape of the graph between 1500 and 2000.

A+I **3** There are three different lines showing the predicted population size in the future. Suggest why.

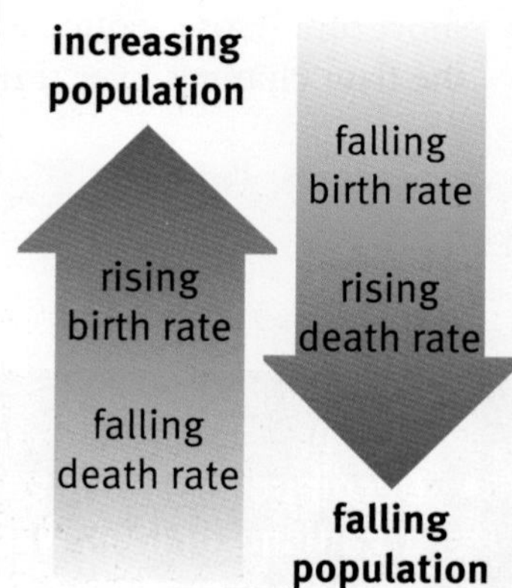

How birth rate and death rate affect population size.

Factors affecting the size of animal populations

We can define a population as the number of organisms of a particular species that are living in the same place at the same time.

Look back at the diagram of the food web in the Southern Ocean, on page **28**. Let's think about the population of penguins.

Food supply

Penguins eat squid and fish. If the numbers of squid or fish fall, then not all penguins will get enough food. More penguins are likely to die. The ones that survive may not be able to have so many young.

If adult penguins cannot get enough food to feed themselves and their chicks, the death rate will increase.

Predators

Penguins are killed by leopard seals and killer whales. If the number of these predators increases, then more penguins will be killed. Their population will fall.

This leopard seal is waiting for penguins to enter the water.

Disease

Some diseases can increase death rate and decrease birth rate. For example, in 2006, researchers in South Africa noticed that some penguins were losing their feathers. They do not know why this is, but they think it may be caused by a pathogen (a disease-causing organism). Although the feathers eventually regrow, penguins without feathers are more likely to die.

Diseases caused by pathogens often become more common when a population is large, because it is easier for the pathogens to spread when animals are crowded together.

Questions

Use the food web on page **28** to answer these questions.

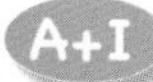

4 Suggest how a decrease in the population of squid and fish could affect the population of leopard seals. Explain your answer.

5 Suggest how a decrease in the population of squid and fish could affect the population of krill. Explain your answer.

6 Food supply, predators and disease affect the sizes of animal populations. Make a list of **three** factors that you think might affect the size of a plant population.

Summary

- A population is all the organisms of one species living in the same place at the same time.
- A population increases in size if the number of births per year is greater than the number of deaths per year.
- A population decreases in size if the number of deaths per year is greater than the number of births per year.
- A decrease in food supply, an increase in predators or an increase in disease can reduce the size of a population.

2.7 Pollution

In Stage **7**, you learnt about **pollution**. Pollution means adding things to the environment that harm living organisms.

Let's look at one example of pollution, and think about how it affects food webs, decomposers and the populations of living organisms.

Effects of fertiliser pollution in water

Step 1 Fertiliser added to a lake

A farmer sprays fertiliser onto a field to help his crops to grow better. By mistake, some of the fertiliser gets into a lake.

Step 2 Increased growth of water plants and algae

The fertiliser makes the algae and plants in the lake grow faster. (Algae are very simple plant-like organisms.) Their populations increase. This is known as an **algal bloom**.

Step 3 Plants die

The big populations of plants and algae cover the water. They stop light getting to the plants underneath them. Many plants die.

Step 4 Increase in decomposers

All the dead plants provide extra food for decomposers. The numbers of decomposers increase. Populations of bacteria get very large. The bacteria all respire, using up most of the dissolved oxygen in the water.

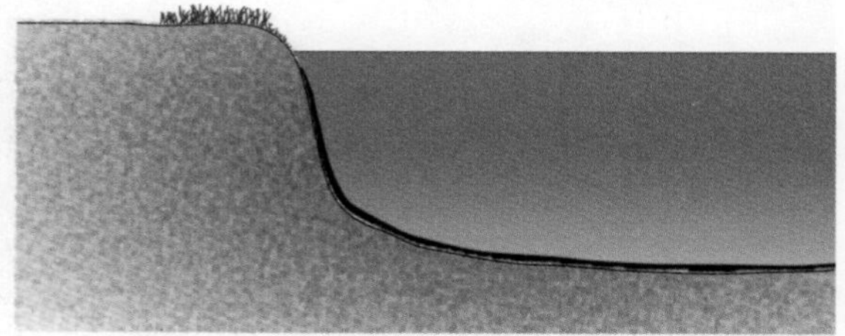

Step 5 Death of fish

Now there is so little oxygen in the water that most animals cannot live there. Fish die. Only animals that are adapted to live in low oxygen concentrations can survive.

The algae that cause algal blooms often produce toxic chemicals. Animals that drink the water may be poisoned.

This photo was taken by a NASA satellite. It shows the Black Sea. The green colour around the edges is caused by an algal bloom.

Questions

1 What do fertilisers contain, that make plants and algae grow faster?
2 Explain why the plants die when they do not get enough light.
3 Explain why the population of bacteria in the water increases after the plants die.

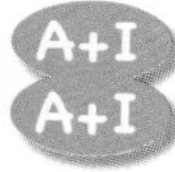

4 Explain why fish die when they do not get enough oxygen.
5 Suggest what happens to the populations of birds that feed on fish.
6 Look at the satellite photograph of the Black Sea. Suggest why the algal bloom is around the edges of the sea, rather than spread all over it.

Activity 2.7

Pollution poster

Most farmers try not to pollute lakes and rivers with fertilisers. Fertilisers are expensive, so they do not want to waste them. But it is easy to make a mistake.

Make a poster to go on the wall of a store where farmers come to buy fertilisers. Your poster should:

- catch the eyes of the farmers
- explain clearly why they should not let fertilisers get into lakes or rivers
- tell them what clues to look out for that would show that pollution may have happened.

Summary

- Pollution is the addition of harmful substances to the environment.
- Adding fertilisers to water can cause algal blooms.
- When the algae die, bacteria feed on them, using up the oxygen that was dissolved in the water.
- Aquatic animals may die, or move away, because they cannot get enough oxygen.

2.8 Habitat destruction

All living organisms have adaptations that help them to live in their habitat. If humans destroy their habitat, then they may not be able to survive. Some species may become **extinct**. This means that all the members of that species will be dead. Once a species is extinct, it cannot ever exist again.

As the human population increases, we are destroying more and more habitats. The main reasons for this are:

- using more land to grow crops and farm animals, to provide food for more people
- building more homes and roads
- cutting down forests to provide firewood and timber for building
- mining, to obtain more minerals from the ground.

Many different kinds of habitats are being destroyed. The ones that contain the most species are wetlands, rainforests and coral reefs.

Wetlands

A wetland is a place such as a swamp, marsh or bog. Some wetlands are inland, and some are next to the sea. Some wetlands stay wet all year round, while others dry out at some times of the year. Many plants and animals are adapted to live in wetlands.

The most important threat to wetlands is that people drain the land. They do this so that they can use it to grow crops, or to build on. Sometimes, wetlands near the sea are dug away to make deep water harbours. This has happened to huge areas of wetlands all over the world.

These wetlands are in Sri Lanka. What can you see in the photograph that suggests that they are not wet all the year round?

This used to be a wetland. Water has been taken away from it to use to irrigate agricultural land. The plants are dying, because they are adapted to live in wet places, not dry ones.

Rainforests

Rainforests grow in the tropics, and also in cooler, temperate regions. They are the habitats for many different species of plants and animals. We say that they have a very high **biodiversity**.

Humans have cut down vast areas of rainforest. Many species of plants and animals that are adapted to live in rainforest habitats have already become extinct. Many others are **endangered**. This means that there are so few left that they may soon become extinct.

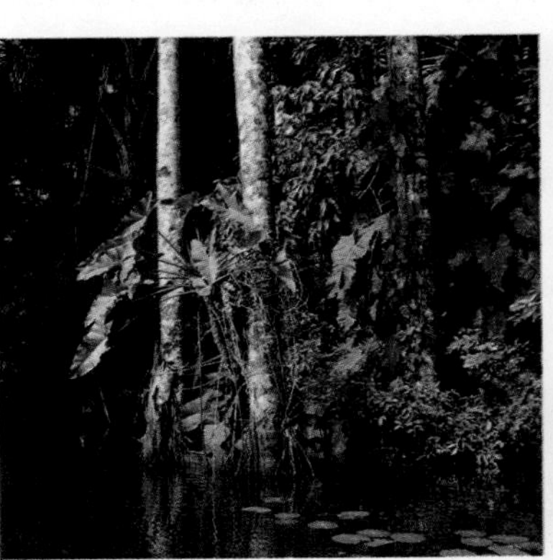

This rainforest in the Amazon in Peru may look undamaged but it has no large trees because they have been logged (cut down).

Orangutans need large areas of rainforest to live and breed. Deforestation in Borneo threatens them with extinction.

This palm oil plantation is growing where there was once tropical rainforest.

Coral reefs

Coral reefs are sometimes called 'the rainforests of the sea'. This is because they have a very high biodiversity.

Coral reefs are built by tiny animals similar to sea anemones. They live together in big colonies, and make hard coverings around themselves. These coverings are made from calcium carbonate.

The coral animals have tiny algae growing inside them. The algae make carbohydrates by photosynthesis. The coral animals use the carbohydrates for food.

Many different species of invertebrate animals and fish live their whole lives in coral reefs. Other animals, such as turtles and sharks, visit coral reefs to feed.

One of the biggest threats to coral reefs is acidification of sea water. Carbon dioxide in the air dissolves in sea water to produce a weak acid. The acidic sea water makes it difficult for the coral animals to build their skeletons.

Coral reefs have a huge biodiversity.

Questions

1 Explain each of these statements:
  - **a** The growing human population on Earth is causing habitat destruction.
  - **b** Habitat destruction can cause species to become extinct.

2 What are the producers in a coral reef?

3 Think about what you learnt about air pollution in Stage **7**. Explain what is happening to the amount of carbon dioxide in the air.

4 Think about what you learnt about the reactions between carbonates and acids in Stage **8**. Explain what might happen to the calcium carbonate in coral reefs, if the sea water becomes more acidic.

Summary

- **Humans destroy the habitats of animals and plants.**
- **Each species is adapted to live in a particular habitat. If that habitat is destroyed, the species may become extinct.**

2.9 Protecting the environment

The growing human population is causing increasing damage to the environment. Much of the damage is caused by pollution and habitat destruction.

What can we do to reduce the damage?

Countries all over the world get together to decide on ways to reduce harm to the environment. Several important international agreements have been signed.

Preserving wetlands

In 1971, representatives from 21 nations met in Iran to discuss the threat to the world's wetlands. They continued their discussions for several years. In 1975, they all signed an agreement called the Ramsar Convention. This listed things that they would all try to do to save the Earth's wetlands.

Since then, more and more nations have signed up to the Ramsar Convention. By 2012, 161 nations had joined.

Each country identifies its important wetlands, and puts measures into place to try to protect them. Representatives from each country meet at regular intervals, to discuss their progress.

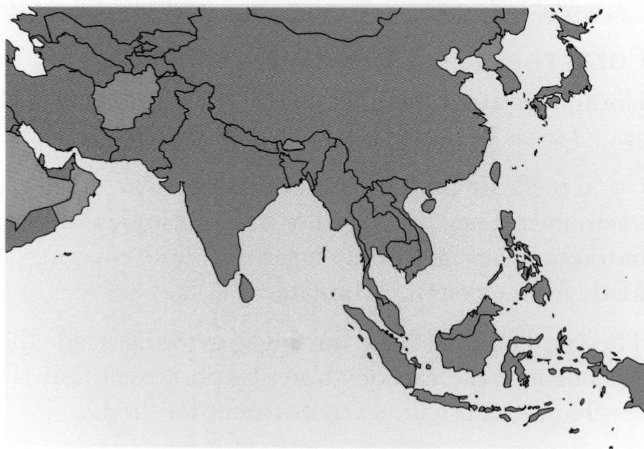

The countries shown in green on this map of Asia have signed up to the Ramsar Convention.

Question

A+I

1 Identify some of the countries that have **not** signed the Ramsar Convention. (You may need to use an atlas to help you.) Can you suggest why they have not signed?

Protecting the ozone layer

In Stage **7**, you learnt about how gases called chlorofluorocarbons (CFCs) damage the ozone layer. In 1989, a treaty came into force that was signed by many countries. They agreed to phase out the use of CFCs.

The combined efforts of so many countries have had an enormous effect. The addition of CFCs to the atmosphere has greatly decreased. Scientists predict that the ozone layer will eventually recover almost completely.

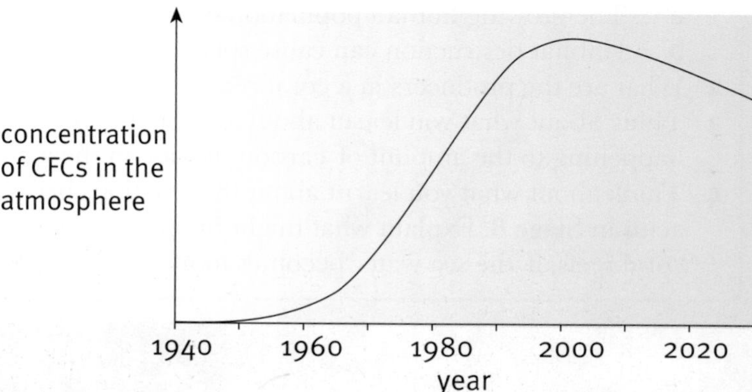

This graph shows how the concentration of CFCs in the atmosphere has changed since 1940, and also how it is predicted to change by 2030.

Questions

You will need to think about your work on ozone depletion in Stage **7** to answer these questions.

2 What is ozone, and where is the ozone layer?

3 Why is the ozone layer important to us?

A+I **4** Look at the graph on the previous page. Suggest why CFC levels began to rise in the 1950s.

A+I **5** Suggest why the level of CFCs did not begin to fall until after 2000, even though the international treaty to reduce CFCs first came into force in 1989.

Reducing carbon dioxide emissions

Countries have signed international treaties promising to reduce the amount of carbon dioxide they produce. However, this has proved very difficult to achieve. Most countries have not managed to meet the targets for reducing carbon dioxide emissions.

This means that carbon dioxide concentrations in the atmosphere are still rising. This is causing the Earth to get warmer. This is called **global warming**.

Global warming will affect the habitats of many different species. Species that are adapted to live in cold places will have to move, or they may become extinct.

Global warming affects climate patterns. Some countries will get less rainfall than they do now. Others may get more. This may make it difficult for people to grow their usual crops. It could also change the habitats of plant and animal species.

Polar bears need to hunt on sea ice to find seals, their main prey. Global warming may cause much of the sea ice in the Arctic to disappear.

Question

6 Suggest why it has proved to be so difficult for countries to reduce their carbon dioxide emissions. (You will need to think about where the carbon dioxide comes from.)

Summary

- Nations all over the world are acting together to try to reduce the harm we do to the environment.
- The Ramsar Convention has helped to save many wetlands.
- There has been great success in reducing CFC emissions.
- It is proving very difficult to reduce carbon dioxide emissions.

2.1 The photograph shows a snowy egret, which is adapted to live in wet places.

Describe **three** adaptations that help the egret to live in its habitat.
For each adaptation, explain how it helps the egret to survive. [6]

2.2 The diagram shows a food web in a forest in Europe.

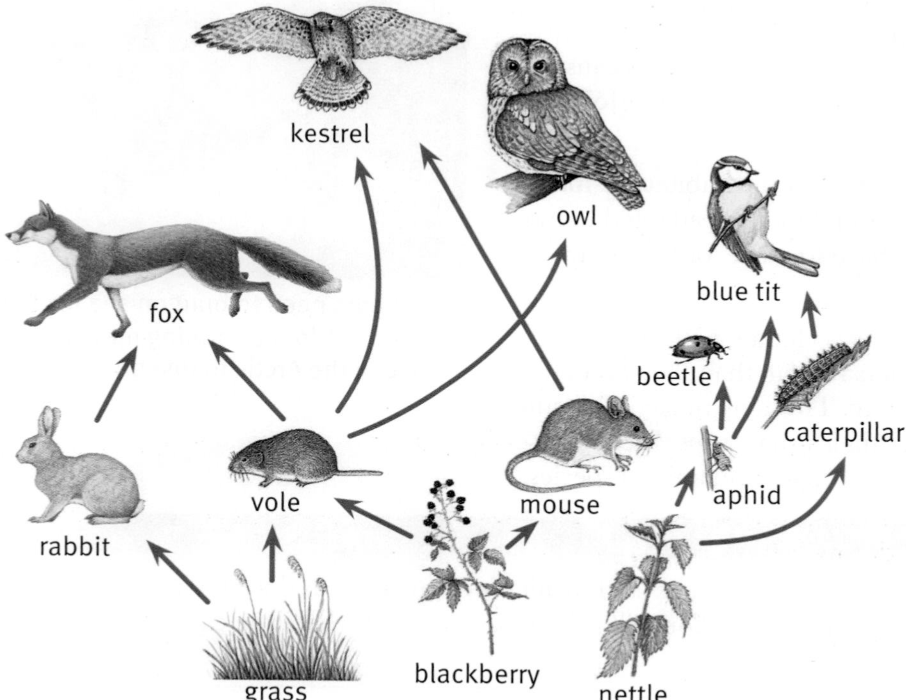

- **a** Name the **three** producers in the food web. [1]
- **b** Name **one** predator in the food web. [1]
- **c** What do the arrows in the food web represent? [1]
- **d** Draw **three** different food chains, from this food web, that contain an aphid. [1]
- **e** Suggest what would happen to the populations of the other animals in the food web, if the voles became extinct. Explain your suggestions. [3]

2.3 The photograph shows a fungus growing on horse dung (faeces).

a What name do we give to organisms like this fungus, that break down organic matter? [1]

b Describe how the fungus breaks down the horse dung. [2]

c Explain why organisms that break down waste materials are important in a habitat. [3]

2.4 The Serengeti Plains is a large area of grassland in Africa. The first graph shows the amount of rainfall on the Serengeti Plains in each month during one year. The second graph shows the mean height of the grass during the same year.

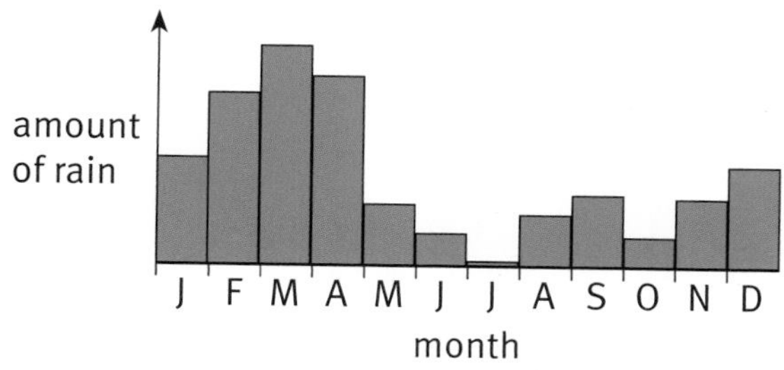

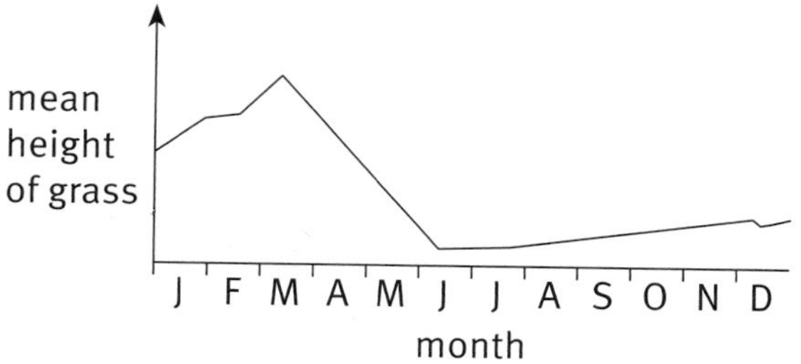

a In which month did most rain fall? [1]

b Is there any correlation between the amount of rainfall and the height of the grass? Explain your answer. [2]

Zebras are herbivores that eat grass. The graph below shows the size of the zebra population during the same year.

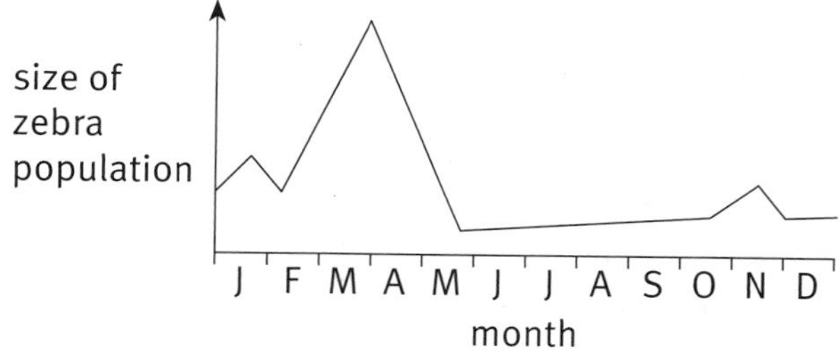

c Using the information in the first two graphs, suggest reasons for the changes in the zebra population during the year. [4]

3.1 Keys

If you did any ecology investigations in Unit **2**, you had to try to identify the organisms that you found. One way of doing this is to look for a picture of an organism that looks like yours, in books or on the internet. Another way is to use a **key**.

A key is a set of questions about the organism you want to identify. The answer to each question takes you to another question. You work through all the questions until you arrive at the name of the organism.

Here is a simple key to help someone to identify an invertebrate. (You will have to imagine you have the whole animal to look at, not just these pictures.)

Does it have legs?

- Yes → Does it have more than six legs?
  - Yes → **crab**
  - No → Does it have four wings?
    - Yes → **dragonfly**
    - No → **housefly**
- No → Is its body made up of rings?
  - Yes → **earthworm**
  - No → **slug**

To use the key:

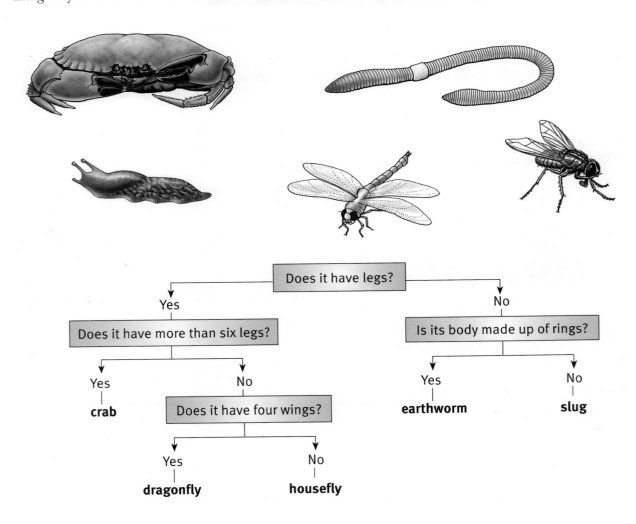

- Choose one organism that you want to identify.
- Starting at the top of the key, answer the first question – yes or no?
- Follow the line to the next question, and keep going until you have the name of the organism.

Some keys are arranged differently. The idea is the same, but in this kind of key you are given two statements, **a** and **b**. You choose which statement describes the organism. Once you have made the choice, this leads you to another pair of choices.

1 **a** has legs .... go to 2
  b does not have legs .... go to 3

2 **a** has six legs .... go to 4
  b has more than six legs .... **crab**

3 **a** body is made up of rings .... **earthworm**
  b body is not made up of rings .... **slug**

4 **a** has four wings .... **dragonfly**
  b has two wings .... **housefly**

For example, to identify the dragonfly, you would work through these statements: 1a, 2a, 4a.

Constructing keys

Imagine you are going to write a key to identify these four students.

Step 1: Think of a way that you can split the students into two groups. For example, you could split them into male and female students. So your first question could be:

Is the student male?

Step 2: Now take just one of these groups – say both of the female students. Think of another way to split them into two. For example, you could use the colour of their hair.

Deidre

Ben

Anna

Ari

Questions

A+I **1** Copy and complete this key. Your key should enable (permit) someone else to identify the four students.

A+I **2** Write another key to identify the four students, but this time use the style of key that has two statements, **a** and **b**, to choose from.
You could use the same features as in the key you wrote for Question **1**, or you could set yourself a challenge and use different pairs of features.

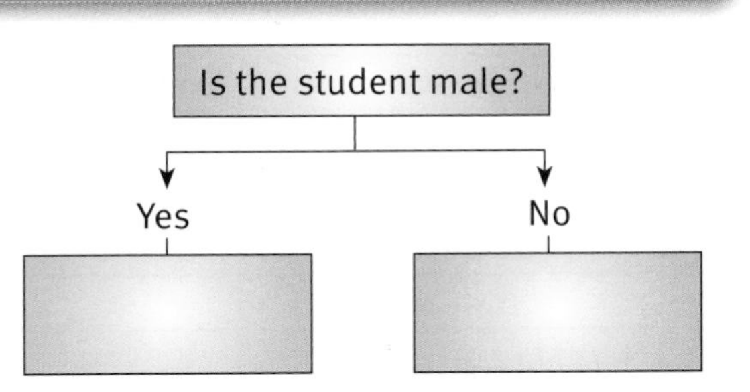

Summary

- A key is a method of identifying an unknown organism.
- A key has a series of questions or statements, which you work through in sequence to find the name of the organism.

3.2 Variation

In Stage 7, you learnt that living organisms are classified into **species**. A species is a group of organisms that share the same features, and that can breed together to produce fertile offspring.

Although all the members of a species share the same features, no two individuals are ever exactly alike. The differences between the individuals within a species are called **variation**.

All of these snails are the same species.

Question

1 The Latin name of the species of snail shown in the photograph is *Cepaea nemoralis*.
   a Why do scientists give species Latin names?
   b Snails are eaten by birds. Snails with plain yellow or cream shells are generally found in dry grass, while snails with stripes are often found in woodland. Suggest why.

A+I

Activity 3.2

Measuring variation in humans

SE

In this activity, you are going to measure and record the variation in wrist circumference in your class. If you have forgotten about tally charts and frequency diagrams, you may need to look back at the work you did in Stage 7.

1 Measure the circumference of the right wrist of every person in your class. Write down your measurements in a list. Remember to write down the units you have used for your measurements.
2 Use your measurements to calculate the mean (average) wrist circumference of the people in your class.
3 Draw a results table like this. You may need to change the numbers in the first column a little, to fit the range of measurements you have found. (Have a look at the smallest and largest measurements you have made.)

Wrist circumference / cm	Tally	Number of people
8.0–8.9		
9.0–9.9		
10.0–10.9		
11.0–11.9		
12.0–12.9		
13.0–13.9		
14.0–14.9		
15.0–15.9		
16.0–16.9		

continued ...

... continued

4 Put a mark in the appropriate 'Tally' column for each wrist circumference you have measured. Add up all the tally marks for each row, and write the number in the 'Numbers' column.
5 Now you are ready to draw a frequency diagram of your results. The wrist circumference should go on the horizontal axis, and the number of people on the vertical axis.
6 Draw bars to show the number of people in each size range. The bars should touch each other.

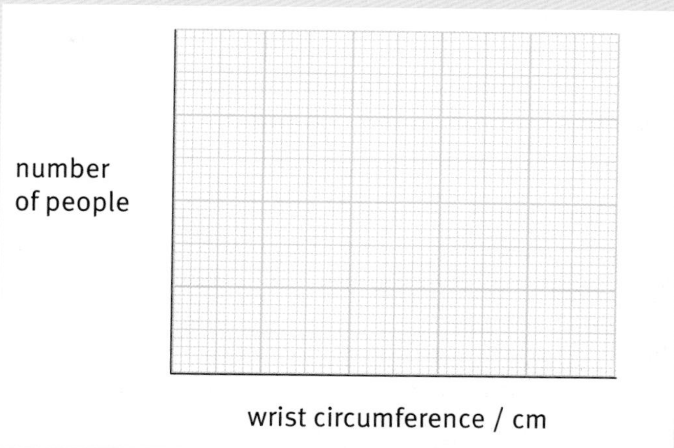

Questions

A1 What is the overall range of wrist circumference in your class (that is, the smallest and the largest measurements)?
A2 Which wrist circumference is the most common in your class?
A3 Describe any patterns that you can see in your results.

What causes variation?

Why do the people in your class have different sizes of wrist?

Part of the reason is that you have different **genes**. Your genes determine many different things about you – such as whether you are male or female, or what colour hair you have.

Another reason is your **environment**. This means anything around you that affects you or the kind of lifestyle that you live. For example, a person who uses their hands and arms to do heavy work may have very large wrists. Someone who did not get enough to eat when they were growing up may have very small wrists.

Questions

2 Suggest **two** features of humans that are caused by their genes, and are **not** affected by their environment.

A+I **3** Suggest **two** features of humans – other than wrist circumference – that are affected by both genes and environment.

Summary
- The differences between the individuals in a species are called variation.
- Variation is caused by genes and by environment.

3.3 Inheritance

Everyone knows that offspring tend to be like their parents. But why is this? And why are they not ever **exactly** the same?

Each of the animals in the photographs has inherited many of its features from its parents. **Inheritance** is the passing of features from parents to their offspring.

A family of cats.

A family of elephants.

Giraffes always give birth to giraffes, not to horses or tigers.

Questions

1 List **three** features that the young giraffe has inherited from its parents.
2 List **three** features that the kittens have inherited from their parents.

Genes

You are human because you inherited human features from your parents. An animal that belongs to one species always gives birth to young that belong to the same species.

This happens because each animal has a set of instructions in its cells. These instructions are called **genes**. The genes determine the characteristics of the animal. They provide a set of instructions for building an animal belonging to a particular species.

All organisms have genes. Plants, bacteria and fungi all have genes.

Genes are passed on (transferred) to offspring from parents. Half of your genes came from your father, and half from your mother. This is why children tend to have some characteristics like their father, and some like their mother.

In each generation, children inherit genes from both of their parents.

Genes and environment

As we have seen, your genes are not the only reason for why you are you. Your environment also has a big effect.

For example, a child might inherit the genes to grow tall from his parents. But if he does not get enough to eat while he is a small child, then he may not grow tall.

Some of your characteristics are to do with your behaviour, not what you look like.

Uggh
Hola! Me llamo Rafaela.
Hi! My name's Brad.

The gorilla cannot speak words. She does not have genes to build a brain and vocal chords that can produce speech. Rafaela and Brad do have these genes, so they can both talk. But they speak in different ways because they have grown up in different environments. Rafaela's family speak Spanish. Brad has grown up in an English-speaking family.

Questions

3 The twins in the photograph have identical genes.

Describe **three** features of the twins in the photograph that are caused by their genes.

4 Describe **three** of their features that are caused by their environment.

Summary

- Genes are passed on from parents to offspring.
- Genes provide a set of instructions that determine some of the characteristics of an organism.
- Some characteristics are caused by an organism's environment.

3.4 More about inheritance

Genes and chromosomes

Your genes are found inside the nucleus of every cell in your body. The genes are found on long threads called **chromosomes**. Genes and chromosomes are made of a chemical called **DNA**.

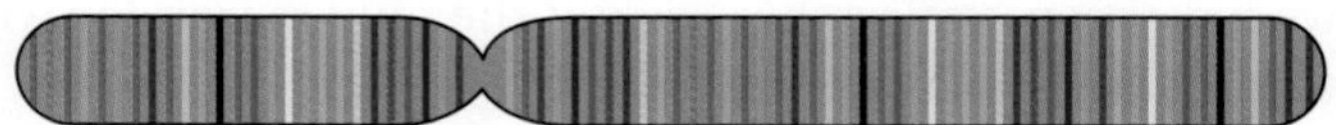

Each chromosome is a long chain of hundreds of different genes.

Each gene is a set of instructions for the cell. The gene tells the cell how to make a particular substance. All the cells in your body have the same genes, so they all have the same sets of instructions.

For example, one of your genes has instructions for making the pigment (colour) of your hair. Another one has instructions for making the shape of your nose.

Most genes have two or more different forms. For example, the gene with the instructions for making hair pigment in humans has many different forms. There are forms that produce blonde hair, brown hair, red hair and black hair.

The gene that gives instructions for growing hair in guinea pigs has two forms. One form produces smooth hair, and the other produces rough hair.

Questions

1 In which part of a cell is DNA found?
2 Explain the difference between a gene and a chromosome.
3 Which form of the hair colour gene do you have?

Activity 3.4
Modelling genes and chromosomes

You are going to design and make a model of a cell containing chromosomes. Here are some decisions to make before you begin.

- Will you make a 2D model (for example, sticking things onto a sheet of paper) or a 3D model?
- How will you show the outside of the cell – the cell surface membrane?
- How will you model the nucleus of the cell?
- What will you use to model the chromosomes?
- How many chromosomes will you put into your cell?
- How will you show the different genes on the chromosomes?

Passing on genes

As you grow, your cells divide to make more and more cells. Each time a cell divides, a complete set of chromosomes and genes is passed on to each daughter (new) cell.

But where did your very first cell come from? You began your life as a zygote. This is a cell that was made when the nucleus of your father's sperm cell and your mother's egg cell fused together. The sperm cell contained chromosomes and genes from your father. The egg cell contained chromosomes and genes from your mother. Exactly half of your chromosomes and genes came from each of your parents.

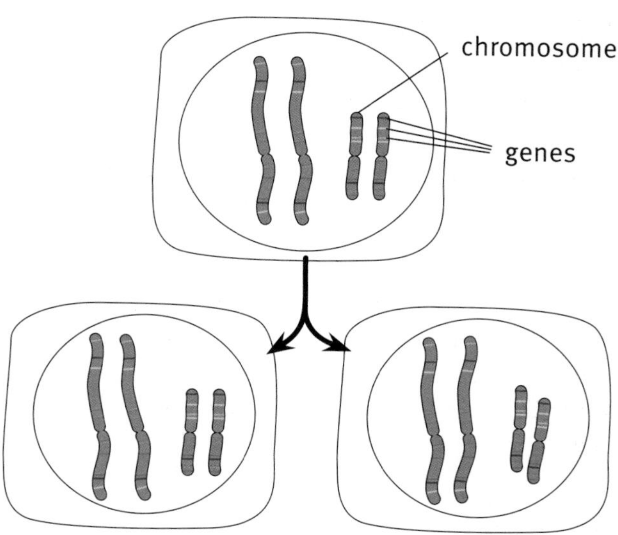

When a cell divides, the daughter cells inherit exactly the same genes as the parent cell.

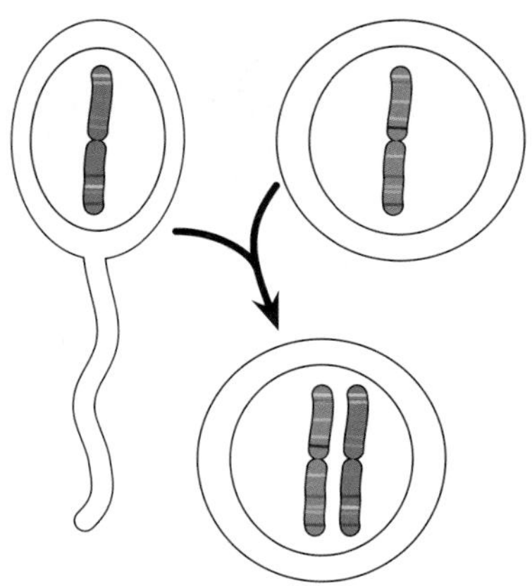

At fertilisation, the chromosomes of the male parent combine with the chromosomes of the female parent.

So your genes are a mixture of ones that came from your father, and ones that came from your mother. They can mix up in almost any combination. You might have a gene from your father that gave you curly hair, and a gene from your mother that helped to make you good at running.

Children inherit half of their genes from each of their parents.

Summary

- Genes are found on chromosomes, in the nucleus of a cell.
- Most genes come in several different forms.
- Offspring inherit half of their genes from each of their parents.

3.5 Selective breeding

Water buffalo are kept in many parts of the world. They are used to pull carts and ploughs, to produce milk and to produce meat.

Originally, water buffalo were wild animals. People began to domesticate water buffalo about 5000 years ago. 'Domesticating' a type of animal means taming it, so that you can keep it and use it.

We think that the people who first domesticated water buffalo took care about which ones they allowed to breed together. Wild buffalo are very large and can be aggressive. People probably chose to breed together buffalo that were not too big, and that were docile (calm) animals. They carried on doing this, generation after generation.

These features of the water buffalo were affected by the forms of genes that they had. The chosen parent buffalo passed on their genes to their offspring.

Of course, the early farmers did not know anything about genes. They just knew that small, calm water buffalo tended to have small, calm offspring. Over time, and many generations, the water buffalo became gradually smaller and more docile.

Wild water buffalo.

A domesticated water buffalo in the Philippines.

Breeding sheep

Let's say that you have a flock of sheep. You want to improve the length of the wool that your sheep produce. This is what you would do.

- Choose the rams (male sheep) and ewes (female sheep) that have the longest wool.
- Breed these rams and ewes together. You would not let any of the other sheep breed together.
- When the offspring of your chosen rams and ewes have grown up, choose the ones with the longest wool. Allow them to breed together.
- You would keep doing this for many generations.

This process is called **selective breeding**. Eventually – with much patience, and after many years – you should end up with a flock of sheep with longer wool than the ones you began with.

We think that the mouflon was the wild sheep from which all today's breeds of sheep have been produced.

The Merino breed has been produced by selective breeding for sheep that produce thick, fine wool.

The Assaf breed has been produced by selective breeding for sheep that produce lots of milk and good quality meat.

Questions

A+I

1 Wheat is a crop that is grown in many different countries. The seed heads of wheat plants are called ears. The seeds are called grain. Wheat grain is used to make flour.

The first photograph shows one of the ancestors of modern wheat. The second photograph shows a modern variety (breed) of wheat.

a What differences can you see between the old type of wheat and the modern wheat?

b Explain how the modern variety of wheat could have been produced.

A+I

2 Imagine you are a farmer with a herd of goats, which you keep to produce milk. You want to build up a herd of goats that produce more milk.

Describe what you would do. (Take care – remember that only females will produce milk! Males do not produce milk.)

This scientist is trying to produce better varieties of wheat. She is rubbing pollen from the flowers of one plant onto the stigmas of another plant. Can you suggest why she is keeping the plants in a laboratory, rather than outside?

Summary

- When people breed animals and plants, they can choose which ones they will allow to breed.
- Animals and plants with desired features are allowed to breed, but those that do not have the desired features are not allowed to breed.
- This is done for many generations. This is selective breeding.

3.6 Natural selection

We have seen how selective breeding can, over time, produce new varieties of animals and plants. Can a similar process happen in the wild, without any involvement of humans?

Let's think about how this might work. We will use an imaginary example.

Long ago, in a population of giraffes, some had long necks and some had short necks. This was because they had different forms of a gene. The giraffes ate leaves on trees.

One year, there was a severe drought. Food was in short supply. When all the lower leaves had been eaten, only the long-necked giraffes could get food.

Most of the short-necked giraffes died. Only the long-necked giraffes survived.

The long-necked giraffes reproduced. Their offspring inherited the genes for long necks.

Question

1 From the giraffe story, give an example of each of the following:

a variation
b adaptation
c a factor affecting the size of a population.

Comparing selective breeding and natural selection

The way in which the length of giraffes' necks may have changed is called **natural selection**.

Natural selection is similar to the process of selective breeding. The table shows some ways in which they are similar – but not quite the same.

Selective breeding	Natural selection
To begin with, there is a population of organisms that show variation. The variation is partly caused by their genes.	To begin with, there is a population of organisms that show variation. The variation is partly caused by their genes.
People choose individuals that have characteristics that they want.	Individuals that have characteristics that provide the best adaptations to their habitat are more likely to survive.
Only the individuals with the characteristics that people want are allowed to breed.	Only individuals with the best adaptations survive long enough to breed.
These individuals pass on their genes, and therefore their characteristics, to their offspring.	These individuals pass on their genes, and therefore their characteristics, to their offspring.

Question

2 Use the table to find **two** differences between selective breeding and natural selection.

Activity 3.6

Mountain hares and global warming

Mountain hares live in places that get very cold in winter. Most mountain hares have coats that are brown in summer and turn white in winter. This camouflages them from foxes and other predators.

Some mountain hares have coats that do not turn white in winter. They stay brown.

In your group, use the theory of natural selection to discuss what might happen to mountain hare coats if global warming happens.

Make a presentation, or construct a poster, to explain your ideas.

A mountain hare in winter.

A mountain hare in summer.

Summary

- Some of the variation between organisms is caused by their genes.
- Individuals that have variations that best adapt them to their environment are most likely to survive and reproduce.
- These individuals pass on their genes to their offspring. The offspring may inherit the genes for these adaptations.
- This process is named natural selection.

3.7 Natural selection in action

The examples of how giraffes might have got their long necks, and how the coats of mountain hares might change, are just theories. We don't have any evidence that this is actually what happens.

However, scientists have now found many examples of natural selection happening. Here are two of them.

Bacteria and antibiotics

In Stage **7**, you learnt that antibiotics are drugs that we can take to kill bacteria that are causing disease in our bodies.

There are many different antibiotics. But doctors are finding that many antibiotics do not work any more. Bacteria have become **resistant** to them.

This is what has happened.

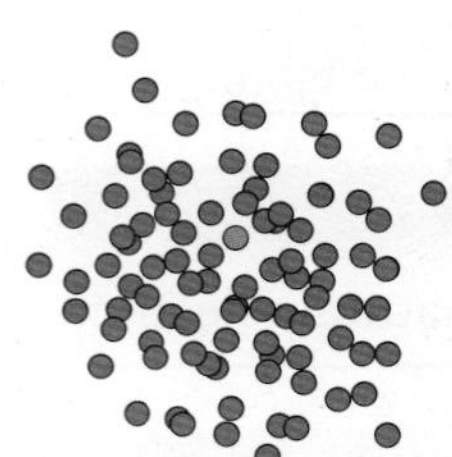

In a population of bacteria, not every one is alike. By chance, one may have a gene that makes it resistant to an antibiotic.

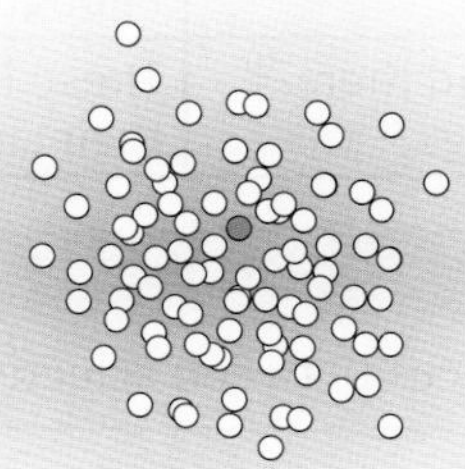

Antibiotic is added, which kills the bacteria that are not resistant.

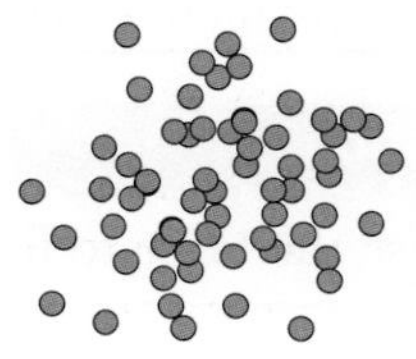

The resistant one can now multiply and form a population of resistant bacteria just like itself.

Questions

1 Explain what is meant when we say that bacteria have become 'resistant' to an antibiotic.

A+I

2 Scientists say that we should try not to use antibiotics for mild illnesses. We should save them for when people have serious illnesses. Suggest an explanation for this advice.

Peppered moths

Peppered moths live in England. Most peppered moths have pale wings, but some have dark wings.

Peppered moths rest on tree trunks. They are hunted and eaten by birds. The pale colour of peppered moths camouflages them perfectly against tree trunks that have lichens growing on them. (Lichen is an organism that grows on rocks and trees, especially where the air is unpolluted.)

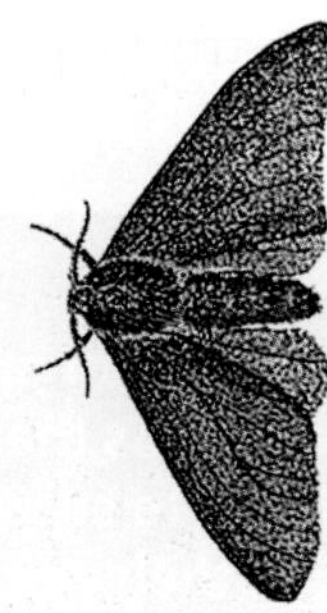

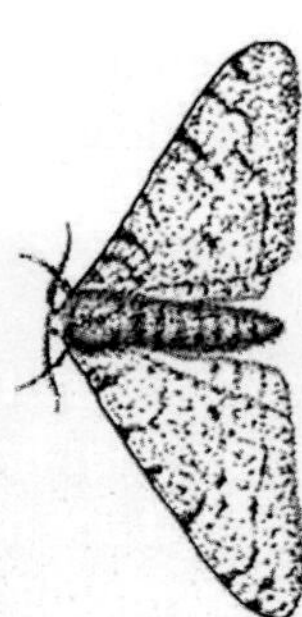

The dark and pale varieties of the peppered moth.

Until the year 1849, almost all peppered moths were pale. Then more and more dark ones began to appear. By 1900, almost all of the peppered moths near some English cities were dark ones.

During this time, industry was developing rapidly in England. Many factories burnt coal, which produced smoke. The smoke polluted the air. It killed lichens, and made tree trunks dark.

Scientists have done experiments which show that birds can see light moths more easily than dark moths, when they are resting on dark tree trunks.

Now we can explain why the dark variety of the moths became more common. As the tree trunks got darker, the pale moths were not well camouflaged. Many of them were killed and eaten by birds.

But the birds could not see the dark moths. The dark moths were more likely to survive than the light ones. The dark moths reproduced, and passed on the gene for their dark colour to their offspring.

Each generation, more dark moths were born and fewer pale moths.

Today, pollution has greatly decreased in England. Factories are not allowed to pollute the air. Tree trunks are covered by pale-coloured lichens again. Almost all peppered moths found today are pale.

Can you spot the moth?

This illustration was drawn in the middle of the nineteenth century. It shows steel factories in the town of Sheffield, England.

Dark and pale varieties of the peppered moth on a dark tree trunk.

Question

3 Use the ideas of natural selection to explain why most peppered moths in England today are pale, not dark.

Summary

- When antibiotics are used, any bacteria that have a gene that makes them resistant to the antibiotic survive and reproduce. Natural selection causes populations of resistant bacteria to be produced.
- Natural selection caused dark varieties of the peppered moth to become more common in England during the nineteenth century.

3.8 Charles Darwin

Charles Darwin was born in Shrewsbury, in England, in 1809. Although he trained to be a doctor, he always had a great interest in the natural world around him. He was very observant, and made records of many of the plants and animals that he saw in his garden and on his travels.

Darwin corresponded with many other scientists, with whom he remained friends for much of his life. One of these was Charles Lyell. In 1830, Lyell published a book called *Principles of Geology*. In this book, Lyell suggested that the mountains and valleys that we see today have not always been there, and they will change in the future. Lyell also thought that the fossils which people found in rocks were remains of different kinds of organisms that had lived millions of years ago. These were both new ideas. Most people thought that rocks and species were unchanging.

In 1831, Charles Darwin began a five-year voyage as the naturalist on board the ship *The Beagle*. He visited many countries in South America, as well as the Galapagos Islands in the Pacific Ocean. He took Lyell's book with him. He began to think that, if mountains and rocks could change over time, then perhaps species of organisms could change, too.

Darwin was particularly interested in the species of birds that he saw in the Galapagos Islands. Each island seemed to have its own set of species, and most of the species were slightly different on each island. Each finch was adapted for a slightly different lifestyle. For example, some had thick, strong beaks for eating large seeds, while others had thinner beaks, better for eating small seeds or insects.

When he eventually arrived home, Darwin began to develop an idea. Perhaps all of the different species of finches on the different islands in the Galapagos had developed from one original species. But at first he could not work out how this could have happened.

In 1855, Darwin took up pigeon breeding. This was a popular hobby in England. Many different varieties of pigeons had been produced, but no-one had kept records of where they all came from. Darwin had the idea that they had all been developed from a species of wild pigeon, the rock dove. He began to see a way in which the different species of finches on the Galapagos Islands might have developed.

A portrait of Charles Darwin made in 1840, when he was 31 years old.

An engraving of *The Beagle*, sailing through the Straits of Magellan.

Darwin thought that all of these different species of finches might all have come from the same ancestor.

3.8 Charles Darwin

In 1859, another book containing new ideas was published. The author was Thomas Malthus. Malthus suggested that the population of humans on Earth could not grow for ever. Eventually, he wrote, there would not be enough food for us all.

This was another important piece in the puzzle. Now Darwin thought that he could see the steps that could lead to the evolution of a new species. In 1859, he published his most famous book, *The Origin of Species*.

These were the main points in his theory:

- The organisms in a species are not all exactly the same as each other. They show variation.
- Many organisms will not survive until adulthood. They may be killed by predators, die of disease, or not be able to get enough to eat.
- The individuals that have variations that make them best adapted to their habitat are the ones that have the best chance of surviving.
- The best-adapted organisms are therefore the ones that are most likely to breed and have offspring.
- The offspring will inherit some of the features of their parents.
- If this continues, generation after generation, then there could be a change in the species over time. Eventually, it could change so much that it would be a different species.

Darwin called his theory **natural selection**. This is the term that we still use today.

This poster, printed in 1891, shows some of the many pigeon breeds that existed in Darwin's time.

Activity 3.8

Darwin's big idea

SE

In your group, look at each of the steps in Darwin's theory. For each step, discuss what you think helped him to think out his theory.

Some people in the group could research some more information about this, using the library or the internet.

Now plan how you can present your ideas to the rest of the class. For example, you could draw a big mind map, or write your ideas down in words.

Summary

- Darwin was the first person to suggest a way in which one species could change into another species.
- Darwin put forward (proposed) the theory of natural selection.
- The theory of natural selection states that the individuals that are best adapted to their environment are the ones that are most likely to pass on their features to the next generation.

Unit 3 End of unit questions

3.1 Choose the word that matches each of these descriptions. You can use each word once, more than once or not at all.

cytoplasm **DNA** **environment** **fertilisation** **gene**
inheritance **nucleus** **protein** **unit** **variation**

a The chemical from which chromosomes are made.
b The part of a cell in which chromosomes are found.
c Part of a chromosome that determines one particular characteristic of an organism.
d The passing on of genes from parents to their offspring.
e Differences between organisms belonging to the same species. [5]

3.2 The photograph shows six flowers A–F.

Complete the key, to allow someone to identify each of the flowers. The Latin names of the flowers are:

A *Limnanthes* **B** *Viola* **C** *Potentilla* **D** *Lunaria*
E *Erodium* **F** *Silene*

1 **a** flower has four petals .... *Lunaria*
b flower has more than four petals ... go to 2

2 **a**
b [5]

3.3 Pedro wants to breed strawberry plants that have larger fruits.
He chooses five of his strongest strawberry plants and plants them in the same part of his garden. When they produce fruits, he collects the fruits and finds the mean mass of the fruit from each plant.
These are his results.

	Plant A	Plant B	Plant C	Plant D	Plant E
Mean mass of one fruit / g	23.8	24.2	21.3	26.2	25.9

a Explain why it was important for Pedro to plant all five plants in the same part of his garden. [2]
b Describe how Pedro could find the mean mass of one fruit on Plant **A**. [2]
c Which two plants should Pedro breed together? [1]
d Pedro breeds the two plants together by taking pollen from one of them and brushing it onto the stigma of the other one. Explain why he does this. [3]
e Suggest what Pedro should do next. [3]

3.4 A bacterium called *Staphyloccus pneumoniae* is a major cause of a serious infection of the lungs, called pneumonia. The graph shows the percentage of cases of pneumonia in which the bacteria were resistant to penicillin (an antibiotic).

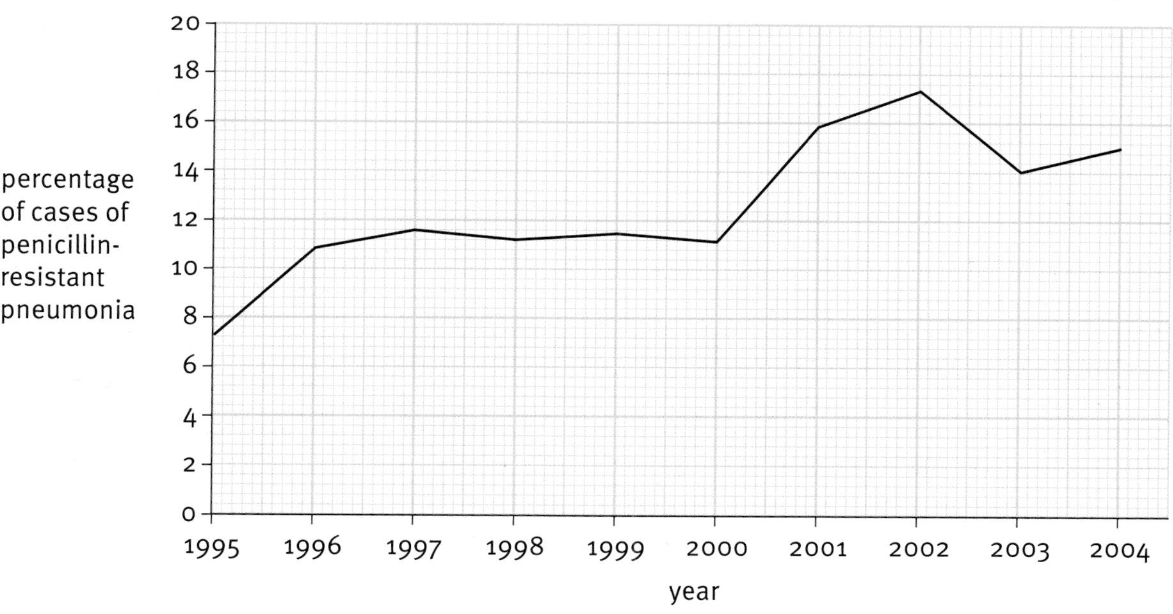

a What is an antibiotic? [1]
b Describe the trend shown in the graph. [1]
c Suggest how natural selection has caused this trend. [3]

4.1 The structure of the atom

Atoms

In Stage **8** you learnt that **atoms** are so small that you cannot see them without using the most powerful microscopes yet invented. The word 'atom' comes from a Greek word that means 'cannot be split'.

All the atoms in a particular element are the same. Different elements have different atoms. For example the atoms in sodium are all the same as one another. They are different from the atoms in potassium.

What is an atom like?

Scientists have discovered that atoms are made up of even smaller particles. Atoms are made up of three kinds of particles: **protons**, **neutrons** and **electrons**.

These particles are arranged in a similar way in every atom.

The protons and neutrons are grouped closely together in the centre of the atom. They form the **nucleus** of the atom. (Take care not to confuse the nucleus of a cell with the nucleus of an atom!)

The electrons move around the nucleus.

The three different particles in an atom have different properties.

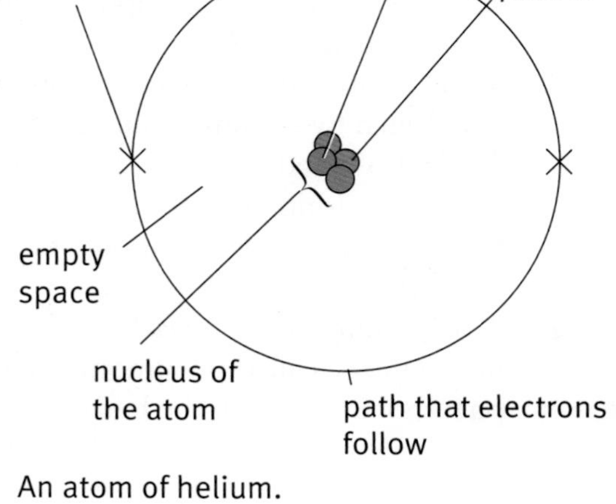

An atom of helium.

- Protons and neutrons have much more mass than electrons. In fact, electrons have almost no mass at all.
- Protons have a positive electrical **charge**.
- Neutrons have no electrical charge.
- Electrons have a negative electrical charge.

There is a lot of empty space between the parts of the atom. This space really is completely empty – there is nothing in it at all.

Questions

1 Which particle in an atom has a positive electrical charge?
2 Which of the three particles that make up an atom has the smallest mass?
3 Which particles make up the nucleus of an atom?

A+I
4 The size of the negative charge of an electron is exactly the same as the size of the positive charge of a proton. What is the overall charge of the helium atom shown in the diagram?

How did scientists come up with this model of the atom?

Scientists from different parts of the world have worked on a number of different ideas that have led to the model of the atom which we use today.

In the late 1890s a British scientist called J.J. Thompson discovered the electron. His model for the atom was that the different parts of the atom were scattered throughout the structure.

One of Thompson's research students originally came from New Zealand. His name was Ernest Rutherford. Rutherford discovered the proton in 1909 and the nucleus in 1911. Rutherford's most famous experiment was the gold foil experiment.

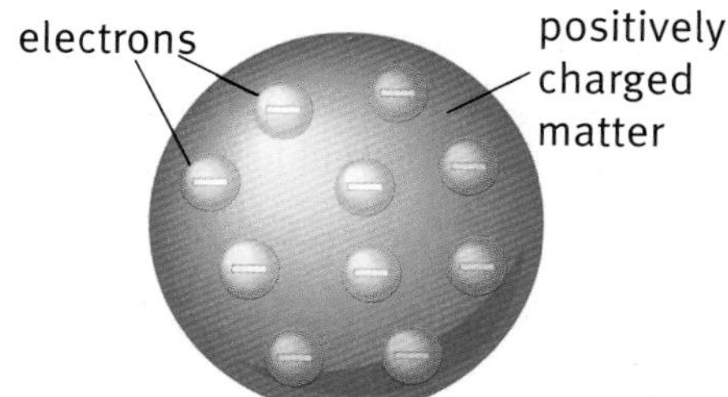

Thompson's model of the atom.

In this experiment Rutherford fired fast-moving particles – smaller than an atom – at very thin gold foil. Most of the particles passed straight through the foil. Only a few of these particles (about 1 in 8000) were deflected in various directions. ('Deflected' means that their direction was changed.) This led Rutherford to have the idea that gold atoms must be mostly empty space, with their particles packed into a dense nucleus at the centre. This helped to move towards the model of the atom we use today.

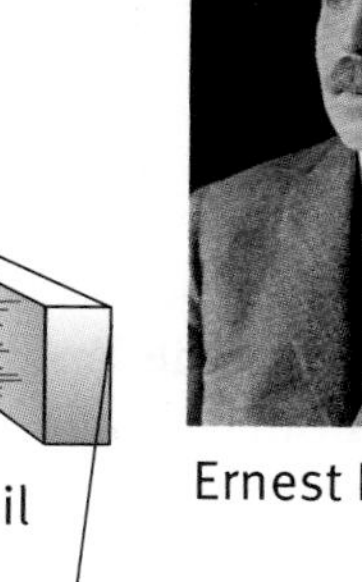

Ernest Rutherford.

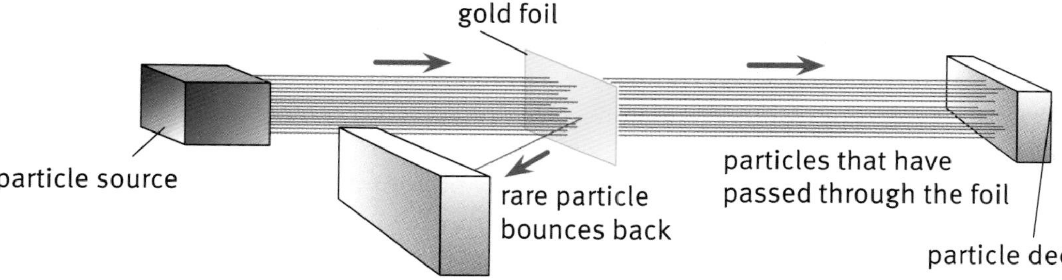

Rutherford's gold foil experiment.

James Chadwick worked with Rutherford and Thompson. In 1932, he proved that neutrons exist.

The stories of these men show how scientists from all over the world work together and develop their ideas. Each scientist builds on the discoveries of others. These scientists won Nobel prizes for their work. Their experiments and ideas have helped us to understand the structure of the atom.

There is still a lot that we do not know about atoms. Scientists continue to work to improve our understanding of the structure of the atom. For example, scientists from all over the world are using the Large Hadron Collider in Switzerland to further understand the structure of matter.

Tunnel in the Large Hadron Collider.

Summary

- Atoms are made up of protons, neutrons and electrons.
- The nucleus of an atom is made up of protons and neutrons.
- Electrons move around the nucleus of an atom.
- Scientists from around the world have helped us understand the structure of the atom.

4.2 More about the structure of the atom

Different sorts of atoms

In Stage **8** you learnt about the first 20 elements and their symbols in the **Periodic Table**. Now you will learn more about the structure of the atoms of these elements.

metals

non-metals

1 H hydrogen 1

1 – atomic number; 1 – mass number

																	2 He helium 4
3 Li lithium 7	4 Be beryllium 9											5 B boron 11	6 C carbon 12	7 N nitrogen 14	8 O oxygen 16	9 F fluorine 19	10 Ne neon 20
11 Na sodium 23	12 Mg magnesium 24											13 Al aluminium 27	14 Si silicon 28	15 P phosphorus 31	16 S sulfur 32	17 Cl chlorine 35	18 Ar argon 40
19 K potassium 39	20 Ca calcium 40																

- The atoms of the elements increase in mass as you progress from left to right and downwards in the Periodic Table. For example, an atom of hydrogen has less mass than an atom of sodium.
- Each element has an **atomic number**. This tells you how many protons it contains. The atomic number increases by one with every element.
- Each element has a **mass number**. This tells you how many protons and neutrons each atom in the element has in total.
- Protons have a **positive charge**. Electrons have a **negative charge**.
- An atom has no overall charge, because the number of protons is the same as the number of electrons.

Let's take lithium as an example.

- Atomic number = 3
- Mass number = 7
- Number of protons = 3
- Number of electrons = 3
- Number of neutrons = ?

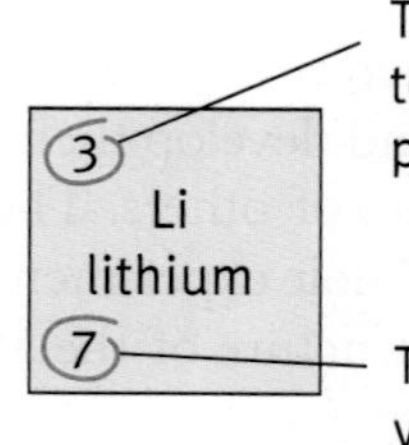
3
Li
lithium
7
The atomic number tells you how many protons there are.
The mass number tells you how many protons plus neutrons there are.

The mass number tells you that for lithium the number of protons and neutrons is seven. We know there are three protons so we can work out that there are four neutrons.

Arranging the electrons.

The electrons are arranged in electron **shells** or **orbits** around the nucleus. This is the **electronic structure**. The first shell has only room for two electrons. The second and third shells each have room for up to eight electrons. A Danish scientist called Niels Bohr first had the idea that the electrons move in different shells around the nucleus. He was awarded a Nobel prize for his work.

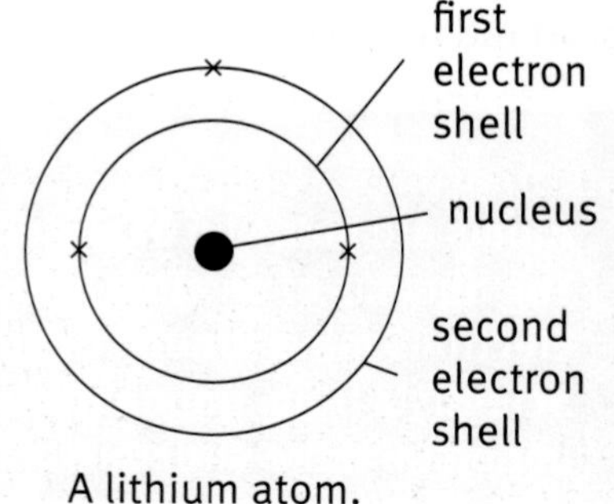
first electron shell
nucleus
second electron shell

A lithium atom.

Look carefully at the diagrams as the atoms get bigger.

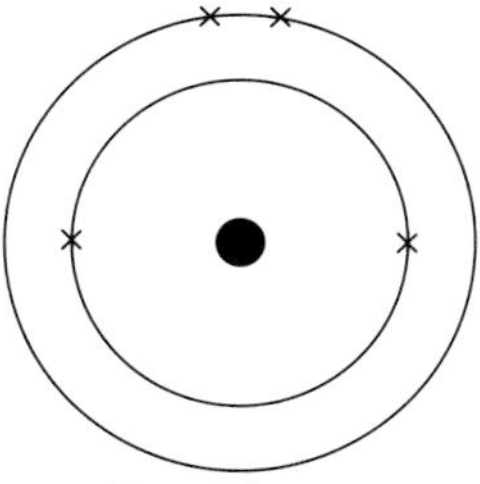

Beryllium.

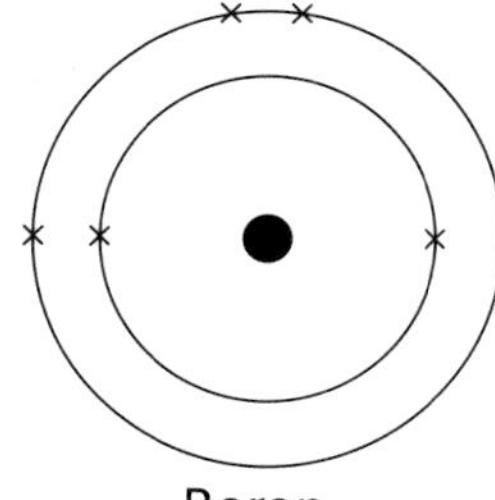

Boron.

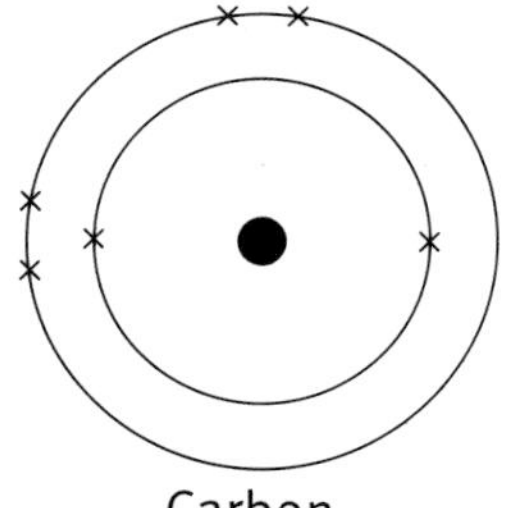

Carbon.

The arrangement of electrons in an atom is often written as numbers. For example, the electron arrangement for an atom of boron can be written as 2,3. This means there are two electrons in the first shell and three in the next shell. The first shell always fills up before electrons go into the second shell.

Questions

1 How many electrons are there in an atom of carbon?
2 How many protons are there in an atom of beryllium?

You will need to look at the Periodic Table to answer the following questions.

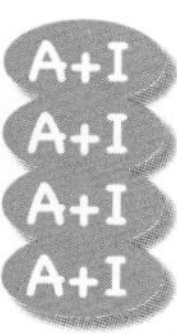

3 How many neutrons are there in an atom of boron?
4 Draw a diagram to show the structure of an atom of magnesium.
5 What is the name of the element that has electrons arranged 2,8,2?
6 Draw a labelled atomic diagram of the element fluorine.

Activity 4.2

A model of an atom

In this activity you will build a model of an atom of a particular element.

1 Cut a circle of card about 6 cm diameter; this will act as the base for the nucleus.
2 Cut out enough small circles of about 1.5 to 2 cm in diameter to represent twice the number of protons in red coloured paper or card, and twice the number of neutrons in blue coloured card. Stick these onto both sides of the nucleus.
3 Cut out concentric rings of card to represent the shells of electrons. The circles should be about 2 cm wide.
4 Cut out small circles, in green coloured paper, to represent twice the number of electrons. Stick these on both sides of the appropriate ring. Assemble the model as shown in the diagram. Make a label for your atom.

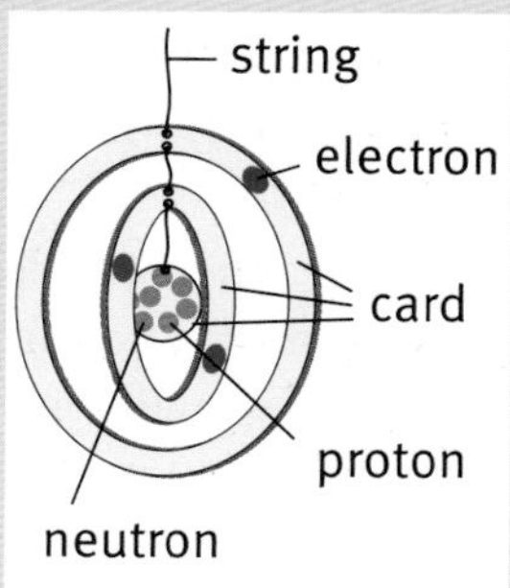

Summary

- The atomic number tells you how many protons are in the atom.
- The mass number tells you how many protons + neutrons there are.
- Electrons are arranged in shells. A shell must be filled before starting on the next one.

4.3 Trends in Group 1

Groups in the Periodic Table

In Stage **8** you learnt that the columns in the Periodic Table are called groups. The first group, also known as the **alkali metals**, includes the elements lithium, sodium and potassium. These elements have some properties in common.

The table below contains data about three of the metals in Group 1.

Group 1
(alkali metals)
Li
Na
K

Element	Atomic number	Mass number	Melting point / °C	Boiling point / °C
lithium, Li	3	7	180	1360
sodium, Na	11	23	98	900
potassium, K	19	39	63	777

As you can see, the atomic number increases as you go down the group. The mass number also increases as you go down the group. These increasing numbers show you that the size of the atom is increasing.

When you look at the melting points you can see that they go down as you go down the group. The next metal down in the group is rubidium. We can predict it would have a melting point lower than 63 °C.

Questions

1 Where in the Periodic Table do you find the metals?

2 What is the trend shown in the boiling points of Group 1 elements?

A+I **3** What prediction can you make about the boiling point of rubidium?

4 How many more electrons than lithium does an atom of sodium have?

Activity 4.3

Reactions in Group 1 metals

SE

Your teacher will demonstrate the reactions of lithium, sodium and potassium with water. The three elements are stored in a particular way and your teacher will cut a small piece of the metal to react in a trough (bowl) of water. Watch carefully and record your observations.

Questions

A1 Describe the safety precautions your teacher took.

A2 Describe what you saw happen when each of the metals reacted with the water.

A3 Write the word equation for each reaction.

A4 What similarities do you notice about the reactions of these metals?

A5 What differences do you notice about the reactions of these metals?

A6 List the properties that these elements share.

A7 Suggest why the next element in this group, rubidium, is not used in schools.

The structure of the Group 1 elements

Lithium has an atomic number of 3 and a mass number of 7. This atom contains three protons, 3 electrons and 4 neutrons. The electrons are arranged as 2,1. This arrangement of electrons is known as the **electronic structure**.

Sodium has an atomic number of 11 and a mass number of 23. This atom contains 11 protons, 11 electrons and 12 neutrons. The electrons are arranged as 2,8,1.

Potassium has an atomic number of 19 and a mass number of 39.
This atom contains 19 protons, 19 electrons and 20 neutrons.
The electrons are arranged as 2,8,8,1.

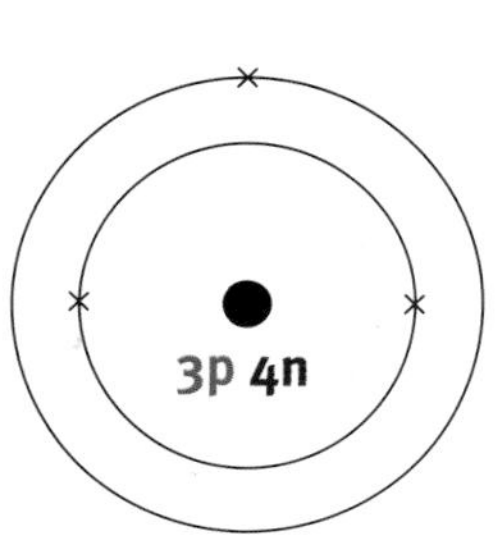

Lithium atom.

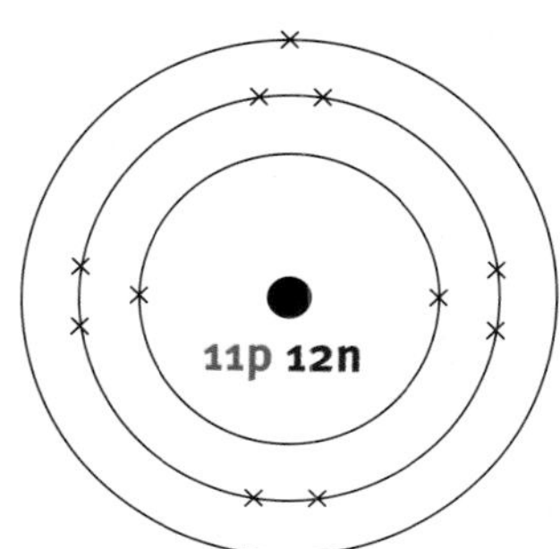

Sodium atom.

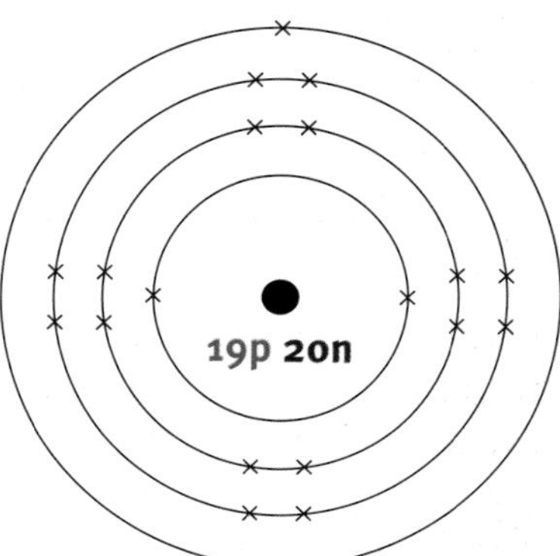

Potassium atom.

Questions

5 What happens to the size of the atoms as you go down this group?

6 What similarity is there in the structure of these atoms? (**Hint**: look at the electron shell arrangements.)

A+I

A+I

7 Suggest why this group of metals is called Group 1.

8 What are the trends in the structure and behaviour of these elements in Group 1?

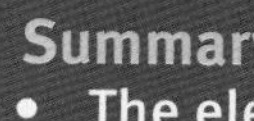

Summary

- The elements in Group 1 share some properties.
- The trend in Group 1 is that the melting points and the boiling points decrease, as you go down the group.
- The elements in Group 1 react more vigorously with water as you go down the group.

4.4 Trends in some other groups

Group 7 – the halogens

The group you are going to look at next is Group 7. This group is sometimes called the **halogens**. The group includes fluorine, chlorine and bromine.

The elements in Group 7 have a number of properties in common. The first two elements are gases at room temperature and bromine is a liquid. The most reactive of these elements is fluorine, then chlorine. Bromine is the least reactive of the three.

Group 7 (halogens)
F
Cl
Br

Element	Atomic number	Electronic structure	Mass number	Colour	Melting point / °C	Boiling point / °C
fluorine, F	9	2,7	19	pale yellow	−220	−188
chlorine, Cl	17	2,8,7	35	yellowish green	−101	−34
bromine, Br	35	2,8,18,7	80	brown	−7	59

Questions

1 Are the halogens metals or non-metals?
2 What is the trend (pattern) in melting points of this group?
3 What is the trend in boiling points in this group?
4 What is the trend in colour in this group?
5 What would you predict about the boiling and melting points of iodine, the next element in this group?
6 Would you expect iodine to be more or less reactive than bromine?

The structure of fluorine and chlorine atoms.

Fluorine has an atomic number of 9 and a mass number of 19. This atom contains 9 protons, 9 electrons and 10 neutrons. The electrons are arranged as 2,7.

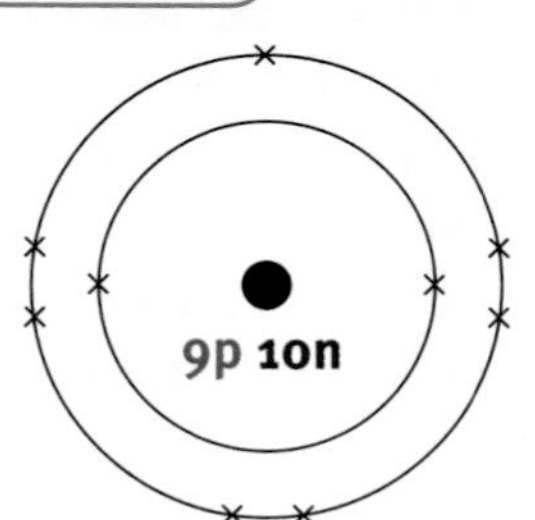

Fluorine.

Chlorine has an atomic number of 17 and a mass number of 35. This atom contains 17 protons, 17 electrons and 18 neutrons. The electrons are arranged as 2,8,7.

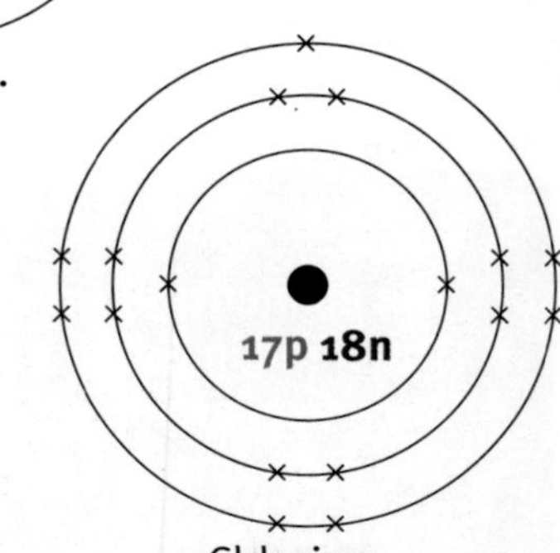

Chlorine.

Questions

7 What happens to the size of the atoms as you go down this group?

8 What similarity is there in the structure of these atoms? (**Hint**: look at the electron shell arrangements.)

9 Suggest why this group is called Group 7.

Group 8 – the noble gases

Group 8 includes the elements helium, neon and argon. They are all gases. They are **inert** (unreactive) and do not form compounds. They are called **noble gases**.

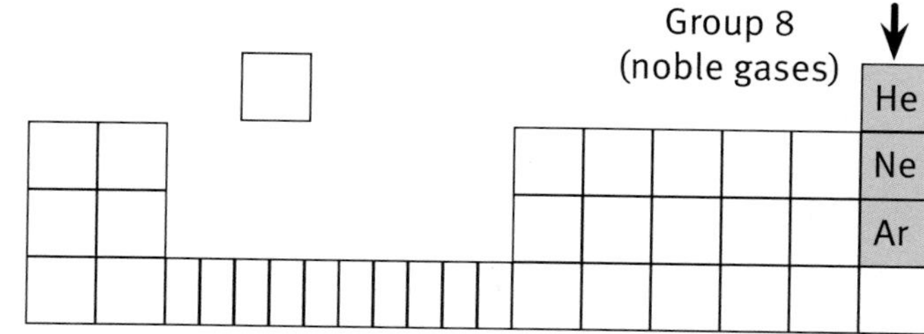

Element	Atomic number	Electronic structure	Mass number	Melting point / °C	Boiling point / °C
helium, He	2	2	4	−270	−269
neon, Ne	10	2,8	20	−249	−246
argon, Ar	18	2,8,8	40	−189	−186

Helium has an atomic number of 2 and a mass number of 4. This atom contains 2 protons, 2 electrons and 2 neutrons. The electrons are arranged with 2 in the first shell. The shell is full.

Neon has an atomic number of 10 and a mass number of 20. This atom contains 10 protons, 10 electrons and 10 neutrons. The electrons are arranged with 2 in the first shell and 8 in the second shell. The outer shell is full.

Argon has an atomic number of 18 and a mass number of 40. This atom contains 18 protons, 18 electrons and 22 neutrons. The electrons are arranged with 2 in the first shell and 8 in the second and third shells. The outer shell is full.

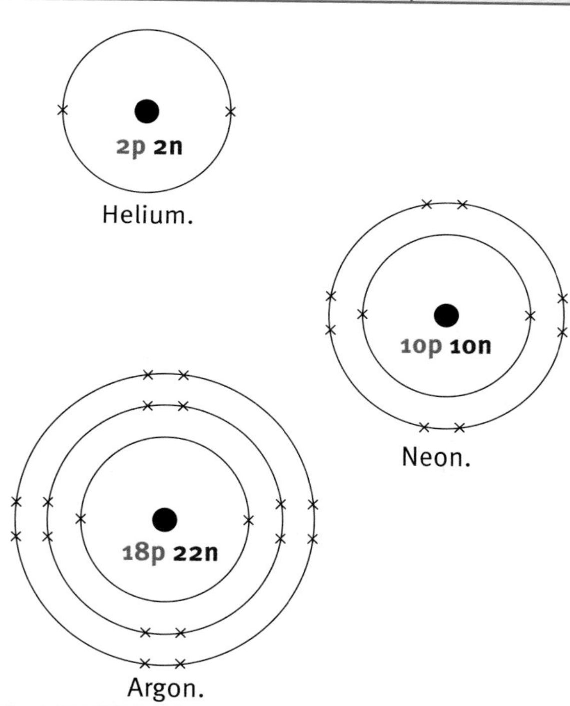

Questions

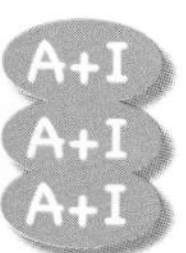

10 What trend in melting points can be seen in Group 8?
11 What happens to the size of the atoms as you go down Group 8?
12 What similarity is there in the structure of these atoms?
13 Suggest why this group is called Group 8.

Summary

- The elements in each group share some properties.
- The elements in Group 7 react less vigorously as you go down the group.
- The elements in Group 8 have all their electron shells full and do not react to form compounds.

Unit 4 End of unit questions

4.1 The table shows some information about four elements. These elements are from the same group in the Periodic Table. They are given in the same order as in the Periodic Table.

Element	Melting point / °C	Boiling point / °C	Reaction with water
lithium	180	1342	Fizzes (gives off bubbles of gas) and gives off heat
sodium		883	
potassium	63		Fizzes and gives off so much heat it catches fire
rubidium	39	688	Explodes with such force that the container cracks

There is a trend in the melting and boiling points of these elements. Use the trend to predict the following:

a the melting point of sodium [1]

b the boiling point of potassium. [1]

c The elements all react with water to produce a gas. Name the gas. [1]

d Use the information about the reaction with water to predict the reaction between sodium and water. [1]

e The following are the mass numbers of the four elements in the table above. They represent the relative size of the atoms.

23 **7** **39** **85**

Match the numbers with the elements. [1]

f Lithium has 2 electron shells. The electronic structure is 2,1. This can be seen in the diagram below.

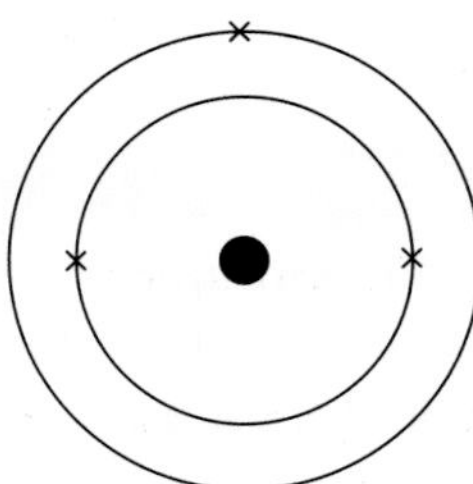

Sodium has the electronic structure 2,8,1. Draw a similar diagram to show the electronic structure of sodium. [3]

4.2 Many scientists contributed to the model of the atom that is shown in the diagram below.

a Copy the diagram and label it using the following words:

electron **nucleus** **proton** **neutron**

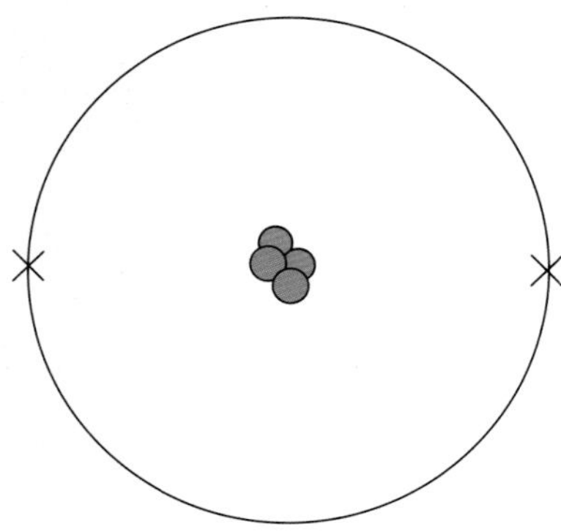

[4]

Name the particle that:

b has a positive charge [1]

c has no charge [1]

d has the least mass [1]

e is present in the same numbers as the protons in an atom. [1]

4.3 **a** Neon is a noble gas. It has the electronic structure 2,8.
Which of the diagrams, **A**, **B**, **C** or **D**, shows the electronic structure of neon?

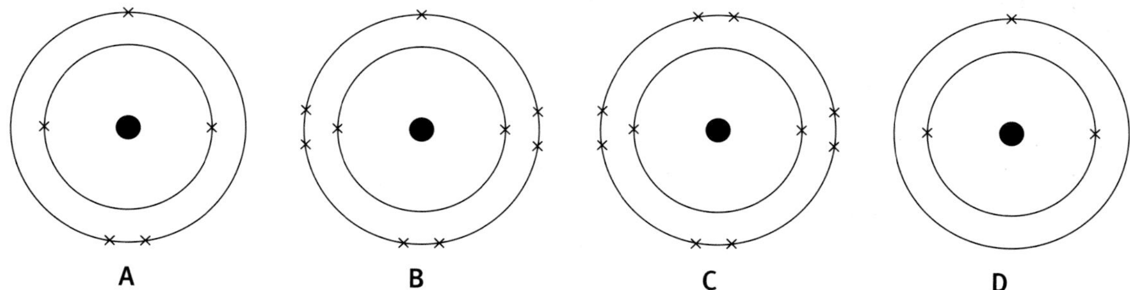

[1]

b How many protons does the atom of neon have? [1]

Neon is in Group 8 of the Periodic Table. Other gases in this group are helium and argon.

c The elements in Group 8 are sometimes called the noble or inert gases. Helium has only one shell of electrons, neon has two and argon has three. What do the shells of this group have in common? [1]

d How are elements in Group 8 different from all other elements in the Periodic Table? [1]

5.1 Burning

When something burns, a chemical reaction is taking place. Burning is a chemical reaction in which a substance combines with oxygen.

In Stage **7** you learnt about different types of energy and how energy can be changed from one form to another. In a burning reaction there are energy changes.

The substance that combines with oxygen is called a fuel. Fuels store energy in the form of chemical energy. Charcoal, wood, coal, natural gas and oil are examples of fuels.

When you burn a fuel, such as charcoal, for cooking or to keep warm, heat energy is given out (released). The chemical energy in the fuel is changed to heat energy and light energy. Sometimes you can hear the fire burning so you know that some of the chemical energy is also changed to sound energy.

Combustion is another term used for burning. Combustion is often a fast reaction.

Combustion of coal.

Reactants and products of combustion

Here is the word equation for the reaction that takes place when charcoal burns. Charcoal is a form of carbon.

There is oxygen in the air around us. About 20% of the air is oxygen. The oxygen is in the form of oxygen molecules, each made up of two oxygen atoms bonded together.

When charcoal burns, the oxygen and carbon atoms rearrange themselves and new bonds are created to form molecules of carbon dioxide. When this rearrangement happens, energy is given out and the temperature rises.

A chemical reaction in which energy is given out is called an **exothermic reaction**.

Questions

1. What is needed for combustion to take place?
2. What is an exothermic reaction?
3. How can you tell that burning is an exothermic reaction?

Burning other substances

Hydrogen can be used as a fuel in a model rocket. The combustion of hydrogen is an exothermic reaction. The hydrogen and oxygen combine to form water.

hydrogen + oxygen → water

When the atoms of hydrogen and oxygen rearrange themselves and combine together, energy is released. This chemical energy is changed to kinetic energy, heat energy, sound energy and light energy.

In this experiment, a large soda bottle filled with hydrogen and air is attached to a string across the room. The stopper in the bottle has wires that allow a spark to be generated. The hot spark provides energy to start the reaction. The hydrogen and oxygen then react together.

string
mixture of hydrogen and air
paper clips
stopper
plastic bottle
to spark generator

Burning hydrogen can propel a plastic bottle like a rocket.

The reaction releases a lot of energy and pushes the stopper out. This energy makes the bottle shoot (move quickly) along the string.

The reactions of other substances burning in air are also exothermic reactions. In Stage **8** you burnt magnesium and saw the formation of magnesium oxide. Energy is given out as heat and light as the magnesium and oxygen atoms rearrange themselves.

magnesium + oxygen → magnesium oxide

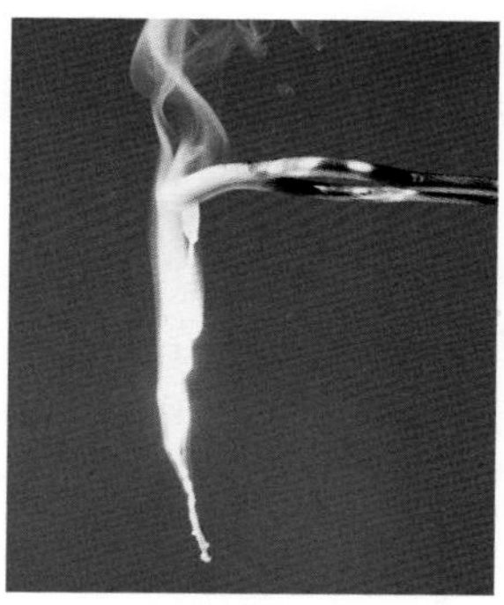

Burning magnesium.

Oxidation reactions

When a substance burns, it combines with oxygen and a new substance called an oxide is formed. Any reaction where a substance combines with oxygen is also known as an **oxidation reaction**. Combustion is an oxidation reaction.

When iron rusts, it combines with oxygen from the air. Iron oxide is formed. Although rusting is a much slower and less vigorous reaction than combustion, it is also an oxidation reaction.

Questions

4 What sort of reaction is rusting?
5 Which compound is formed when copper reacts with oxygen?
6 When magnesium burns in air what types of energy is the chemical energy changed into?

Summary

- An exothermic reaction is one in which heat energy is given out.
- Burning (combustion) is an exothermic reaction.
- Burning is a reaction in which a substance combines with oxygen.
- When a substance combines with oxygen, we say that oxidation has taken place.

5.2 More exothermic reactions

Reactions of metals with water

In Stage **8** you observed the reaction of potassium in water. In Unit **4** you compared the reactions of lithium, sodium and potassium in water. In all of these reactions heat energy is released to the environment and the reaction temperature increases. They are exothermic reactions.

Potassium reacting with water.

Here is the word equation for the reaction of potassium with water.

potassium + water → potassium hydroxide + hydrogen

Water is made of molecules containing hydrogen and oxygen. In this reaction, the bonds between the atoms of oxygen and hydrogen in the water break. The atoms rearrange to form potassium hydroxide and hydrogen. Heat energy is released.

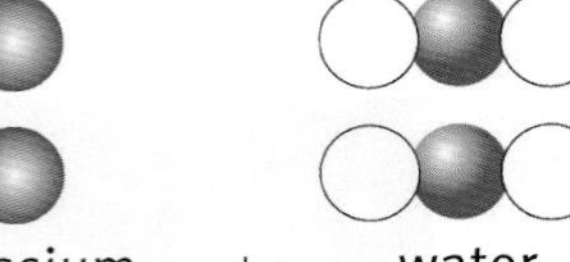

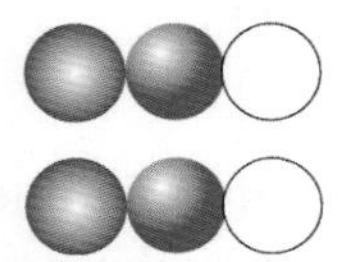

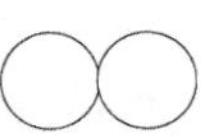

potassium + water → potassium hydroxide + hydrogen

Reactions of metals with acid

You may have noticed that when you put magnesium in dilute hydrochloric acid the test tube got hot. The reaction between hydrochloric acid and magnesium is an exothermic reaction.

magnesium + hydrochloric acid → magnesium chloride + hydrogen

Measuring rise in temperature during a reaction

Noor and Hanif each poured 10 cm^3 of hydrochloric acid into a test tube and measured the temperature. Then they added identical pieces of magnesium ribbon. When the reaction stopped they measured the temperature again.

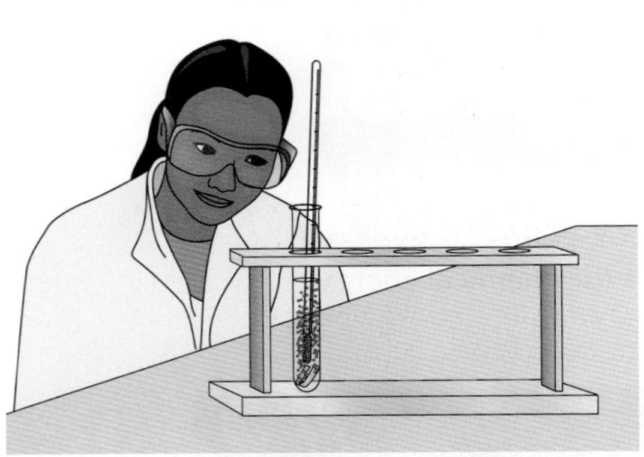

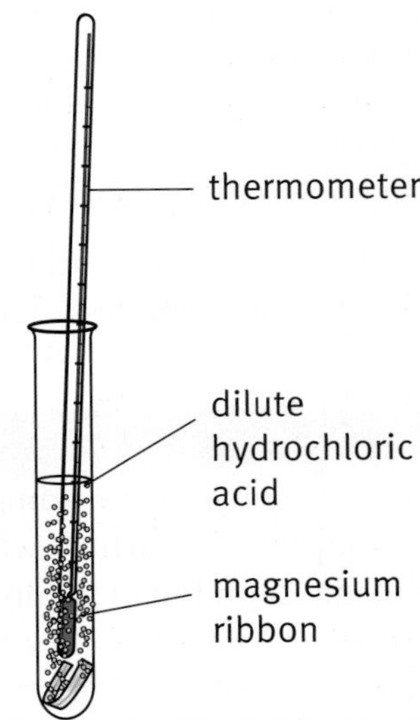

Measuring the rise in temperature when magnesium reacts with hydrochloric acid.

Noor's results	
Start temperature / °C	**End temperature / °C**
18	42

Hanif's results	
Start temperature / °C	**End temperature / °C**
21	45

Questions

1 What are the products when magnesium and hydrochloric acid react?
2 How did Noor and Hanif know when the reaction had finished?
A+I 3 Hanif thought that more heat energy had been given out by his reaction because in his experiment the end temperature was higher. Noor thought that both reactions gave out the same amount of heat energy. Whose idea was correct? Explain why.
SE 4 Explain why it was a good idea to wear safety glasses.
SE 5 Noor and Hanif wondered how they could produce a higher temperature change. Their ideas included adding more magnesium, using a different metal and using a different acid.
Write each of these three ideas as a scientific question to be investigated.

Activity 5.2

Planning an investigation into the reaction between acid and magnesium

SE 1 Choose one of the questions from question **5** (or one of your own) and write a plan for your investigation.
- Before you write your plan, try out the reaction between magnesium and an acid. In this **preliminary work** you should practise measuring the temperature change.
- You also need to find out how big a change in the variable (for example, the length of magnesium ribbon) is needed to make a change in temperature that you can measure.
- When the reaction takes place and heat energy spreads out into the environment, are you sure that you are accurately measuring the temperature change? What could you do to reduce this heat loss?
- Decide on how you will record and present your results.

2 Ask your teacher to check your plan.
3 Carry out your plan. You may find that you want to make changes to it once you begin doing the experiment. If so, write down the changes that you have made, and explain why you made them.

Questions

A1 What can you conclude from your results?
A2 Compare your results with others in the class. Are your results in agreement with others who carried out the same investigation?
A3 How could you improve your investigation?

Summary

- When metals react with water or acids, heat energy is given out.
- The reaction of a metal with water or with an acid is exothermic.

5.3 Endothermic processes

Endothermic reactions

Some chemical reactions take heat from their surroundings and store it as chemical energy. These are called **endothermic reactions**. When an endothermic reaction takes place, the temperature decreases.

Activity 5.3

Carrying out an endothermic reaction

1 Place some citric acid or lemon juice in a test tube.
2 Measure and record the temperature.
3 Add three spatulas of sodium hydrogencarbonate and stir.
4 Measure and record the temperature.

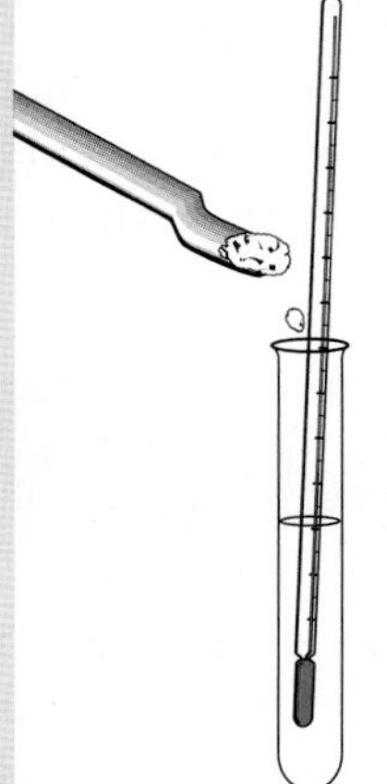

Questions

A1 What was the difference between the temperatures at the start and the end of the experiment?

A2 Is heat energy given out or taken in during this reaction?

This is the word equation for the reaction between sodium hydrogencarbonate and citric acid.

sodium hydrogencarbonate + citric acid → sodium citrate + water + carbon dioxide

During this reaction, energy is taken from the environment. This results in the contents of the tube having a lower temperature.

When we eat refreshing sweets we use this reaction. Inside sherbet sweets there is a mixture of dry citric acid and sodium hydrogencarbonate. When you eat them, these substances dissolve in the water in your saliva, and react together. This gives a cool 'fizzy' feeling in your mouth, which is refreshing.

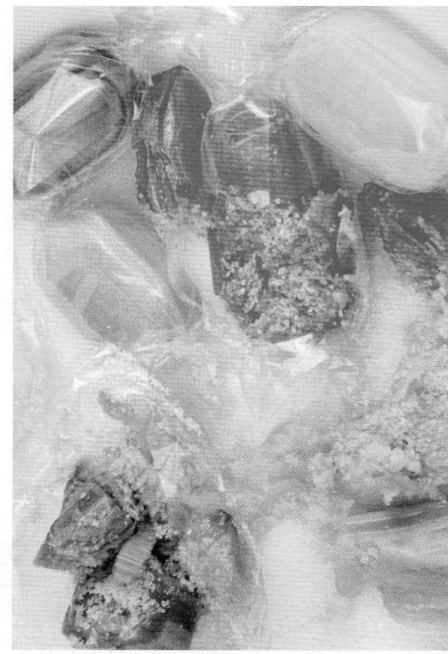

Sherbet sweets.

Questions

1 What are the reactants in the reaction shown in the word equation above?
2 Which are the products in the reaction shown in the word equation above?
3 What is an endothermic reaction?
4 Explain why eating sherbet sweets makes your mouth feel cooler.
5 You may also get a 'fizzy' feeling in your mouth when you eat sherbet. Why is this? (A+I)

Another way to cool down

If you put about 25 cm^3 of water in a beaker and then stir in three spatulas of potassium chloride, you will find that the beaker gets cold. In this case no chemical reaction has taken place. The potassium chloride has just dissolved. A solution of potassium chloride has been formed. Potassium chloride is the solute and the solvent is the water.

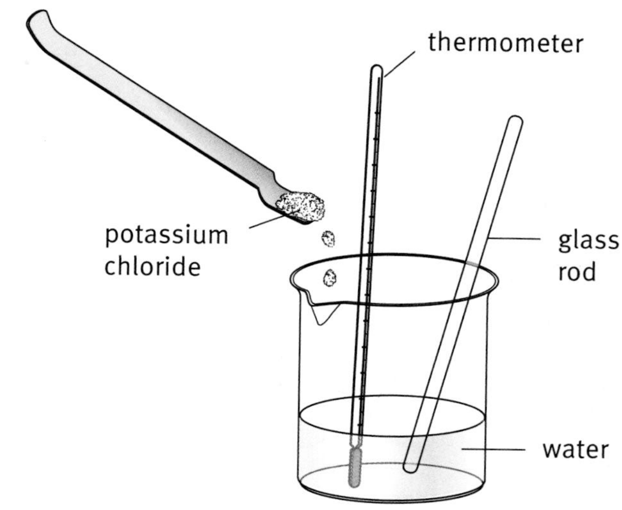

When potassium chloride dissolves in water, heat energy is taken in (absorbed) from the surroundings. This is why the beaker feels cold. This is an **endothermic process**.

Ice melting is another endothermic process. Heat energy from the environment is taken in as the solid ice changes to liquid water. Think about what happens to the particles when water changes state. The particles in the ice are lined up in rows and can only vibrate about fixed positions – they cannot move around inside the ice. The forces between the particles are strong.

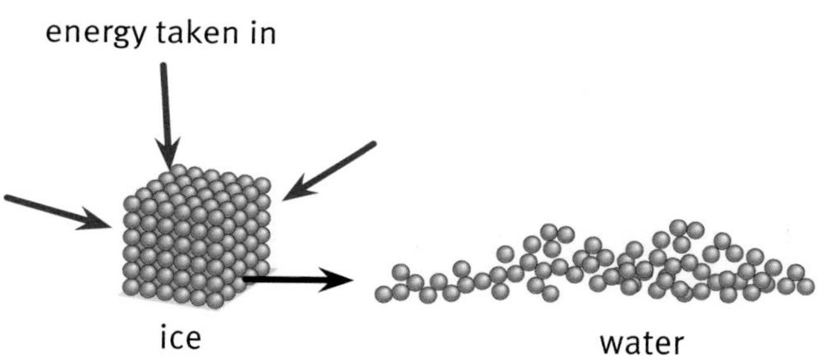

As the particles gain energy from the surroundings they vibrate more and more. The ice begins to melt. When the particles have enough energy they can move and overcome the forces holding them in place. The particles are now able to slide past one another. The water is now in a liquid state.

Questions

6 Why is ice melting called an endothermic process and not an endothermic reaction?

A+I

7 Suggest a change of state, other than ice melting, that is an endothermic process.

A+I

8 When you have been swimming and you come out of the pool, you may feel cold. Use your understanding of endothermic processes to explain why.

A+I

9 Suggest whether water freezing is an endothermic or exothermic process. Can you explain your suggestion?

Summary

- An endothermic reaction is a chemical reaction in which energy is taken in.
- An endothermic process is a process in which energy is taken in, for example dissolving.
- During an endothermic reaction or process, the temperature decreases.

5.4 Exothermic or endothermic?

In exothermic reactions and processes, heat energy is given out. In endothermic reactions and processes, heat energy is taken in.

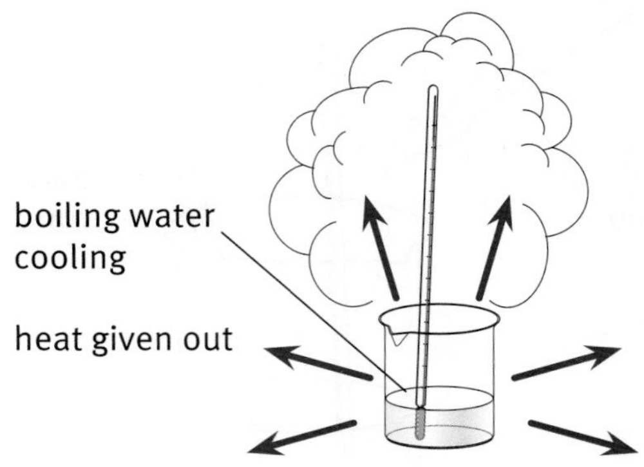

Exothermic processes give out heat.

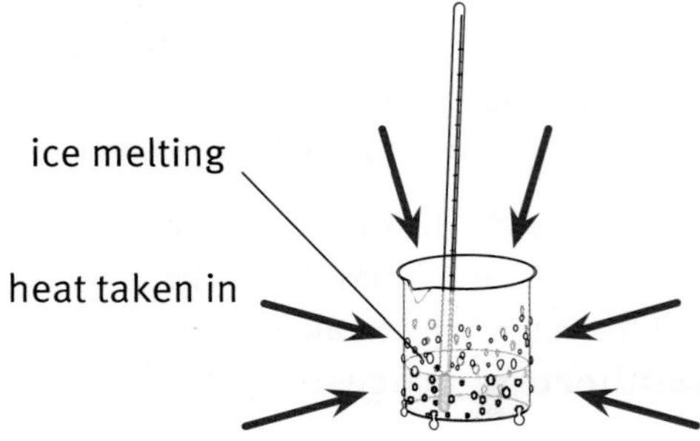

Endothermic processes take in heat.

Activity 5.4
Exothermic or endothermic

SE

Carry out each of the reactions or processes provided for you.

1. Place one of the solutions in the polystyrene cup.
2. Measure and record the temperature.
3. Add the other substance.
4. Allow the substances to react and then measure and record the temperature.

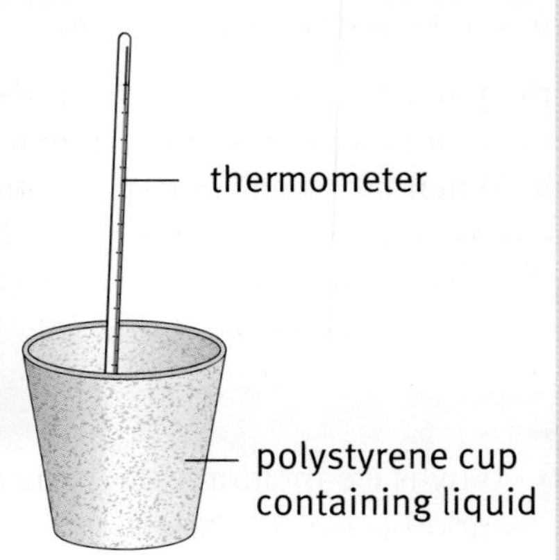

Questions

A1 Why is a polystyrene cup used rather than a glass beaker?
A2 Which reaction gave out the most heat energy?
A3 Which reaction took in the most heat energy?

Using exothermic reactions

Some exothermic reactions are used to produce self-heating cans of food or drink. For example, a can of self-heating coffee or self-heating food contains two chemicals, which are in separate compartments. When you press a button, the two chemicals mix with each other and react. The reaction warms up the food or drink.

The chemicals used are calcium oxide and water. When the water and calcium oxide are mixed together they react, and heat is given off.

calcium oxide + water → calcium hydroxide

This is an expensive idea because of the difficulty of making the compartments in the tin, so that the food or drink is not contaminated.

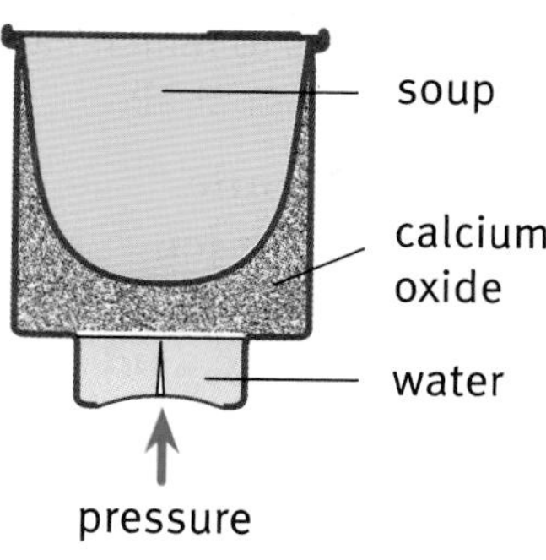

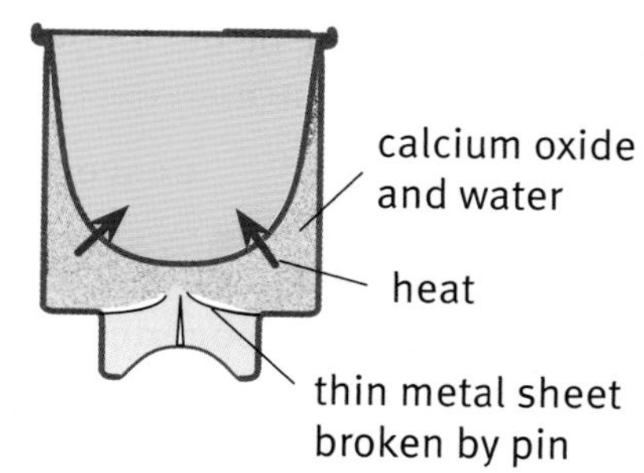

A self-heating can of soup.

Using endothermic reactions and processes

People sometimes use ice packs when they injure themselves. These packs are stored in a fridge or freezer until they are needed. When the ice pack is placed on the injured area, the melting ice takes in heat from the injured area. This is an endothermic process. It means that the injured area is cooled and this often prevents it from swelling up. After use, the ice pack can be placed back in the freezer and used again.

Some 'ice' packs are made using substances that undergo an endothermic process when they mix together. These packs can be used even when you don't have a refrigerator or freezer. The pack has two compartments inside, each containing a different substance. These substances are usually ammonium nitrate and water. When you push on the pack and break the compartment containing ammonium nitrate, the water mixes with it and the ammonium nitrate begins to dissolve. This is an endothermic process, so the temperature drops.

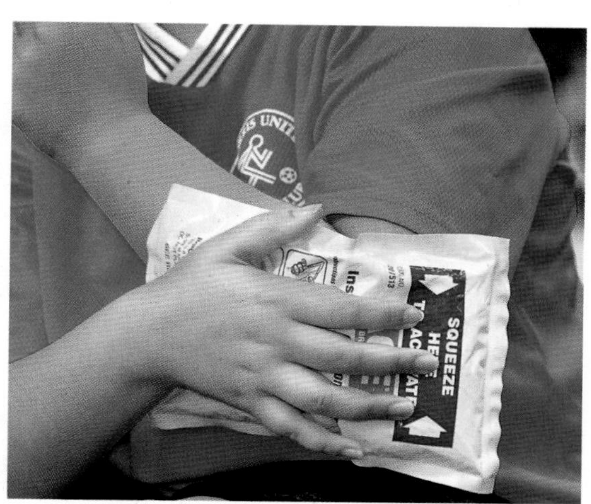

A chemical ice pack being used to treat an injury.

Questions

1 Explain why self-heating cans are very expensive.

2 Explain why a self-heating can can only be used once.

A+I

3 Describe **one** advantage and **one** disadvantage of each of the two types of ice pack described above.

Summary

- Exothermic and endothermic reactions can be identified by taking the temperature at the start and the end of the reaction.
- Exothermic and endothermic reactions and processes can be used to produce useful items.

Unit 5 End of unit questions

5.1 Choose one of the following words or phrases to match each description. Each may be used once, more than once, or not at all.

burning **decreases** **endothermic** **evaporation**
exothermic **increases** **melting ice**
magnesium ribbon placed in hydrochloric acid
sodium hydrogencarbonate added to citric acid

a An example of a chemical reaction where heat is given out.
b An example of an endothermic reaction.
c The temperature in an endothermic reaction.
d An example of an endothermic process.
e The type of reaction between calcium and water. [5]

5.2 Vishal and Manish are carrying out an investigation into the heat given off when they add pieces of calcium to water.
They both use 10 cm^3 water and add pieces of calcium.
These are Vishal's results:

Mass of calcium added / g	Start temperature / °C	Final temperature / °C
1	19	20
2	19	21
3	19	22
4	19	23

These are Manish's results:

Mass of calcium added / g	Start temperature / °C	Final temperature / °C
1	21	22
2	21	22
3	21	24
4	21	25

a What trend is shown by both sets of results? [1]
b Predict what would happen if 5 g of calcium were added. [1]
c Using Vishal's results, calculate the temperature change for each mass of calcium used. Then do the same for Manish's results. [2]
d Now construct a summary table, showing the mean (average) temperature rise for each mass of calcium. (Your table does not need to show the start and final temperatures.) [2]
e Vishal and Manish plot a graph of their results. Which variable and unit should they put on the horizontal axis? [1]
f Which variable and unit should they put on the vertical axis? [1]
g The boys carried out a third set of experiments, using 20 cm^3 of water instead of 10 cm^3. Could they use these results to add to the first two sets, to calculate an average temperature change? Explain your answer. [2]

5.3 Some students carried out four reactions and took the temperatures at the start and end of each reaction.

Reaction	Start temperature / °C	Final temperature / °C
A	20	25
B	19	16
C	20	23
D	18	24

a Which reactions are exothermic and which are endothermic? [4]
b Explain how you worked out your answer to **a**. [1]
c Which reaction had the largest energy change? [1]

5.4 Burning is a chemical reaction where heat energy is given out. It is an exothermic reaction. Lisa has four fuels to investigate to find out which one gives out the most heat. She uses apparatus like this.

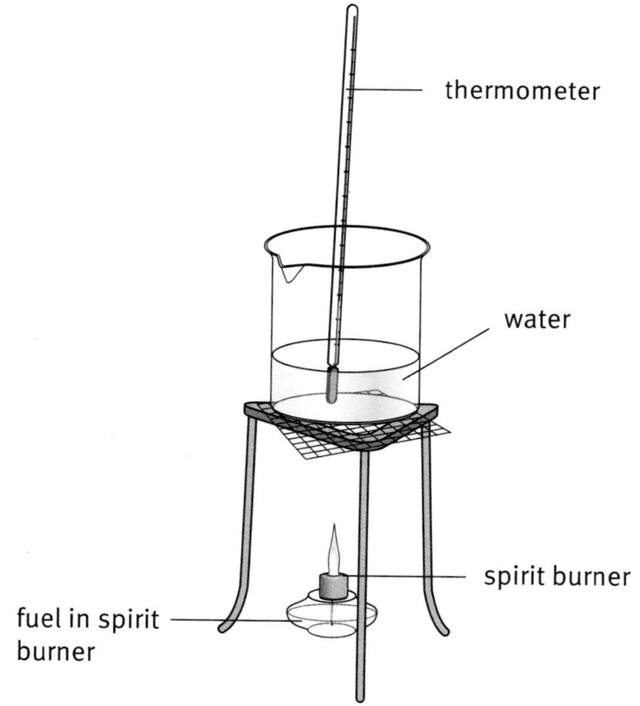

a Which variable will Lisa change? [1]
b Name **two** variables Lisa must keep the same. [2]
c Explain what she must do in order to be able to identify which fuel gives out the most energy. [2]
d Name one safety precaution she should take whilst carrying out this investigation. [1]

6.1 Metals and their reactions with oxygen

In Stages **7** and **8**, you learnt about some of the properties of metals. Now you are going to investigate how different metals react with oxygen.

Activity 6.1
Heating metals in air

SE

In this activity, you will heat several different metals in air. Air contains oxygen, and some of the metals will react with this oxygen.

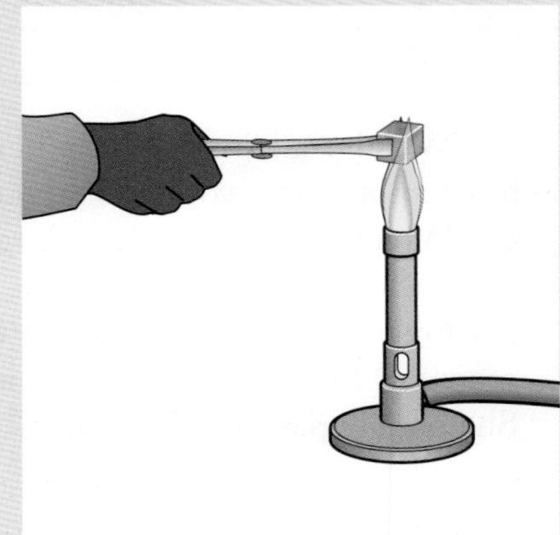

Read through the instructions and decide on the safety precautions you will need to take. Discuss these with your teacher before you carry out the investigation.

1. Take a small piece of one of the metals provided for you.
2. Place it in the tongs and heat it in a Bunsen flame.
3. Record your observations in a table and explain what has happened.
4. Repeat steps **1** to **3** for each of the other metals your teacher has provided.

Questions

A1 Which was the most reactive of the metals you were given? What evidence do you have for this?

A2 What safety precautions did you take whilst carrying out this investigation?

A3 Are the reactions of Group 1 metals with oxygen more or less vigorous than the ones you tested? What evidence do you have for this?

Looking at the reactions of metals with oxygen

Many metals react with oxygen if they get hot enough. You have seen magnesium react with oxygen when you heat it. You have also seen the effect of iron reacting with oxygen when it rusts.

When you look carefully at the reactions of metals with oxygen, it is possible to identify which metals are more reactive. We can say that magnesium is more reactive than iron because we can see that iron reacts much more slowly than magnesium.

Metals and the Periodic Table

When you looked at the elements in Stage **8**, you learnt that there are 118 different elements. Most of these are metals.

metals

non-metals

H hydrogen

Group 1	Group 2	Group 3	Group 4	Group 5	Group 6	Group 7	Group 8
							He helium
Li lithium	Be beryllium	B boron	C carbon	N nitrogen	O oxygen	F fluorine	Ne neon
Na sodium	Mg magnesium	Al aluminium	Si silicon	P phosphorus	S sulfur	Cl chlorine	Ar argon
K potassium	Ca calcium						

The first twenty elements in the Periodic Table.

Each of the elements has a different atomic structure with a different number of electrons, protons and neutrons. The atoms of the different elements are different sizes.

Metals have some properties in common and some properties that are slightly different. For example, iron is hard and strong but sodium is much softer and can be easily cut with a knife.

Reactions of Group 1 metals with oxygen

The metals in Group 1 of the Periodic Table are softer than other metals. They are also more reactive than other metals. They must be stored under oil because they react vigorously with the moisture in the air and can explode.

When pieces of lithium, sodium or potassium are taken out from their containers, they appear dull (not shiny). When the pieces are cut, the surface is shiny. The shiny surface soon becomes dull because the metal reacts with the oxygen in the air. The surface becomes covered with a new substance – the oxide of the metal. These metals are so reactive that they react with oxygen even when they are not heated.

The general word equation for the reaction of a metal with oxygen is:

metal + oxygen → metal oxide

Questions

1 Name **two** metals that have atoms larger than those of sodium.
2 Which property of sodium is not typical of a metal?

3 Suggest why it might be difficult and dangerous to test sodium for electrical conductivity.
4 Write the word equation for the reaction of sodium with oxygen.

Summary

- When a metal reacts with oxygen a metal oxide is formed.
- Metals have different levels of reactivity.

6.2 Reactions of metals in water

Activity 6.2
Reactions of metals in water

SE

1 Take a small piece of one of the metals provided for you. Use sandpaper to clean the surface of the metal. You need to do this because some of the metals may have reacted with the oxygen in the air and formed a layer of metal oxide on the surface. This would prevent the metal from being in direct contact with the water.
2 Place the metal into a test tube of water.
3 Record your observations in a table and explain what has happened. You may need to leave the metal to react for some time. If nothing happens, you could try testing the metal again using hot water.
4 Repeat steps **1** to **3** for each of the other metals your teacher has provided.

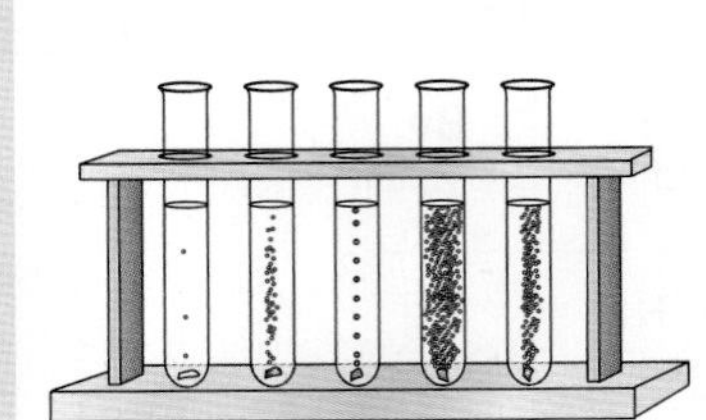

Questions

A1 Which was the most reactive of the metals you were given? What evidence do you have for this?
A2 Use the results of your experiment to arrange the metals in order of their reactivity, starting with the most reactive.
A3 Suggest why some metals will react with hot water but not with cold water.

Reactions of Group 1 metals with water

In Stage **8** you learnt about the reaction of some metals with water. You saw the reactions of lithium, sodium and potassium when pieces of each metal were placed on water.

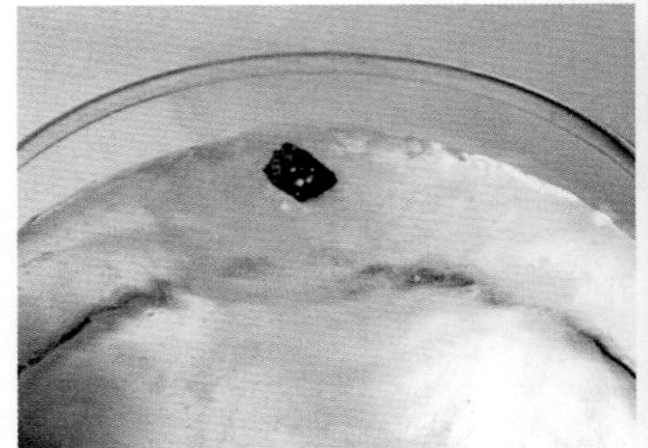

Lithium reacts with water to produce lithium hydroxide and hydrogen.

Sodium is more reactive than lithium with water.

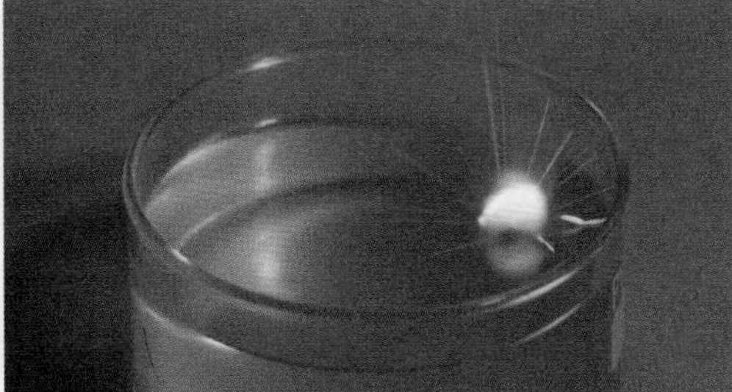

Potassium is even more reactive than sodium. So much heat is generated that the hydrogen gas produced catches fire.

Look at the position of these three metals in Group 1 in the Periodic Table on page **81**. Potassium is the most reactive and is lower down the group. Lithium is the least reactive and is at the top of the group.

In all three of these reactions the metal reacted with water to produce hydrogen and the metal hydroxide.

metal + water → metal hydroxide + hydrogen

Questions

SE

1. Which of these three metals – sodium, lithium and potassium – reacts the most vigorously?
2. Write the word equation for the reaction of sodium with water.
3. What safety precautions must be taken when these reactions take place?
4. Explain why these metals must be stored under oil.

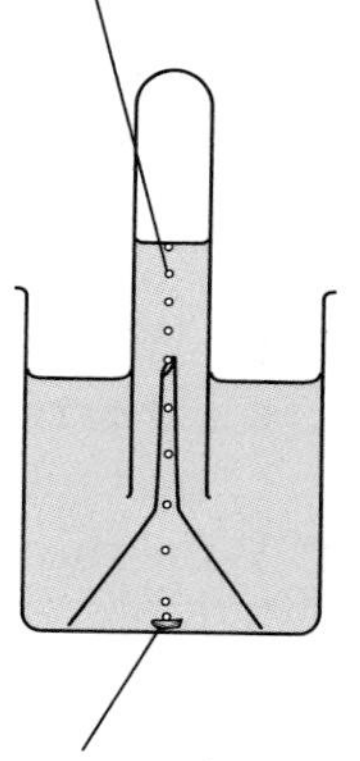

Reactions of other metals with water

Some other metals react less vigorously with water – for example, magnesium and calcium. In the experiment shown in the diagram, a piece of calcium has been placed in the bottom of a beaker and covered with water. A filter funnel has been placed upside down over the metal. The gas given off is collected in a test tube by the displacement of water.

Questions

5. What is the gas that is given off? How would you test for it?
6. How could you tell if calcium or magnesium is the more reactive?
7. What factors should you take into account to make this a fair test?
8. Write the word equation for the reaction between calcium and water.

Some of the metals that do not react with water may react with steam. Even magnesium will react more rapidly with steam than with water.

In the reaction shown on the right, magnesium is heated. From time to time the ceramic wool is also heated. The ceramic wool has been soaked in water, which produces steam. In this reaction the magnesium reacts with water in the form of a gas. Magnesium oxide and hydrogen are formed. The hydrogen gas that is given off can be burnt. The word equation for this reaction is:

magnesium + steam → magnesium oxide + hydrogen

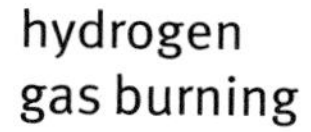

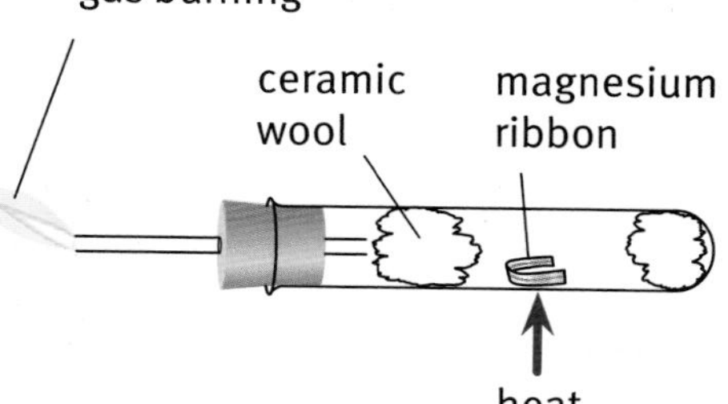

Questions

9. Explain, using particle theory, why the reaction between steam and magnesium is more vigorous than that between liquid water and magnesium.

Summary

- Group 1 metals react vigorously with water.
- The metals nearest the bottom of Group 1 in the Periodic Table react more vigorously than those at the top.
- Some metals will react with hot water or steam, but not with cold water.

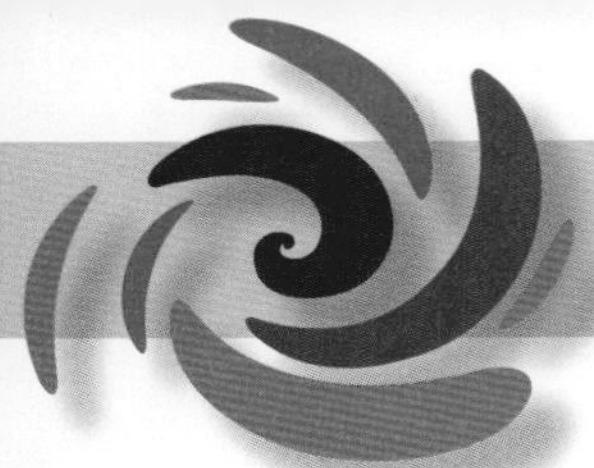

6.3 Reactions of metals with dilute acid

You will probably remember seeing the reaction of magnesium with hydrochloric acid. This is the word equation for this reaction:

magnesium + hydrochloric acid → magnesium chloride + hydrogen

Magnesium chloride is an example of a **salt**. When a metal reacts with an acid, the products are a salt and hydrogen.

Questions

1 **a** Write the word equation for the reaction between magnesium and sulfuric acid.

b What is the salt that is produced in this reaction?

c Describe what you would observe if this reaction took place in a test tube.

2 Write the word equation for the reaction between zinc and nitric acid.

Priya and Rohit have been asked to investigate the reactivity of metals with acids. The equipment and reagents that are available in the laboratory are shown below. Their first task is to plan their investigation. They need to choose which items they will use. They need to decide how they will carry out the investigation.

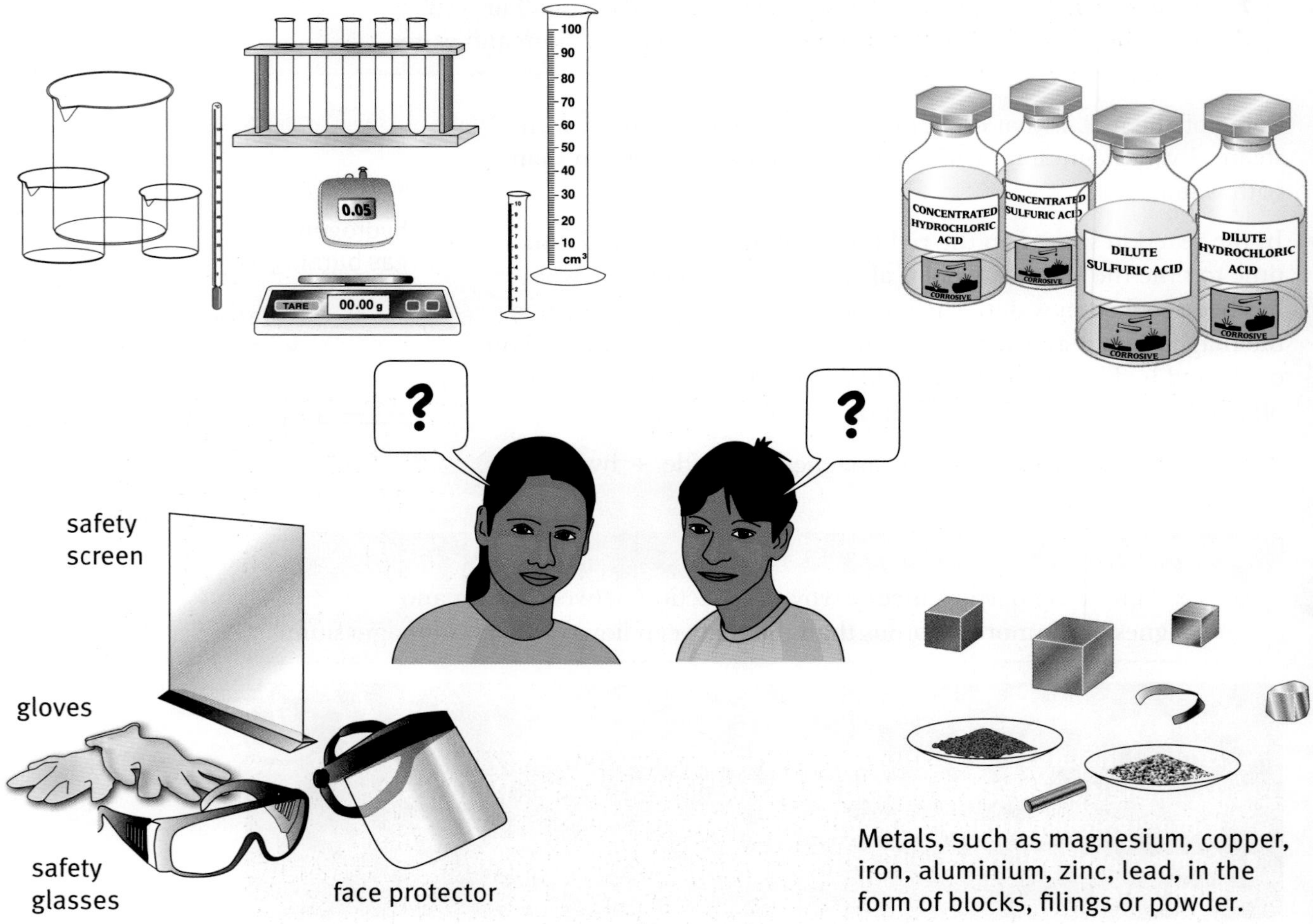

100
90
80
70
60
50
40
30
20
10
cm³
0.05
TARE
00.00 g
CONCENTRATED HYDROCHLORIC ACID
CONCENTRATED SULFURIC ACID
DILUTE SULFURIC ACID
DILUTE HYDROCHLORIC ACID
CORROSIVE
?
?
safety screen
gloves
safety glasses
face protector
Metals, such as magnesium, copper, iron, aluminium, zinc, lead, in the form of blocks, filings or powder.

Activity 6.3A

Plannning an investigation into the reactivity of metals in acid

SE

Use the information and ideas on the previous page to plan the investigation for Priya and Rohit. Choose which of the items in the diagrams they need to use. Some of the items shown are not appropriate to use.

Discuss in your group how you will answer these questions.

- What will they change?
- What will they keep the same?
- How will they measure the reactivity and decide which is the most or least reactive metal?
- How will they keep safe?
- What equipment will they use?

Remember to include a results table and an idea of what they should be looking for in order to identify which are the most reactive.

Write your plan and show your teacher.

Questions

A1 Which metals should **not** be used by the students in this investigation? Give reasons for your answer.

A2 Explain which measuring cylinder they should choose to measure out enough acid to use in this investigation.

Activity 6.3B

Investigating the reactivity of metals in dilute acid

SE

Your teacher will provide you with the items you need to carry out this investigation. Your task is to find the order of reactivity of the metals you are given. Remember to work in a methodical way and keep an accurate record of your results.

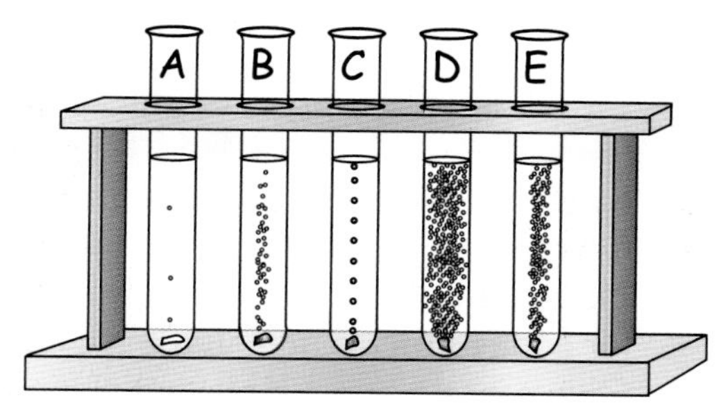

Summary

- When a metal reacts with dilute acid, the products are a salt and hydrogen.
- Different metals have different levels of reactivity in dilute acid.

6.4 The reactivity series

You have seen that some metals are more reactive than others by looking at the reaction of the metals with oxygen, water (or steam) and dilute acid. Using the results of all of these investigations, we can place the metals in order of their **reactivity**.

This list is called the **reactivity series**. It has the most reactive metals at the top and the least reactive at the bottom.

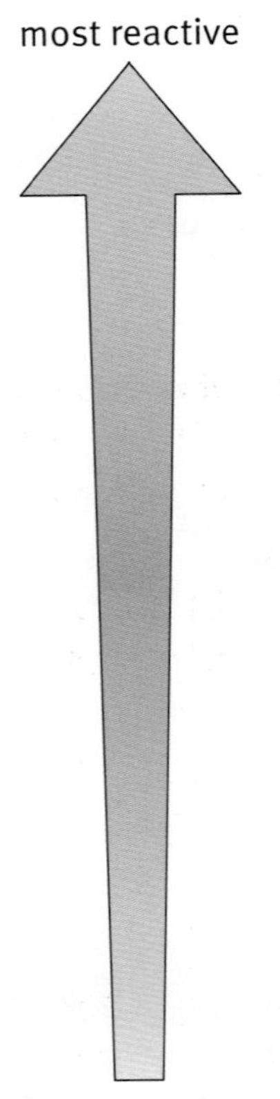

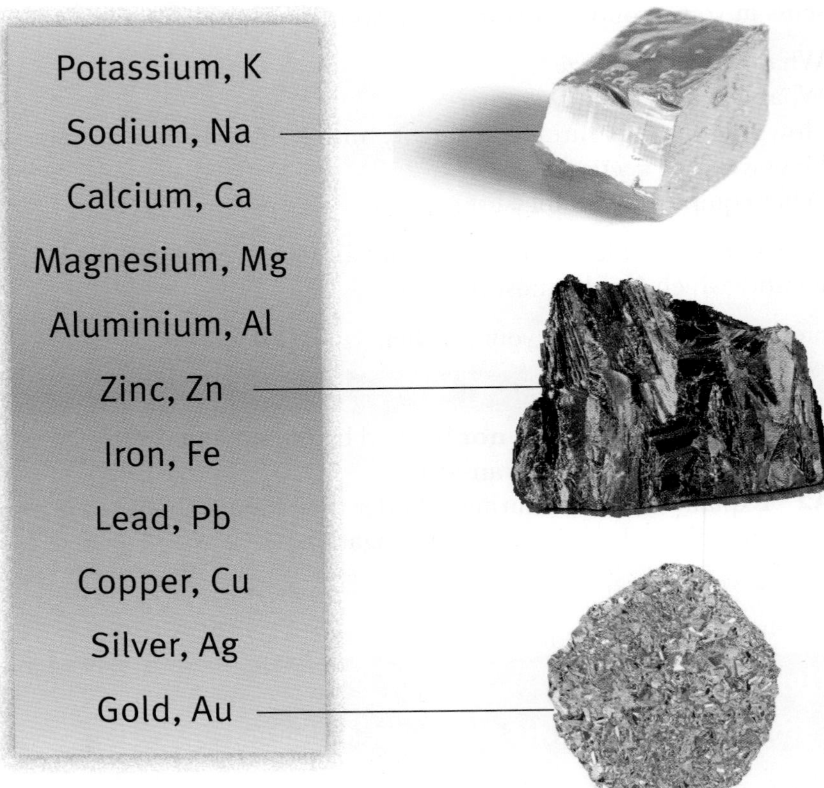

Potassium, K
Sodium, Na
Calcium, Ca
Magnesium, Mg
Aluminium, Al
Zinc, Zn
Iron, Fe
Lead, Pb
Copper, Cu
Silver, Ag
Gold, Au

Questions

A+I **1 a** Suggest where the metal lithium should be placed in this list.

b Give your reasons for placing lithium in this position.

A+I **2 a** Platinum is a precious metal that is used for jewellery. Platinum stays shiny for a long time. Where in the list would you place the metal platinum?

b Give your reasons for placing platinum in this position.

3 Make up a mnemonic to help you to remember the sequence of the metals in the reactivity series. (A mnemonic is a sentence in which the first letter of each word is the same as the first letter of the things you want to remember.) You could either use the first letters of the names of the metals, or their symbols.

This table shows a summary of the reactions of the metals in the reactivity series.

Metal	Reaction with oxygen	Reaction with water	Reaction with dilute acid
potassium	burns brightly when heated to form an oxide	very vigorous reaction in cold water. The hydroxide is formed	violent reaction and very dangerous
sodium			
calcium	burns brightly in air when heated to form an oxide	slow reaction in cold water to form the hydroxide	
magnesium			reaction, which becomes less vigorous as you go down the list
aluminium	slow reaction when heated to form an oxide	reacts with steam but not water to form an oxide	
zinc			
iron			
lead		no reaction with steam or water	
copper			no reaction
silver	no reaction		
gold			

Summary

- Metals have different levels of reactivity.
- The reactivity series is a list of metals with the most reactive at the top.

6.5 Displacement reactions

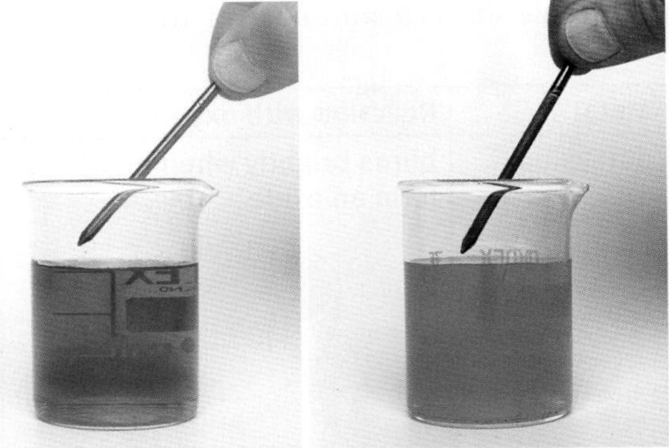

An iron nail is placed in a solution of copper sulfate. When the nail is removed it is covered in copper.

If you place a clean iron nail into a beaker of copper sulfate there is an interesting reaction.

The blue copper sulfate solution changes to a slightly paler colour. The most remarkable thing that happens is that the nail looks a different colour. It has become a copper colour. What has happened in this reaction?

This is the word equation for this reaction.

copper sulfate + iron → iron sulfate + copper

The iron nail has become coated with copper. Iron is more reactive than copper and it has 'pushed out' the copper from the copper sulfate and has reacted to form iron sulfate. This 'pushing out' is called displacement, so this type of reaction is named a **displacement reaction**. A more reactive metal can replace a less reactive one in a salt.

If a copper nail was placed in a solution of iron sulfate there would be no reaction because copper is less reactive than iron. Copper cannot displace the iron in the iron sulfate.

Questions

Use the reactivity series on page **86** to help you answer the following questions.

1 Which is the more reactive metal – zinc or lead?

A+I 2 Can zinc displace the lead in lead nitrate?

3 Which is more reactive – silver or aluminium?

A+I 4 Can silver displace the aluminium in aluminium sulfate?

Activity 6.5A
Displacing metals

SE

In this activity you will use four different metals and four different solutions of salts. The solutions are copper sulfate, magnesium sulfate, iron sulfate and lead nitrate. The metals are iron, lead, copper and magnesium.

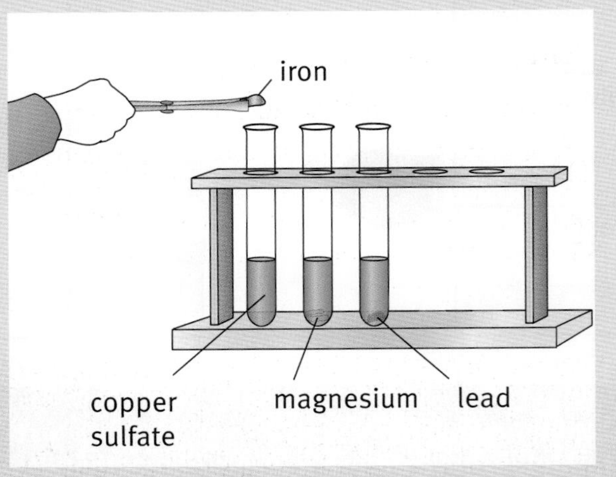

1 Read through these instructions and prepare a results table. (You will need to think about this quite carefully – there are a lot of different results to record.)

2 Pour copper sulfate solution into three test tubes so that each is about a third full.

3 Add a small piece of iron into one test tube, a small piece of magnesium to the second and a small piece of lead to the third test tube.

continued ...

... continued

4 Leave the test tubes for a few minutes.
5 Observe carefully and record your observations.
6 Repeat steps **2** to **5** using magnesium sulfate solution and the three metals copper, iron and lead.
7 Repeat steps **2** to **5** using iron sulfate solution and the metals copper, magnesium and lead.
8 Repeat steps **2** to **5** using lead nitrate solution and the metals copper, magnesium and iron.

Safety: Lead is toxic. Do not touch the lead metal with your fingers. Use forceps. If you do touch the lead, wash your hands carefully.

Questions

A1 How did you know that one metal had displaced another from its salt?
A2 Which metal was the most reactive?
A3 Which metal was the least reactive?

Activity 6.5B
Mystery metal

SE

In this activity you have to identify a mystery metal. It is one of the metals from the reactivity series. You are going to investigate which metal it could be.

Remember your safety!

You do not know what the metal is, so treat it with care and pick it up with forceps.

Add a piece of your mystery metal to each of the solutions provided, and decide if a reaction has taken place or not.

Record your observations.

After each test you will be able to cross some metals off your list.

Questions

A4 What do you think the mystery metal is?
A5 Give your reasons for your answer.

Summary

- More reactive metals can displace less reactive ones from solutions of salts.
- Metals can be identified by observing their reactions.

6.6 Using displacement reactions

Aluminium is more reactive than iron. Aluminium will displace iron from solid iron oxide if it is heated.

aluminium + iron oxide → aluminium oxide + iron

This reaction releases a lot of energy. It is an exothermic reaction. The temperature gets so high that the iron that is produced is molten (in a liquid state). The melting point of iron is 1535 °C. This reaction is very useful and is used by railway companies to weld rails together.

Welding railway rails using an exothermic reaction.

In the photograph you can see the reaction being used to weld railway rails together. Often, rails need to be welded where the railway lines are. The iron oxide and aluminium powder react in a container placed on the rails. The molten iron produced in the reaction is shaped and used to join the rails together. This reaction is called the **thermite reaction**.

In order for the reaction to take place, the iron oxide and aluminium mixture has to be ignited. This is done using another exothermic reaction – this time between magnesium powder and barium nitrate. This provides the energy to start the displacement reaction between the aluminium and iron oxide.

Questions

1 Can iron displace aluminium from aluminium oxide? Explain your answer.
2 Why is the thermite reaction useful for welding rails?

Displacement using carbon

Carbon is not a metal, but it can be used to displace some metals from their compounds. Carbon will displace zinc, iron, tin and lead from their **ores**. An ore is a rock that contains a metal compound.

People discovered that carbon could displace iron around 3500 years ago. They discovered that iron ore heated with charcoal (a form of carbon) at very high temperatures produced molten iron. Today this displacement reaction is still carried out, but on a large scale, in a **blast furnace**.

The iron ore is mainly iron oxide. This reacts with carbon to form iron and carbon dioxide.

iron oxide + carbon → iron + carbon dioxide

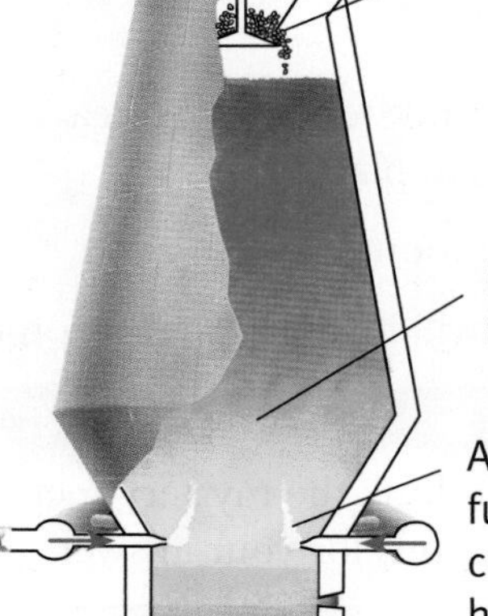
Iron ore and coke (a form of carbon) are added.
iron being displaced from its ore by carbon
Air is blown into the furnace to burn the coke and create the high temperatures needed for the reaction.
molten iron collects at the bottom

A blast furnace.

Questions

A+I

3 The early blast furnaces were in areas where there were supplies of iron ore and a lot of coal mining. Why do you think this was?

Activity 6.6

Extracting metals using carbon

SE

In this activity you will use carbon to try to displace a metal from its oxide. Remember that carbon will only displace a metal that is less reactive than itself. Wear safety glasses for both these experiments.

Experiment 1

1. Place a spatula of lead oxide in a container, such as a small beaker. Avoid touching the lead oxide, but if you do, wash your hands as soon as possible.
2. Add a spatula of charcoal powder and mix the two powders together thoroughly.
3. Place the mixture in a test tube and heat strongly in a Bunsen flame for five minutes.
4. Allow the tube to cool. Tip the cooled contents of the tube onto a heatproof mat.
5. Record your observations.

Questions

A1 Has there been a reaction between the lead oxide and the carbon? Give reasons for your answer.

A2 If there has been a reaction, write a word equation for it.

A3 What evidence does this experiment give you about the reactivity of carbon?

Experiment 2

1. Place a spatula of copper oxide in a test tube.
2. Add a spatula of charcoal powder on top of the copper oxide. Do not mix the powders together.
3. Heat the two layers strongly in a Bunsen flame for five minutes.
4. Allow the tube to cool and then look carefully where the layers meet.
5. Record your observations.

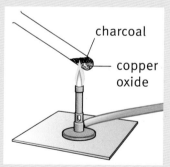

charcoal
copper oxide

Questions

A4 Has there been a reaction between the copper oxide and the carbon? Give reasons for your answer.

A5 If there has been a reaction, write a word equation for it.

A6 What evidence does this experiment give you about the reactivity of carbon?

A7 Where would you place carbon in the reactivity series?

Summary

- The thermite reaction is a displacement reaction which can be used to weld railway lines together.
- Displacement reactions are used to extract some metals from their ores.

Unit 6 End of unit questions

6.1 Hana placed five metals in water. She also placed four of the metals in dilute acid. Her observations are recorded in the table.

Metal	Reaction with water	Reaction with dilute acid
aluminium	No reaction.	Bubbles of gas are given off.
sodium	There is a very vigorous reaction. Sodium gives off bubbles of gas and the gas ignites.	
magnesium	Bubbles of gas are given off.	Bubbles of gas are given off very rapidly.
gold	No reaction.	No reaction.
tin	No reaction.	Bubbles of gas are given off very slowly.

a Name another metal that has a similar reaction to sodium. [1]
b Suggest why Hana did not place sodium in dilute acid. [1]
c Use Hana's results to place the five metals in order of reactivity, starting with the most reactive. [4]
d Write a word equation for the reaction between sodium and water. [2]
e Write a word equation for the reaction between magnesium and hydrochloric acid. [2]

6.2 Rafa places a piece of aluminium metal into a test tube of copper sulfate.

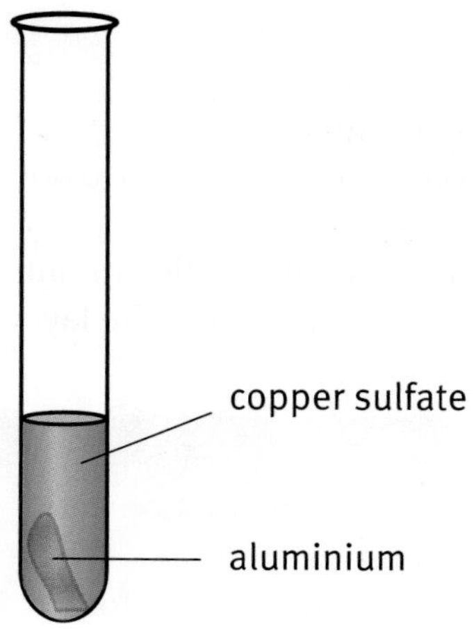

A reaction takes place.
The word equation for this reaction is:

aluminium + copper sulfate → aluminium sulfate + copper

a How can Rafa tell that a reaction has taken place? [1]
b Why is this reaction called a displacement reaction? [1]
c Rafa then places some zinc in a solution of lead nitrate. A displacement reaction takes place. Write the word equation for this reaction. [2]
d He then places some copper into a solution of sodium chloride. No reaction takes place. Give a reason for this. [1]

6.3 The word equations below represent some displacement reactions.

aluminium + copper sulfate → aluminium sulfate + copper
aluminium + lead nitrate → aluminium nitrate + lead
lead + copper sulfate → lead sulfate + copper
lead + silver nitrate → lead nitrate + silver

a Use the word equations to decide which of the four metals – aluminium, copper, lead and silver – is the most reactive. [1]

b Decide if a reaction will take place when lead is placed in a solution of magnesium sulfate. If you think there will be a reaction, write the word equation for it. [1]

c Decide if a reaction will take place when iron is placed in a solution of lead nitrate. If you think there will be a reaction, write the word equation for it. [1]

6.4 **a** The following equations show four reactions.

A carbon + oxygen → carbon dioxide
B iron sulfate + zinc → zinc sulfate + iron
C sodium hydroxide + hydrochloric acid → sodium chloride + water
D magnesium + oxygen → magnesium oxide

Give the letter A, B, C or D of the reaction that is:

i a neutralisation reaction [1]
ii a displacement reaction [1]
iii a reaction in which a metal oxide is formed [1]

b What does the reaction in equation B tell you about the reactivity of the two metals involved? [1]

c When magnesium or zinc metal are placed into dilute hydrochloric acid, bubbles of a gas are given off.

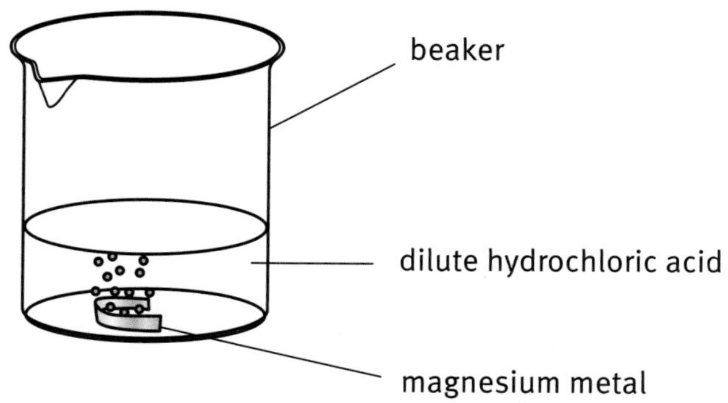

What is the name of the gas? [1]

7.1 What is a salt?

When you think about salt you probably think of the salt you put in your food, as a flavouring. This is sodium chloride. But there are many other kinds of salts, for example, copper sulfate, potassium nitrate and calcium carbonate.

Many salts have important uses in everyday life. The photographs show some examples.

Calcium sulfate is a salt that is used to make blackboard chalk.

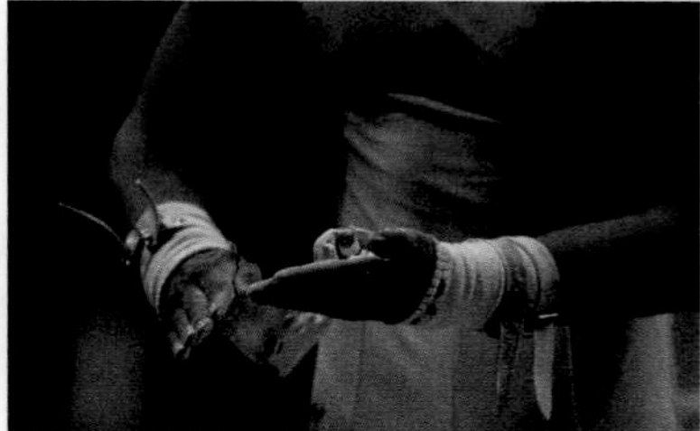

In sport you can use magnesium carbonate to keep your hands dry, so they do not slip.

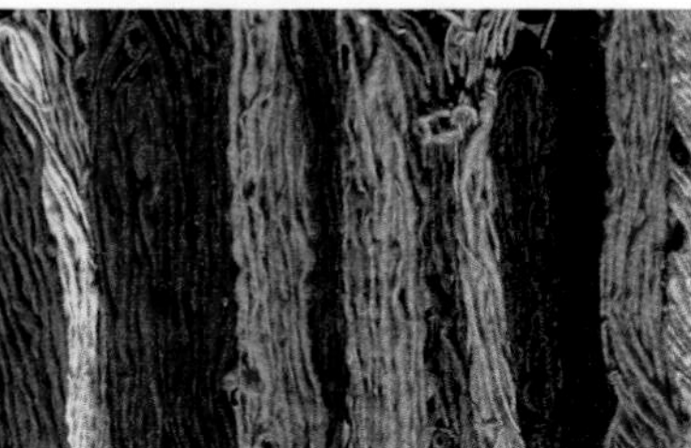

Aluminium sulfate is added to dyes to help them to stick to fibres.

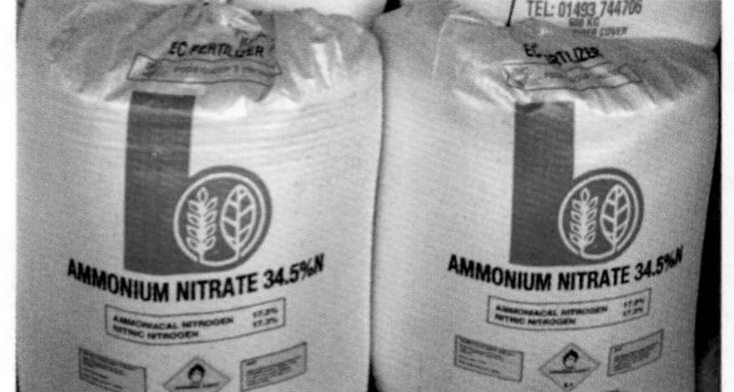

Ammonium nitrate is used as a fertiliser to help crops grow well.

Copper sulfate is used to stop fungi growing on these soya seeds when they are planted.

Sodium chloride is used to preserve food and, as table salt, to flavour food.

Acids and salts

Every day, the chemical industry makes hundreds of thousands of tonnes of different salts. Many methods for making salts start with acids.

All acids contain hydrogen. The table below gives the formulae of the three common acids that you find in the laboratory. The table also shows some examples of the salts that can be formed from these acids.

Two other acids that you may meet are carbonic acid and citric acid. Carbonic acid is a weak acid that is formed when carbon dioxide reacts with water. Salts made from carbonic acid are called carbonates.

Citric acid is found in citrus fruits, such as oranges and lemons. Salts formed using citric acid are called citrates.

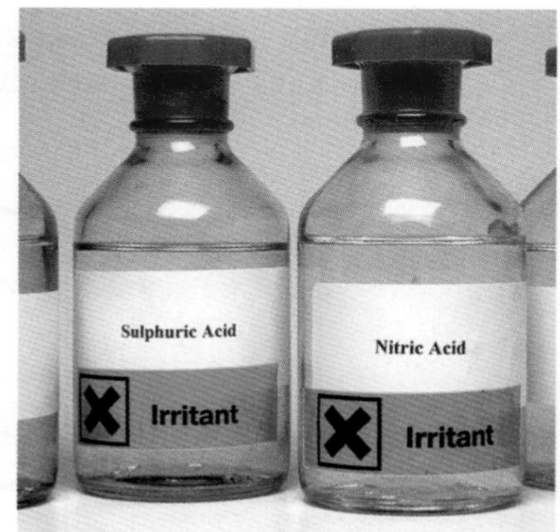

Bottles of laboratory acid.

Name of acid	Formula	Salts formed from the acid	Example of salt	Formula of salt
hydrochloric acid	HCl	chlorides	sodium chloride	$NaCl$
sulfuric acid	H_2SO_4	sulfates	copper sulfate	$CuSO_4$
nitric acid	HNO_3	nitrates	potassium nitrate	KNO_3

Questions

1 Think about what you have already learnt about acids.
  a What are the properties of acids?
  b Name some everyday products that contain acid.

2 Look at the formulae of the compounds in the table on the opposite page.
  a What is similar about the formula for hydrochloric acid and that for sodium chloride?
  b What is different about these two formulae?

A+I

3 The illustration below shows a label on a jar of orange preserve.

> **Allergy advice**: No nuts.
> Suitable for vegetarians.
> **Ingredients**: Sugar, oranges, water, concentrated lemon juice, sodium citrate, citric acid, bitter orange oil.
> Prepared with 30 g of fruit per 100 g.

  a Which ingredient is a salt?
  b Use the internet to find out why this ingredient is added to some kinds of food.

Activity 7.1

Researching a salt

Choose a salt to research. Your teacher will give you some suggestions.

Use the library or the internet to find the answers to these questions:

- How is this salt obtained or made?
- What is the salt used for?

Present what you have found out in an interesting way. You could make a poster, give a short talk or make a slide show.

Summary

- Salts are compounds that have hundreds of different uses in everyday life.
- Salts are formed when the hydrogen in an acid is replaced by a metal or ammonium.

7.2 Preparing a salt using metal and acid

In Topic 6.3, you investigated how metals react with dilute acids. This is often a good way of making a salt.

The general equation for the reaction of metals with acid is:

acid + metal → salt + hydrogen

The equation for the reaction between zinc and hydrochloric acid is:

zinc + hydrochloric acid → zinc chloride + hydrogen

Zinc reacting with an acid.

Questions

1 Which of the compounds in the equation above is a salt?

A+I 2 Which acid would you add to the metal magnesium to make the salt magnesium sulfate?

A+I 3 Write the word equation for the reaction of iron with hydrochloric acid.

A+I 4 Why would it be dangerous to prepare sodium chloride by reacting sodium with hydrochloric acid?

Activity 7.2A

Making the salt zinc sulfate

SE **Safety**: Be careful when heating the evaporating basin (dish) as the solution may spit and burn you.

1 Pour about 50 cm^3 of sulfuric acid into a 250 cm^3 beaker.
2 Add zinc metal (1–5 g) to the acid in the beaker.
3 Once the mixture stops fizzing pour it into an evaporating dish. Heat the evaporating dish very gently until you see crystals forming at the edge of the solution.
4 Remove from the heat and leave for a few days to form crystals.

step 3

Questions

A1 Write the word equation for this reaction.

A2 What are the important practical points you need to consider when you evaporate the solution?

A3 Which do you think is the better way to produce large crystals – heating the evaporating dish until there is very little liquid left or leaving it to evaporate slowly?

Using a metal oxide to make a salt

Some metals will not react with acids to make salts. For example, silver and copper are too unreactive to displace hydrogen from an acid.

So we have to find another way of making salts from unreactive metals. We can do this by starting with a metal oxide.

Activity 7.2B
Making the salt copper sulfate

SE

Safety: Remember not to boil the acid. Be careful when heating the evaporating basin as the solution may spit and burn you.

1 Pour about 100 cm^3 of sulfuric acid into a 250 cm^3 beaker. Add black copper oxide powder to the acid in the beaker.
2 Heat the mixture very gently, stirring all the time. **Safety**: Do not boil the mixture. Harmful fumes may be given off.
3 When the mixture changes colour to blue turn off the heat. Allow the mixture to cool.
4 Filter the mixture. The filtrate is a solution of copper sulfate. Pour this into an evaporating basin.
5 Heat the evaporating basin very gently until you see crystals forming at the edge of the solution. Remove from the heat and leave for a few days to form crystals.

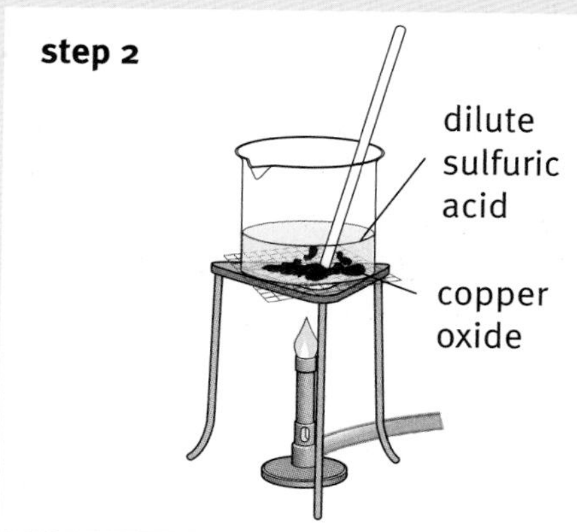

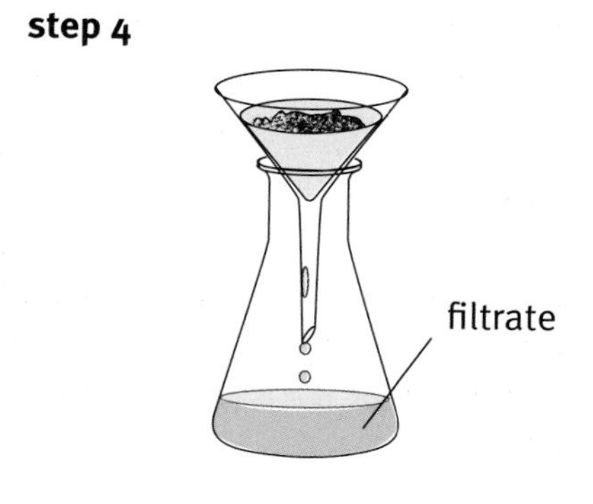

Questions

A4 Suggest why the mixture was filtered.
A5 Suggest how you could use a similar method to make copper chloride.

Summary

- Salts can be prepared by reacting metals with acids.
- To obtain a dry sample of the salt, you must allow the water to evaporate from the solution of the salt.
- Unreactive metals will not react with acids, so you cannot make their salts in this way.

7.3 Metal carbonates and acids

Carbonates – such as calcium carbonate – are salts. Carbonates can be formed by the reaction of a metal with carbonic acid.

We can use carbonates to form other salts by reacting them with an acid.

For example:

sulfuric acid + calcium carbonate → calcium sulfate + water + carbon dioxide

hydrochloric acid + calcium carbonate → calcium chloride + water + carbon dioxide

nitric acid + calcium carbonate → calcium nitrate + water + carbon dioxide

You may remember about the reactions of acids and carbonates from Stage **7**, where you learnt about limestone. Limestone is composed of calcium carbonate. It is damaged when it reacts with acid rain and erodes.

The general equation for these reactions is:

acid + carbonate → salt + water + carbon dioxide

Coral skeletons are made of calcium carbonate. This piece of coral is reacting in hydrochloric acid. How can you tell that a reaction is taking place?

Questions

A+I

1 Write the word equation for the reaction between magnesium carbonate and nitric acid.
2 How could you check that the gas given off in these reactions is carbon dioxide?

Activity 7.3

Preparation of a salt from acid and carbonate

SE

You are going to prepare copper chloride, using the reaction between copper carbonate and hydrochloric acid.

1 Place 25 cm^3 of hydrochloric acid in a small beaker.
2 Add a spatula of copper carbonate.

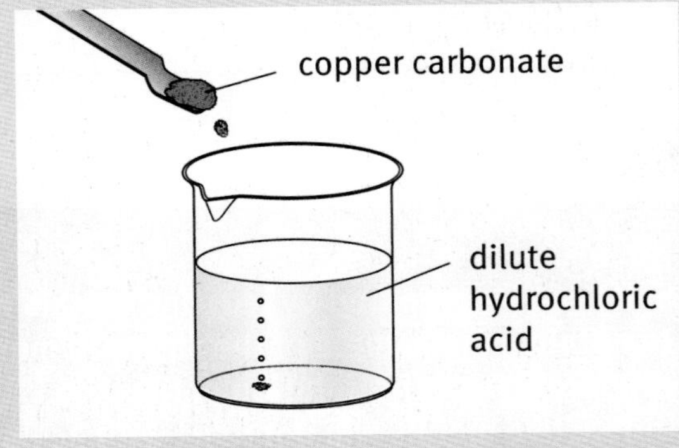

continued ...

... continued

3 Add more copper carbonate until it stops reacting. You should have a small amount of unreacted copper carbonate left in the beaker. (This is called adding excess copper carbonate. It makes sure that all the acid has reacted.)

4 Filter the mixture. The unreacted copper carbonate will be trapped in the filter paper.

5 Pour the filtrate into an evaporating basin and heat it gently. **Safety:** Take care while you heat this as the solution may spit and burn you.

6 Stop heating the dish when you see some crystals around the edge of the solution.

7 Leave the solution for a few days to cool and evaporate slowly.

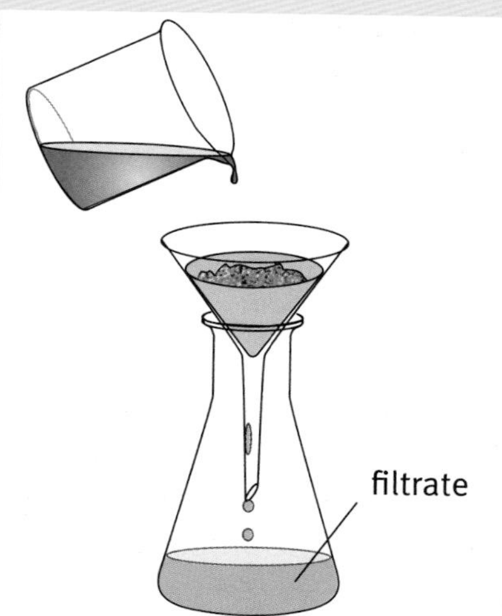

Questions

A1 What did you observe when you added copper carbonate to the hydrochloric acid?

A2 Which gas is given off during this reaction?

A3 Describe the appearance of the copper chloride that you have made.

A4 Write the word equation for your reaction.

A5 Which substances in your word equation are salts?

A6 Using your observations from this experiment, what can you say about the solubility of copper carbonate and copper chloride? (Think about what happened when you filtered the liquid from the beaker.)

A7 Suggest how you could use copper carbonate to make copper sulfate.

Blue-green colours in these rocks in the Atacama Desert in Chile tell you that they contain copper salts. This bright blue-green mineral in the rock is called malachite. It is made from copper carbonate.

Summary

- Salts can be formed by the reaction of acid on a carbonate.
- acid + carbonate → salt + water + carbon dioxide

7.4 Forming salts by neutralisation

You will remember that alkalis react with acids and neutralise them. When an acid is neutralised by an alkali, a salt is produced. For example, when sodium hydroxide reacts with hydrochloric acid, the salt sodium chloride is formed. The other product is water.

sodium hydroxide + hydrochloric acid → sodium chloride + water

The general equation for **neutralisation** reactions is:

acid + alkali → salt + water

Questions

1 How can you test to see if a liquid is an acid or an alkali?
2 What word is used to describe a solution that is neither acid nor alkaline?
3 What are the properties of alkalis?

Activity 7.4

Preparing a salt by neutralisation

SE

1 Place hydrochloric acid in a burette.
2 Measure out 20 cm³ of sodium hydroxide in a small flask.
3 Add a few drops of Universal Indicator solution.
4 Add the acid from the burette slowly, swirling the flask (moving it gently round) as you add the acid.
5 When the Universal Indicator changes to green you have produced a neutral solution.
6 Add a spatula of charcoal powder to the green solution. Mix it with a glass rod. The charcoal takes the green colour of the Universal Indicator out of the solution.
7 Filter the mixture.
8 Place the filtrate into an evaporating dish and heat gently.
Safety: Take care as the solution may spit and burn you.
9 Stop heating when you see some crystals around the edge of the solution.
10 Leave the evaporating basin for a few days. The water will evaporate slowly, leaving crystals of the salt.

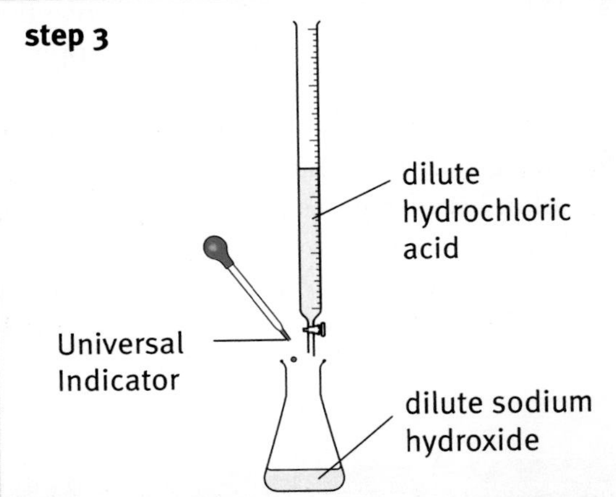

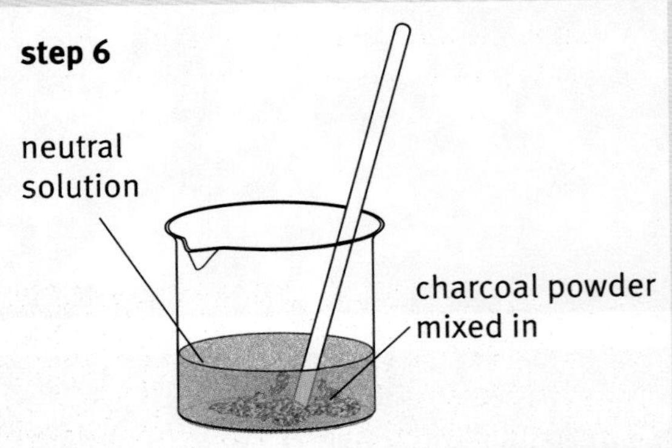

continued ...

... continued

Questions

A1 What colour is the Universal Indicator solution in the sodium hydroxide?
A2 What colour is Universal Indicator solution in a neutral solution?
A3 Why do you need to swirl the flask as you add the acid?
A4 Imagine that you accidentally added too much acid from the burette. What could you do to form a neutral solution?
A5 What salt is formed in this reaction?
A6 Write the word equation for this reaction.
A7 Describe the salt crystals you obtained.

Alkalis and bases

When a metal oxide dissolves in water, it forms an alkaline solution. Metal oxides are called **bases**. Soluble metal bases form alkalis when they dissolve in water.

For example:

sodium oxide + water → sodium hydroxide

Sodium oxide is a base. The sodium hydroxide is an alkali.

Some metal oxides are not soluble in water, for example iron oxide and copper oxide. So they do not form alkalis. But – as you saw if you did activity **7.2B** – they can still react with acids to form salts.

copper oxide + sulfuric acid → copper sulfate + water

Questions

4 What is the difference between a base and an alkali?
A+I **5** Suggest how you could use iron oxide to make iron chloride.

Summary

- Salts are formed when an acid is neutralised by an alkali.
- Metal oxides are called bases.
- Soluble metal bases form alkalis.
- acid + alkali → salt + water

Unit 7 End of unit questions

7.1 The diagram shows an experiment in which hydrochloric acid is added to a calcium salt. The gas carbon dioxide is given off.

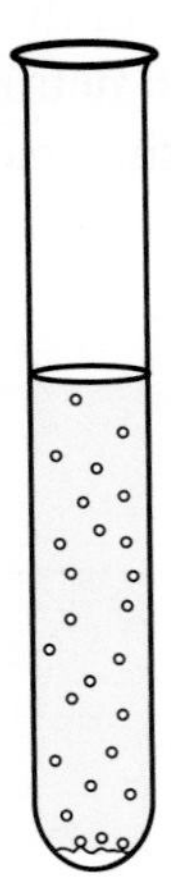

a Use the information to work out which calcium salt is being used. [1]

b How would you test the gas to check it is carbon dioxide? Remember to include the change you would expect to see. [2]

c Name the salt that is produced in this reaction. [1]

7.2 Write the word equations for the following:

a the reaction between magnesium and sulfuric acid [1]

b the reaction between aluminium and sulfuric acid [1]

c the reaction between potassium hydroxide and nitric acid [1]

d the reaction between copper carbonate and hydrochloric acid. [1]

7.3 Name the salt formed in a reaction between the substances given below:

a citric acid and calcium carbonate [1]

b nitric acid and aluminium [1]

c hydrochloric acid and ammonia [1]

d ammonium hydroxide and sulfuric acid. [1]

7.4 **a** Give **two** properties of acids. [2]

b What is a base? Give one example of a base. [2]

c What is an alkali? Give one example of an alkali. [2]

7.5 Carmel is making crystals of the salt potassium chloride by neutralisation. The diagram shows some of her apparatus set up ready to use.

a Copy the diagram and complete the labels.

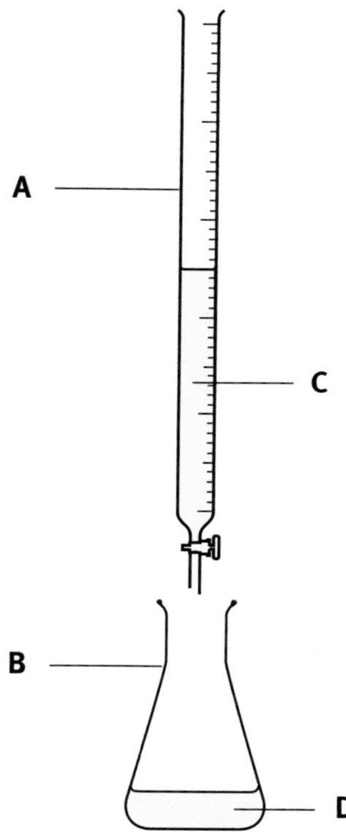

[4]

b How will Carmel be able to tell when she has a neutral solution? [2]

c Describe how she can obtain crystals of the salt. [3]

d List the safety measures she should take to stay safe while she carries out her experiment. [3]

8.1 Measuring the rate of reaction

The rate at which a reaction takes place can be measured by working out how much of one of the products has been made in a given time, or how much of a reactant is used up in a given time.

For example, when you add a piece of magnesium ribbon to hydrochloric acid, hydrogen gas is given off.

Measuring the formation of gas in a reaction.

Question

1 Write the word equation for the reaction of magnesium with hydrochloric acid.

How can you measure how quickly the reaction is taking place?

It is difficult to measure how quickly the reactants are used up or how quickly the magnesium chloride is formed. The easiest way is to measure how quickly the hydrogen gas is produced. You can measure the volume of gas produced in a particular length of time.

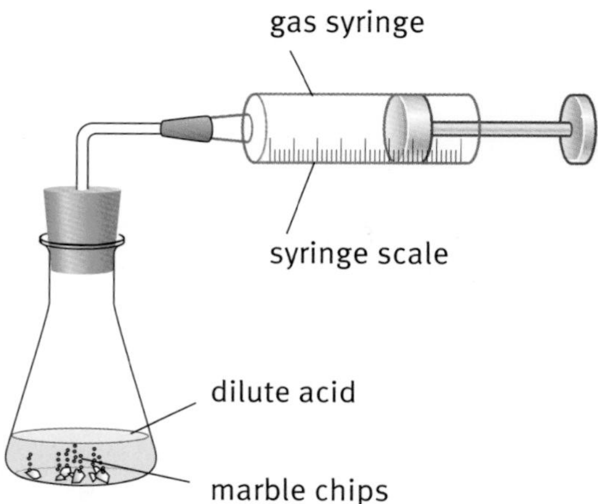

To collect the gas you can attach a syringe to the top of the flask so that no hydrogen can escape. You can use the scale on the syringe to measure the volume of gas produced at different times during the reaction.

The table below shows results obtained using this apparatus.

Time / s	Total volume of hydrogen gas produced / cm^3
0	0
30	10
60	20
90	26
120	40
150	48
180	54
210	60
240	64
270	66
300	66
330	66

Questions

SE **2** How can you tell from the results table that the reaction has finished at 270 seconds?

SE **3** Suggest what might happen to the experiment if you used a lot more magnesium and acid, so that more than 100 cm^3 of hydrogen gas was formed. What could be done to reduce the risk of an accident if more than 100 cm^3 of hydrogen was produced?

When a graph of the results is plotted, it is easier to see the pattern that they make.

The graph shows that one of the results does not fit (correspond with) the pattern. This is called an anomalous result.

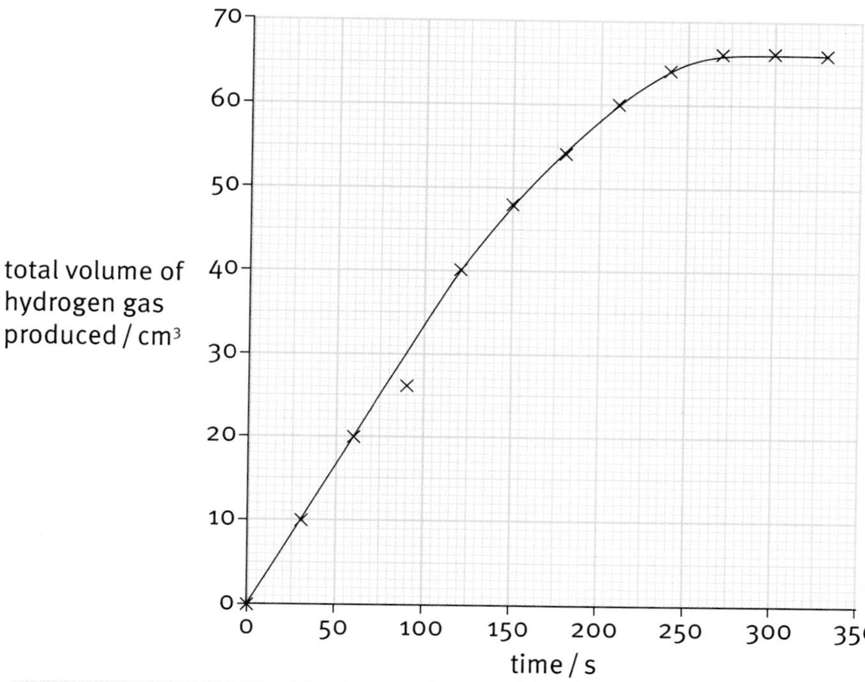

Questions

4 Which of the results is anomalous? Explain how you identified the anomalous result, and say what you would expect the result to be.

5 If you did this experiment and produced an anomalous result, what would you do about it? How would this help you to decide if the result really was anomalous?

Summary

- The rate of a reaction can be measured by the amount of product made in a given time or amount of reactant used.
- If a gas is made in a reaction, measuring the volume of the gas produced in a given time is often the best way to measure the rate of the reaction.

8.2 Changes in the rate of reaction

If you measure the rate of reaction, you find that the rate changes as the reaction proceeds. For example, in a reaction between calcium carbonate and hydrochloric acid, lots of bubbles of carbon dioxide gas are given off at the start of the reaction. As the reaction continues, fewer and fewer bubbles are produced. This shows that the reaction has slowed down.

78.92 g

Measuring the rate of a reaction by finding the loss in mass.

Question

1 Write the word equation for the reaction of calcium carbonate with hydrochloric acid.

As carbon dioxide gas is lost from the flask, the mass of the flask and contents decreases. If you measure the mass of the flask every 30 seconds, you find that the mass decreases quickly at first. But as the reaction continues, the mass decreases more and more slowly.

Using the graph

The graph can be used to measure the rate of reaction at any given time. The slope or gradient of the line tells you how quickly the reaction is taking place.

The steeper the slope, the faster the reaction.

The line is steepest at the start of the reaction. This is when the reaction is fastest. As the slope of the line becomes less steep, the reaction is slowing down. When the line levels out it shows that no more carbon dioxide is being lost. This means that the reaction has ended.

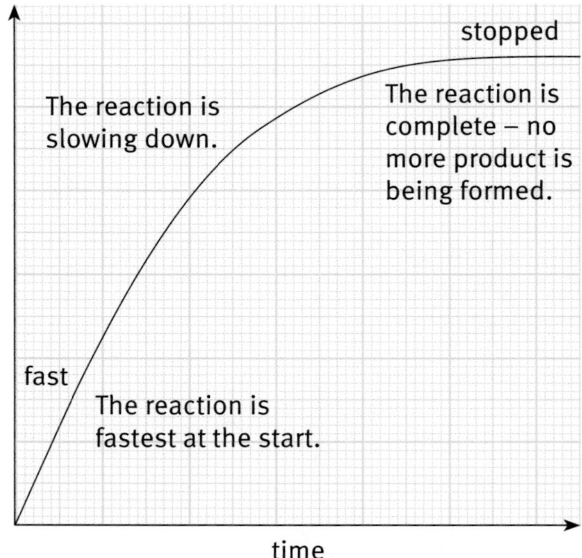

This graph shows the results of an investigation into the rate of reaction between calcium carbonate and hydrochloric acid.

Activity 8.2
Measuring the rate of reaction

SE

In this activity you are going to measure the rate of reaction between calcium carbonate and hydrochloric acid. You could do this by measuring the mass of carbon dioxide lost, using a top pan balance as in the diagram at the top of this page. Or you could collect the carbon dioxide and measure the volume produced either using a gas syringe, as shown on page **104**, or using a funnel and measuring cylinder filled with water, as shown here.

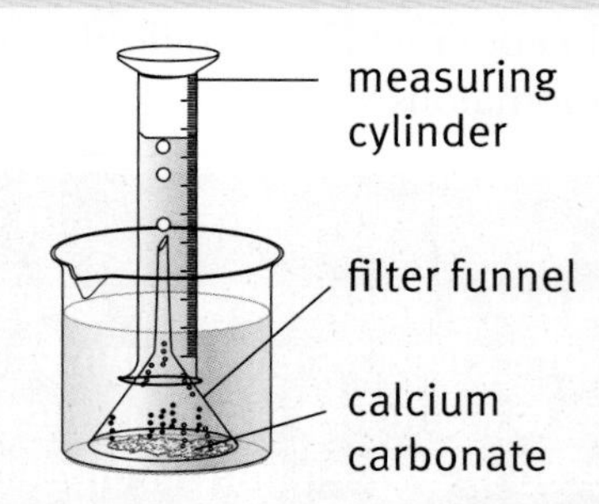

continued ...

... *continued*

1. Prepare a table for your results.
2. Assemble your equipment and put the calcium carbonate into the flask.
3. Add the hydrochloric acid; start the timer and measure the initial mass or volume.
4. After 30 seconds measure again. Repeat this every thirty seconds, until you have three readings that are the same.

Questions

A1 Plot a graph of your results and describe how the rate of reaction changes over time.

A2 What problems did you find when you carried out this reaction? How might these have affected your results?

A3 How could you improve the reliability of your results?

Why does the rate of reaction change?

We can use the ideas about particle theory that you learnt about in Stages **7** and **8** to answer this question.

For a chemical reaction to take place, the particles of the reactants involved have to collide with each other with enough energy to react together. At the start of a reaction there are lots of particles that have not reacted. **Collisions** happen frequently. This means that a lot of carbon dioxide is formed in the first 30 second period.

As the particles react, the number that have not reacted gets lower and lower. The chance of two unreacted particles colliding with each other decreases. This means that less carbon dioxide is formed in the later 30 second periods. This means that the rate of reaction is slower.

Eventually, all the particles have reacted. There are no more collisions that result in the production of carbon dioxide gas. The reaction has finished.

hydrochloric acid
calcium carbonate

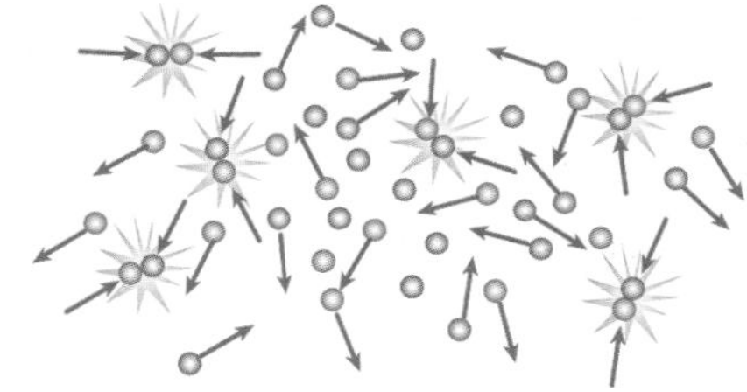

Many particles and frequent collisions.

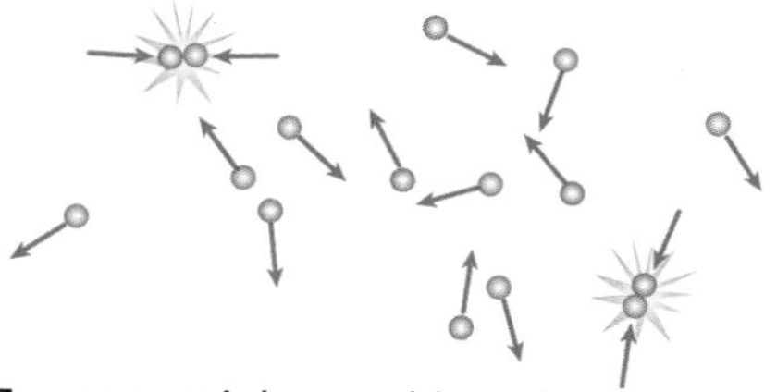

Fewer particles and less frequent collisions.

Summary

- The rate of a reaction changes with time.
- The slope of the graph of the results is a measure of the rate of reaction.
- The more collisions between particles of reactants there are in a given time, the faster the reaction.

8.3 Surface area and the rate of reaction

When you burnt magnesium ribbon in a Bunsen flame it reacted very quickly, with a white flame. But if you place a large piece of magnesium in the Bunsen flame it does not burn. If you place magnesium powder in the Bunsen flame it burns faster than the ribbon.

Why does this happen? Think about what is happening as the magnesium reacts with oxygen in the air. Only the magnesium atoms on the surface can make contact with the oxygen. In the block of magnesium, most of the atoms are inside the block, away from the oxygen. In the magnesium ribbon, most of the atoms are on the surface and react. Magnesium powder has an even larger total **surface area** and, because it has the most atoms available to react, the reaction is quicker.

Small pieces of solids always react faster than larger pieces. Each time you cut a solid into smaller pieces you increase the total surface area.

The slices have a much greater total surface area than the whole loaf.

- atom at the surface
- atom inside

Only the magnesium atoms on the surface can react with oxygen in the air.

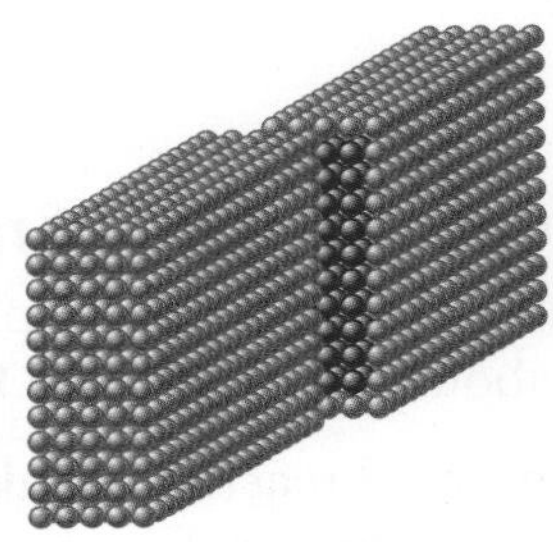

In magnesium ribbon, more of the atoms are on the surface and can react with oxygen in the air.

Activity 8.3A

Burning iron

SE

You are going to compare what happens when you heat an iron nail, iron wool and iron filings in air. Remember to record your observations for each.

1. Grip the nail firmly with tongs and hold it in the flame of a Bunsen burner.
2. Hold the iron wool in tongs and hold it in the flame of a Bunsen burner.
3. Use the end of a spatula to gently sprinkle a few iron filings into a Bunsen flame.

Questions

A1 Compare the reactions of these three forms of iron.

A2 What effect does increasing the total surface area have on the rate of reaction?

A3 Explain the reasons for the change in reaction rate.

Activity 8.3B
The effect of surface area on the rate of reaction

SE

In this activity you are going to investigate the effect of changing the size of pieces of calcium carbonate (marble chips) in the reaction with hydrochloric acid.

You could use any of the methods shown in topic **8.1** and topic **8.2** on pages **104–107** for measuring the rate of reaction. You are going to do the experiment twice, using different sizes of calcium carbonate chips. Whichever method you use, carry out the same one for the two experiments.

Answer these questions before you start the experiment.

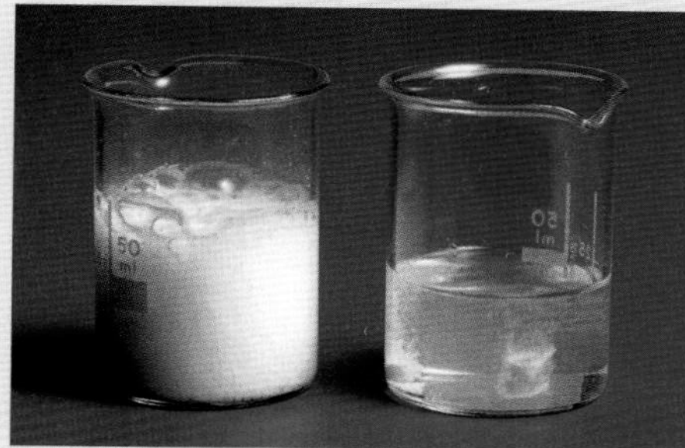

These beakers contain hydrochloric acid reacting with calcium carbonate. You will probably be able to use flasks instead of beakers in your experiment.

Questions

A4 Which reaction do you predict will be the fastest?

A5 The size of the pieces of calcium carbonate will be changed but the total mass of the pieces will be kept the same. Why is it also important to keep the volume, type and concentration of the acid the same?

A6 What are the dependent and independent variables?

A7 Read what you are going to do, and construct a results table.

1. Add 5 g of large marble chips to a measured volume of hydrochloric acid in a conical flask.
2. Start the timer and read the volume or mass every 30 seconds, until you have at least three readings that are the same. Record your results carefully.
3. Repeat, but this time use 5 g of smaller chips.
4. Plot both sets of results on one graph.

Questions

A8 Which line on your graph is steeper?

A9 Which size of marble chip reacts more quickly?

A10 What happens to the rate of reaction as the total surface area increases?

A11 What do you predict would happen if you repeated the experiment using powdered calcium carbonate?

Summary

- When a solid lump is cut into pieces, its total surface area increases.
- An increase in the total surface area gives an increase in the rate of reaction.
- The rate of reaction increases because the reaction can only take place with the particles on the surface of the solid.

8.4 Temperature and the rate of reaction

You are going to investigate how temperature affects the rate of reaction between hydrochloric acid and a salt called sodium thiosulfate. This reaction is a good one to use, because there is an especially easy way to measure its rate.

If you mix hydrochloric acid with a solution of sodium thiosulfate, the mixture becomes cloudy. This is because sulfur is produced. Sulfur is insoluble in water, so it forms a **precipitate**. You can time how long it takes for enough sulfur to be formed to make it impossible to see through the liquid.

As hydrochloric acid and sodium thiosulfate react together, sulfur is formed. The sulfur makes the liquid cloudy.

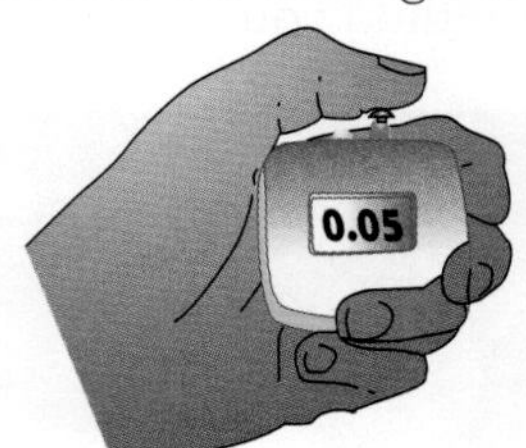

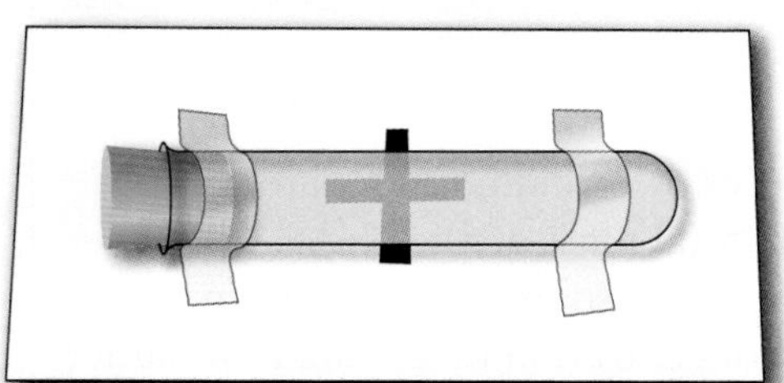

Activity 8.4A

The effect of temperature on the rate of reaction – trial run

SE

You are going to measure the rate of the reaction between sodium thiosulfate and hydrochloric acid at different temperatures. Before you do this you will need to carry out a **trial run**. A trial run means you will carry out a practice experiment to make sure you can do the experiment safely and effectively. You can then be prepared and overcome any problems you find.

Safety: Make sure the room is well ventilated, because sulfur dioxide gas will be produced. Place any reacted solutions into a container with some solid sodium hydrogencarbonate for your teacher to remove later. This will react with the sulfur dioxide.

1. Mark a dark line or a cross on a piece of paper.
2. Place 10 cm^3 of sodium thiosulfate solution in a test tube.
3. Add 1 cm^3 hydrochloric acid and put the stopper into the test tube.
4. Place the test tube horizontally on the paper over the dark cross. (You can hold it in place with some sticky tape or tack adhesive). Time how long it takes for the line to disappear.

Question

A1 What information did your trial run give you?

Activity 8.4B

The effect of temperature on the rate of reaction – preliminary work

SE

The next step is to do some preliminary work to decide which temperatures you will use. To change the temperature of the sodium thiosulfate solution, warm it in a suitable water bath before adding the acid. Make sure there is a stopper in the tube while it is warming.

Discuss in your group how you will do this preliminary work. When you have made your plan discuss it with your teacher.

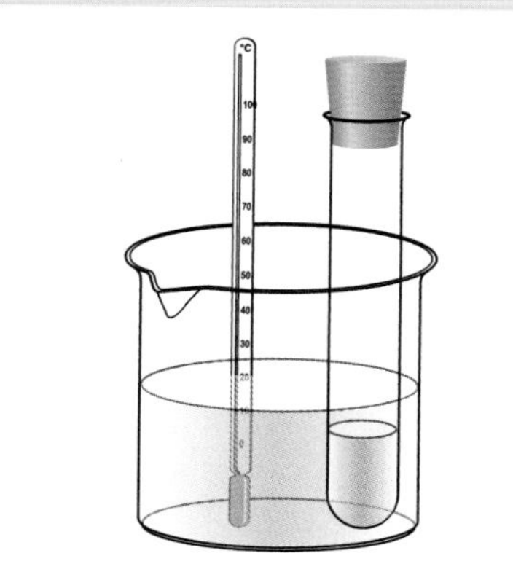

How large a change in temperature is needed to give a reaction time difference we can measure?
How big a range of temperatures will we use?

Will we start the temperatures at room temperature?
Will we increase the temperature by 5 °C or 10 °C or 20 °C?

Questions

A2 Describe what you have decided to do as your preliminary work.
A3 How will this help you with your final investigation?
A4 Write the outline plan for your investigation, including a results table.

Activity 8.4C

The effect of temperature on the rate of reaction – investigation

SE When your teacher has checked your plan, you can carry out your investigation.

Questions

A5 How did you make sure this was a fair test?
A6 Plot a graph of your results.
A7 Describe the relationship between the temperature and the rate of reaction.

Here is a graph of some typical results for the rate of the reaction between marble chips and hydrochloric acid. This was carried out as in the previous topic.

You can see from the graph that you do not get any more of the product (carbon dioxide gas) at the higher temperature. You get the same volume of gas, but in less time.

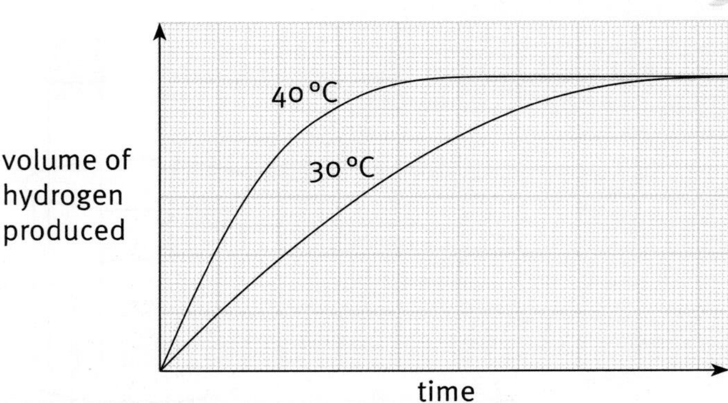

Questions

A+I **1** How can you tell which line shows the faster reaction?
A+I **2** If you did the same experiment at 50 °C what would the line on the graph be like?

Explaining the effect of temperature

Particles move all the time. When the temperature of the reaction is increased the particles move faster. They collide more often, and with more energy.

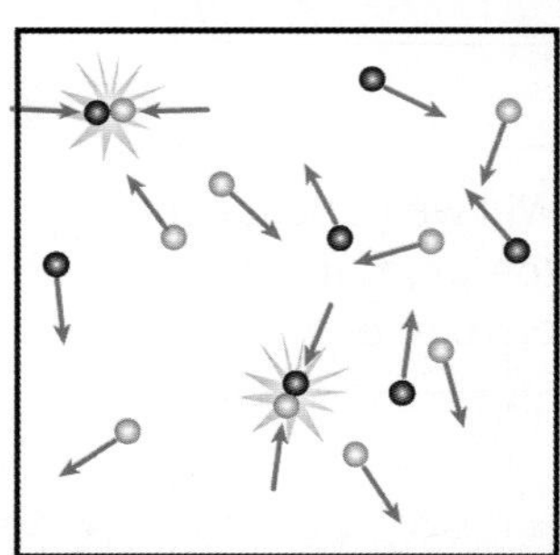
Reaction at 30 °C.

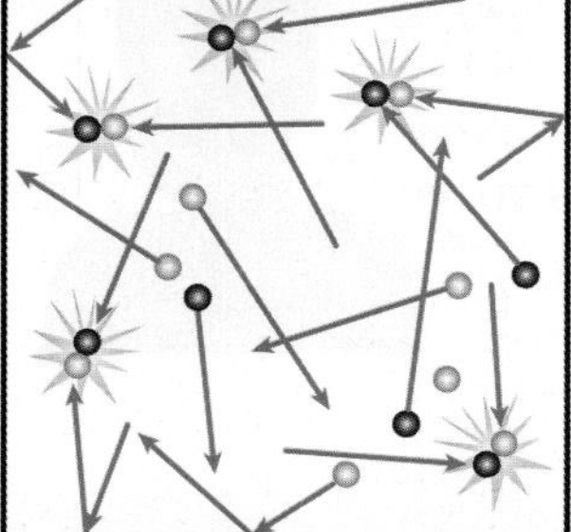
Reaction at 40 °C.

Summary

- As the temperature is increased the rate of reaction increases.
- When particles have more energy they move faster, and collide more often and with greater energy.

8.5 Concentration and the rate of reaction

If you carried out an experiment with marble chips and hydrochloric acid, using the same size and same mass of chips, the same temperature but different concentrations of the acid, what would you expect to happen?

Activity 8.5A

Planning an investigation into the effect of concentration

In this experiment you will change the concentration of the acid used. Instead of measuring the volume of carbon dioxide produced every 30 seconds, you will use a slightly different method of measuring the rate of the reaction – timing how long it takes to collect 25 cm^3 of carbon dioxide in the measuring cylinder.

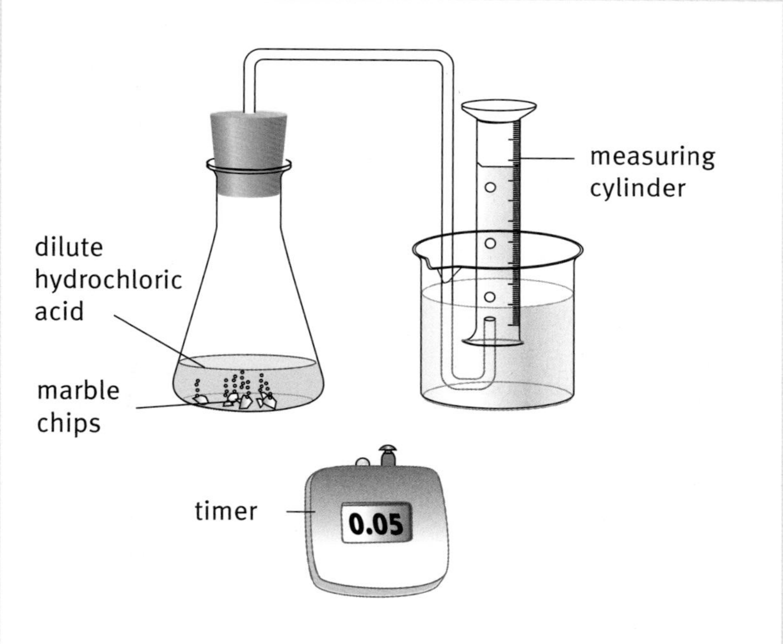

Discuss in your group how you will carry out this investigation. Things to be considered are:

- Which factors will you keep the same?
- What mass of marble chips will you use?
- What volume of acid will you use?
- Which concentrations of acid will you use?
- What safety precautions should you take?
- Do you need to do a trial run or some preliminary work?
- If so what do you want to find out?
- Do you need to repeat any of your readings?

When you have planned your investigation show it to your teacher.

Activity 8.5B

Carrying out an investigation into the effect of concentration

1 Make up your concentrations of acid. You can do this by diluting the acid you have been given. Make up 50 cm^3 each time. Use the following table to help you.

Solution	Acid / cm^3	Water / cm^3	
A	10	40	least concentrated
B	20	30	↓
C	30	20	
D	40	10	
E	50	0	most concentrated

2 Set up the apparatus as in the diagram.
3 Weigh out the marble chips and place them in the flask.
4 Add the acid and time how long it takes to collect 25 cm^3 of carbon dioxide.
5 Repeat with the different concentrations of acid.

Questions

A1 How did you make sure this was a fair test?
A2 How did you make sure the results were reliable?
A3 Plot a graph of your results.
A4 Which concentration of acid gave the fastest reaction?
A5 Describe the pattern in your results.

Here is a graph of some typical results for the rate of reaction between marble chips and dilute hydrochloric acid. In this experiment the volume of carbon dioxide has been measured every 10 seconds.

You can see from the graph that you do not get any more of the product (carbon dioxide gas) at the higher concentration. You get the same volume of gas, but more quickly.

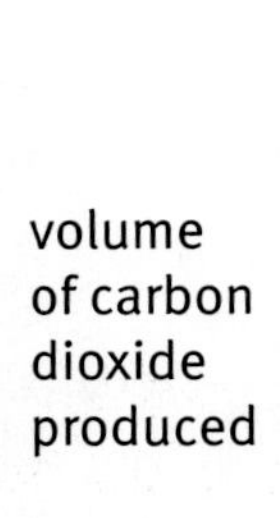

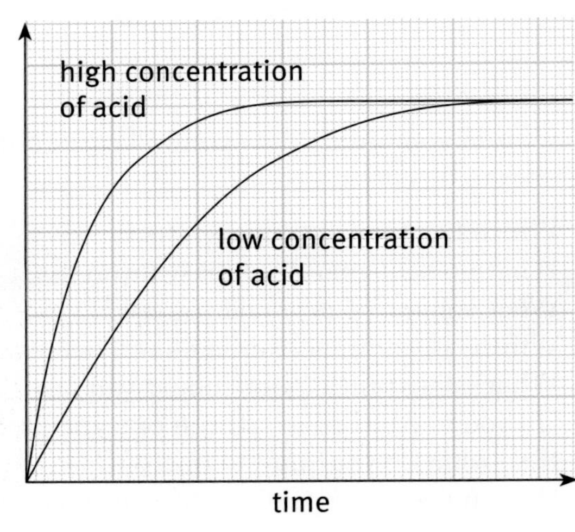

Questions

1 How can you tell which line on the graph shows the faster reaction?
2 If you did the same experiment with even less concentrated acid what would the line on the graph be like?

Explaining the effect of concentration

Again, we can use particle theory to help explain these results.

The higher the concentration of hydrochloric acid, the more hydrochloric acid particles there are in a given amount of space. This means that there will be more frequent collisions between hydrochloric acid particles and calcium carbonate particles.

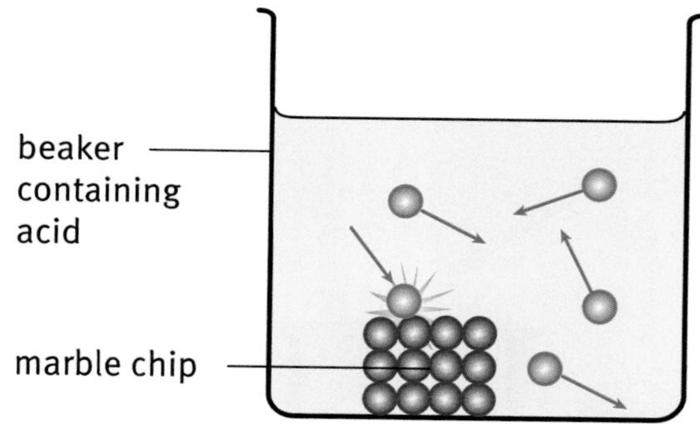

Reaction in dilute acid.

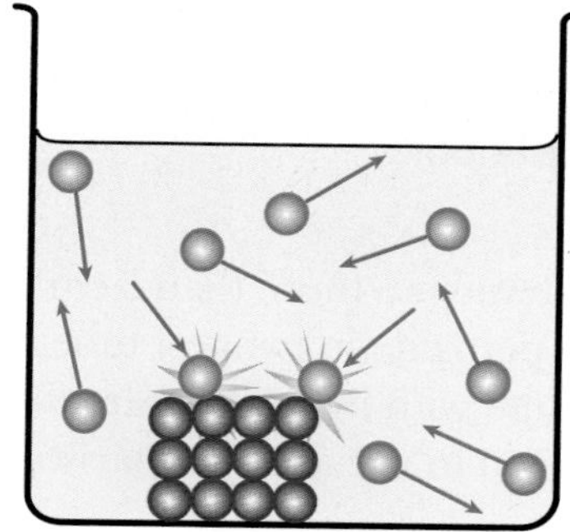

Reaction in acid that is twice as concentrated.

Summary

- As the concentration of reactants is increased, the rate of reaction is increased.
- When there are more particles in a given volume they are more likely to collide with each other.

8.6 Catalysts

When chemical manufacturers make their products, they want to make them as quickly and as cheaply as they can. You have seen that to speed up a reaction you could increase the temperature, concentration or surface area. You could increase all three.

But manufacturers have to balance the costs of the process against the increase in speed of the reaction. Increasing the temperature can be very expensive because energy costs are high. Increasing the concentration can also be expensive. Increasing the surface area may involve a process of crushing solids, which could add to the cost.

Many cars have catalytic converters fitted to their exhaust systems. These have catalysts inside that speed up reactions that help to get rid of harmful gases produced in the engine.

Activity 8.6

Using a catalyst to speed up a reaction

SE

In this activity, you will look at a different way of speeding up a reaction.

Hydrogen peroxide is a colourless liquid. It can decompose (break apart) to produce water and oxygen.

hydrogen peroxide → water + oxygen

You can tell when this reaction is happening because you will see bubbles of oxygen.

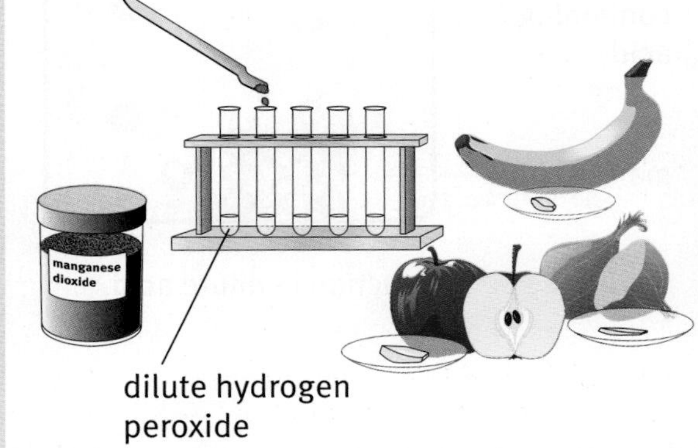

1. Place a small volume (no more than 5 cm^3) of dilute hydrogen peroxide in two test tubes.
2. Leave one test tube with hydrogen peroxide only. This is for you to use as a comparison. It is a control.
3. Add a small amount of manganese oxide to the other test tube. Record your observations.
4. Put the same volume of dilute hydrogen peroxide into four or five other test tubes. Add small pieces of fruit, vegetables and /or meat to each one. Record your observations.
5. Recover the manganese oxide from your second test tube. (Think about how you can do this. **Hint**: manganese oxide is insoluble in water.) Add this manganese oxide to another tube of hydrogen peroxide. Record your observations.

Questions

A1 Which of the items that you added caused the reaction to be quickest? How could you tell?

A2 Did the manganese oxide work for a second time after you had recovered it?

Using catalysts

The manganese dioxide made the reaction happen faster than if the hydrogen peroxide was just left on its own. But at the end of the reaction, the manganese dioxide was still there. A substance that speeds up a reaction, but remains unchanged at the end of the reaction, is called a **catalyst**.

Catalysts are often used to speed up reactions in industrial processes. The same catalyst can be used over and over again. This is usually much cheaper than increasing the temperature.

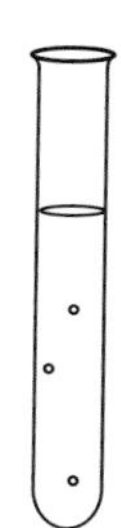

Bubbles of oxygen gas are given off as the hydrogen peroxide breaks down slowly on its own.

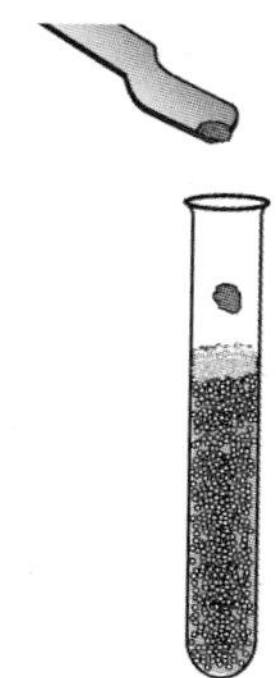

When manganese oxide is added the breakdown of hydrogen peroxide happens much faster.

Enzymes

You learnt about **enzymes** when you studied digestion. Enzymes are **biological catalysts**. Enzymes help to speed up most of the reactions that happen in your body. For example, enzymes are used to speed up the breakdown of the molecules of food in your digestive system so that you can use absorb the small molecules into your blood.

Hydrogen peroxide is formed as a waste product in many reactions in the cells of plants and animals. It is poisonous and if it is not broken down to harmless water and oxygen quickly, it will kill living cells. All living cells have an enzyme, called **catalase**, which speeds up the breakdown of hydrogen peroxide. That is why all the fruits, vegetables and meat you added in your experiment broke down the hydrogen peroxide very quickly.

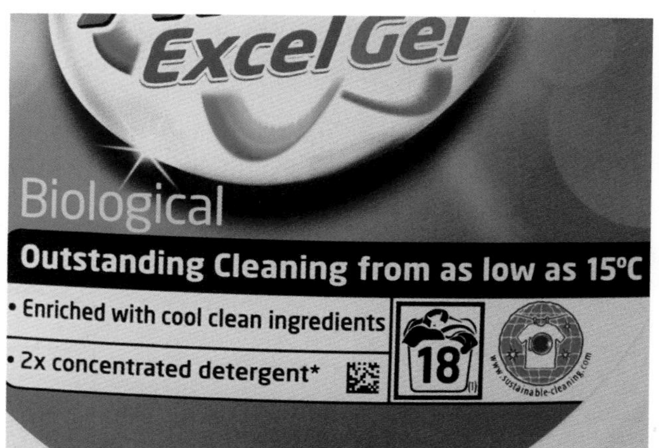

Some washing powders contain enzymes. They are called biological washing powders. They help to break down stains, such as food and blood.

Questions

1 What is another name for a biological catalyst?
2 What sort of washing powder has a catalyst in it?
3 Why do cars have catalytic converters fitted to them?

Summary

- A catalyst is a substance which speeds up a chemical reaction.
- A catalyst is not changed in the reaction and can be recovered and re-used.

Unit 8 End of unit questions

8.1 The chemical name for marble is calcium carbonate. In the experiment shown below, equal masses of marble lumps, small marble chips and powdered marble were placed into equal volumes of dilute hydrochloric acid.

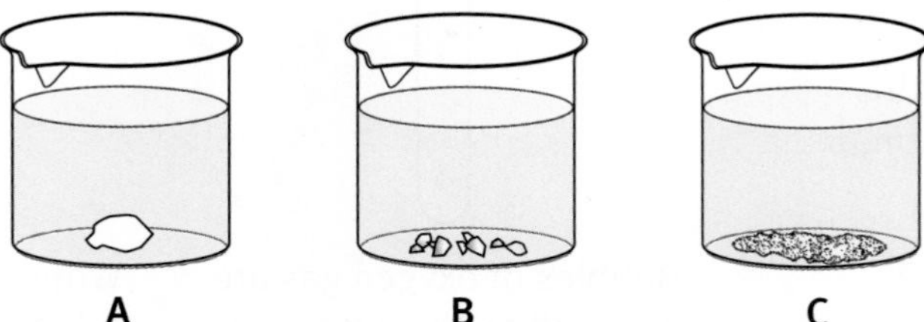

a In which beaker will the reaction be fastest? [1]

b Explain why you think this. [3]

c When the reaction between the calcium carbonate and dilute acid occurs, carbon dioxide gas is given off. How would you test for this gas and what would tell you that the test is positive? [2]

d What is the name of the salt formed in this reaction? [1]

8.2 Samuel was investigating the reaction below. He placed 4 g of magnesium ribbon into a beaker of dilute sulfuric acid. He timed how long it took for the magnesium to 'disappear'. It took 45 seconds.

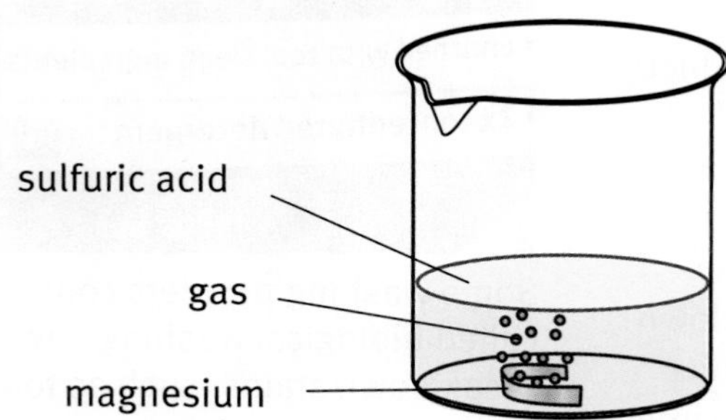

a Write the word equation for the reaction between magnesium and sulfuric acid. [2]

b How would you test for the gas given off in this reaction? (Remember to give the result you would get if the test was positive.) [2]

c Which of the following would result in the magnesium ribbon 'disappearing' in less than 45 seconds?

- warming the acid
- using 2 g magnesium ribbon
- stirring the mixture
- adding water to the acid

[2]

8.3 Bahula investigates the rate of reaction between magnesium and dilute hydrochloric acid.

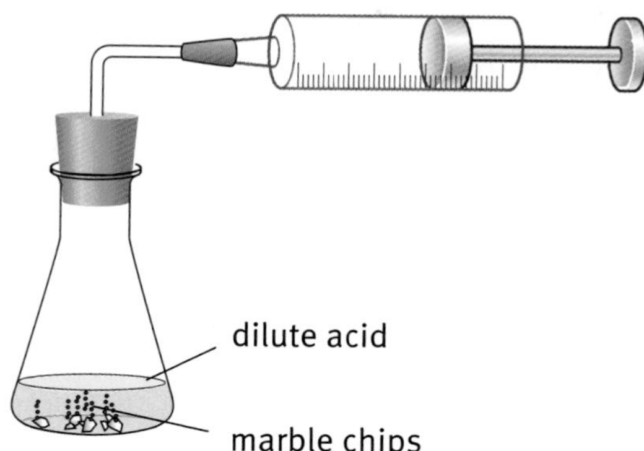

She measures how much gas is given off every 30 seconds. The graph shows her results.

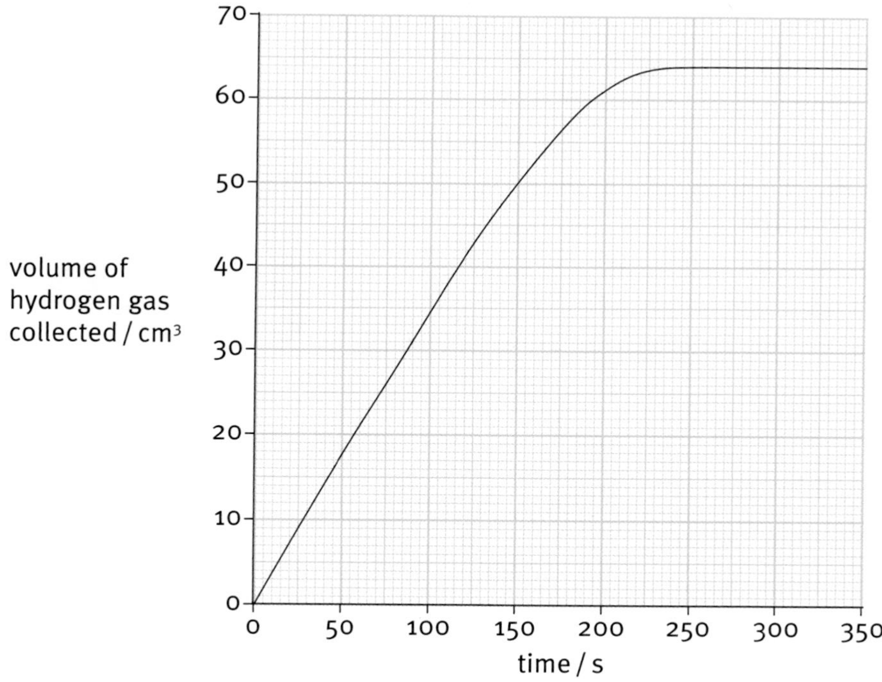

a How long does it take to collect 30 cm^3 of the gas? [1]

b How long does it take for the reaction to finish? [1]

c Describe how the rate of reaction changes over the period that the reaction is taking place. [3]

d Predict what would happen to the rate of the reaction if Bahula increased the temperature of the acid. [1]

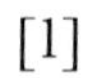

e Explain your answer to **d** using particle theory. [3]

9.1 The idea of density

Your teacher might try to trick you with a question like this: Which is heavier, a tonne of lead or a tonne of feathers?

Everyone knows that lead is heavier than feathers, but that is not the right answer. The answer is that a tonne of feathers is just as heavy as a tonne of lead.

The reason is that a tonne of anything weighs the same – it has a **mass** of one tonne, or 1000 kilograms.

1 tonne of feathers will balance 1 tonne of lead.

Question

1 a The mass of an object tells us how much matter it is made of. What is the unit of mass?

b Which has more mass, 1 kg of water or 1 kg of air?

Taking up space

The reason we can easily be tricked by the question about lead and feathers is that we know that feathers are 'lighter' than lead. But what does this mean?

If you look at the picture above, you will see that one tonne of feathers occupies much more space than one tonne of lead. One tonne of lead has the same mass as one tonne of feathers, but it is squashed into a much smaller **volume**.

If you took two identical boxes and filled one with lead and one with feathers, the box full of lead would be much heavier than the box of feathers. There would be much more mass squashed into the volume of the box.

Feathers are lighter than lead.

Comparing materials

In science, we don't say that lead is heavier than feathers. We say that lead has a greater **density** than feathers.

The density of a material tells us the mass of 1 cubic centimetre (1 cm^3) of the material. This is like a fair test, a way of comparing two materials. For each material we find the mass of 1 cm^3.

A 'heavier' material is more dense than a 'lighter' material. It has a greater density. In the picture, each cube has a volume of 1 cm^3, but the cubes have different masses.

We state the density of a material like this:

Density of water = 1.0 g/cm^3

This tells us that 1 cm^3 of water has a mass of 1.0 g. The unit of density is g/cm^3 (grams per centimetre cubed). Density can also be given in kg/m^3 (kilograms per metre cubed).

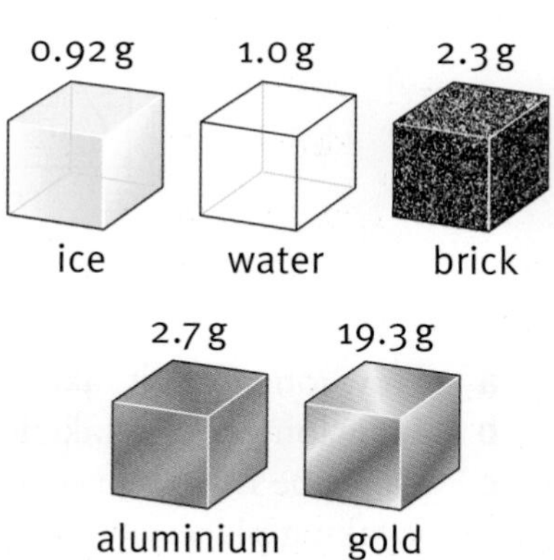

The mass of 1 cm^3 of a material tells us its density.

Question

2 Look at the picture of different materials on the previous page.
  a What is the density of gold?
  b Which is denser, water or ice?

Explaining density

Air has a very low density, about 0.0013 g/cm^3. You can understand this by thinking about the particle model of matter.

Air is a gas. Its particles are spread out, far apart from each other. There is a lot of empty space in between them. So air occupies a lot of space but its particles, which have mass, occupy only a tiny fraction of that space.

Lead is a solid. Its particles are packed closely together, and each particle has more mass than a particle of the air. This is why lead is so dense.

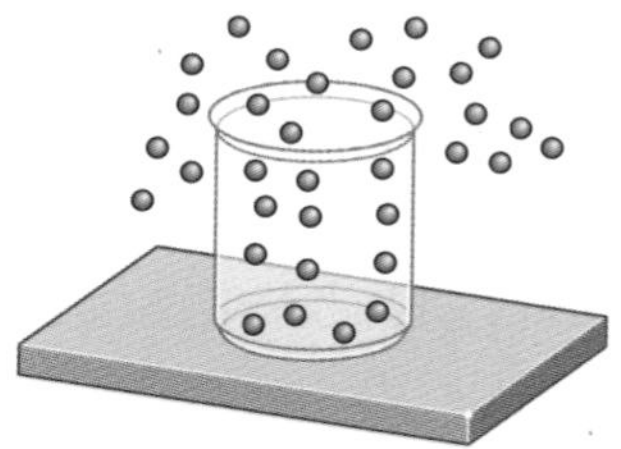

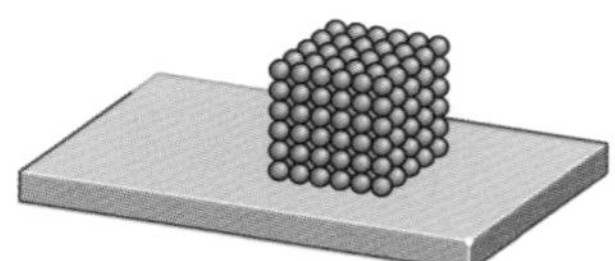

The particle model tells us why lead has a greater density than air.

Question

3 When water boils, it becomes steam. Its particles spread out and occupy a greater volume. Has its density increased or decreased? Explain your answer.

Activity 9.1
Judging density

SE

Sometimes you can tell if one material is denser than another simply by holding samples of the two materials in your hands.

Your teacher will give you some samples of different materials. Your task is to put them in order according to their densities.

Take two samples and hold one in each hand. Use your judgement to decide which is denser. Can you arrange all the materials from the least dense to the most dense?

Compare your answer with others in the class. Discuss how to improve this method for comparing materials.

Summary
- Density is a measure of how light or heavy a material is.
- Density is the mass of 1 cm^3 of a material.

9.2 Measuring density

If you want to know the density of a material, here is what you do. You take a sample of the material and measure two things:

- its mass in grams (g)
- its volume in centimetres cubed (cm^3).

Then you calculate its density like this:

$$\text{density} = \frac{\text{mass}}{\text{volume}}$$

Example: The diagram shows a block of cast iron. Its volume is 30 cm^3 and its mass is 210 g.

$$\text{density} = \frac{\text{mass}}{\text{volume}} = \frac{210\,\text{g}}{30\,\text{cm}^3} = 7.0\,\text{g/cm}^3$$

The picture shows that we can think of the block as being made up of 30 small cubes, each of volume 1 cm^3 and mass 7.0 g.

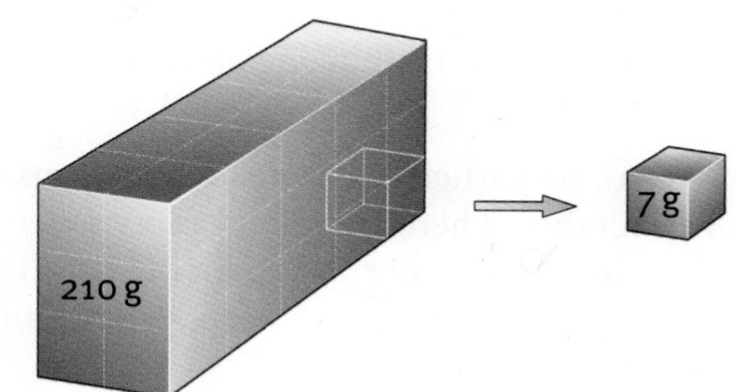

The big iron block measures 5 cm × 3 cm × 2 cm.

Measuring mass

Mass is measured using a balance. There are different designs of balance; check that the scale gives mass in grams.

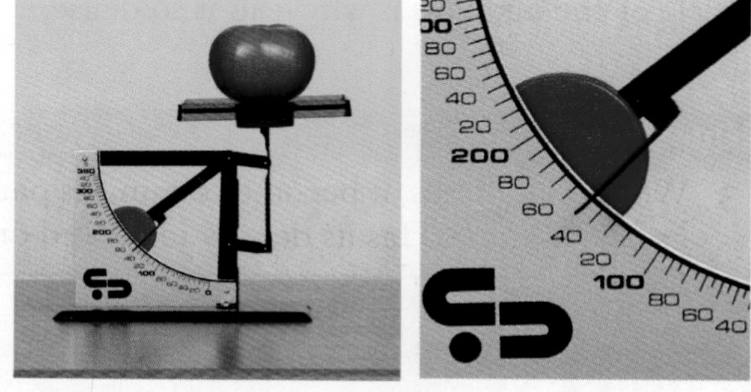

A balance like this can be used to measure mass.

Question

1 What is the mass of the tomato shown in the photograph?

Measuring volume

There are several ways to measure the volume of something. Two are shown below and one on the next page:

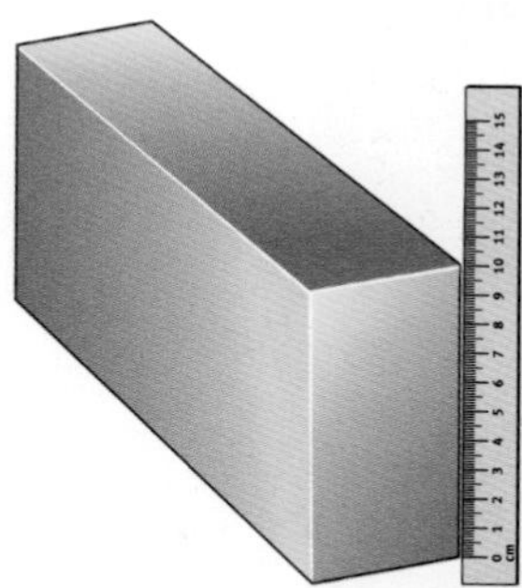

Find the volume of a solid with a regular shape by measuring each side and calculating its volume.
For a rectangular block:
volume = length × width × height

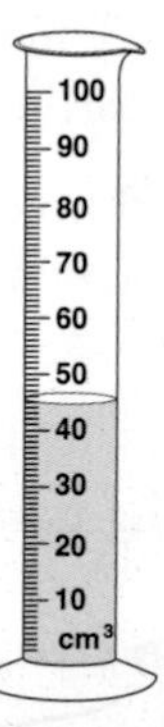

Measure the volume of a liquid by pouring the liquid into a measuring cylinder. Read the volume from the scale.

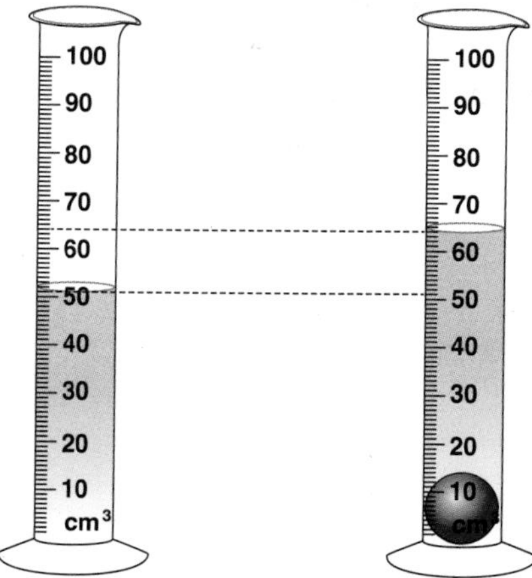

Find the volume of an irregular solid object by submerging the object in water in a measuring cylinder. Calculate the increase in volume.

Question

2 Here is a description of an experiment to measure the density of salty water.

Step 1: An empty measuring cylinder was placed on an electronic balance. The reading on the balance was recorded (54.0 g).

Step 2: Salty water was poured into the measuring cylinder. The new reading on the balance was recorded (115.2 g).

Step 3: The volume of the salty water was read from the measuring cylinder (60 cm^3).

a Draw diagrams to show the three steps described above.

b Calculate the mass of salty water.

c Calculate the density of the salty water.

Activity 9.2

Density measurements

Your task in this activity is to measure the densities of several different materials, some solids and some liquids.

You will have to choose the best method for measuring the mass, and the best method for measuring the volume.

When you have made your measurements, calculate the density.

Add notes to say which methods you used for measuring mass and volume, and why you consider these to be the best.

Summary

- To determine the density of a material, we measure mass and volume.
- $\text{density} = \dfrac{\text{mass}}{\text{volume}}$

9.3 Density calculations

Here is the equation which is used to calculate the density of a material, written in words and in symbols:

$$\text{density} = \frac{\text{mass}}{\text{volume}}$$

$$D = \frac{M}{V}$$

where D = density, M = mass, V = volume.

Question

A+I

1 A rectangular block of steel measures 4 cm × 2 cm × 1.5 cm. Its mass is 93.6 g.

- **a** Calculate the density of steel.
- **b** Steel is made almost entirely of iron atoms, but it is denser than iron. Suggest a reason for this.

Calculating mass

We can rearrange the equation for density like this:

$$\text{mass} = \text{density} \times \text{volume}$$

$$M = D \times V$$

A fish tank.

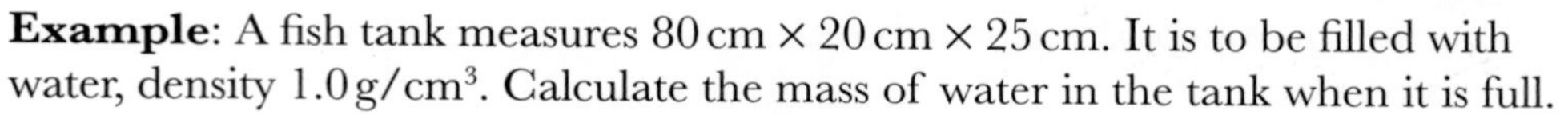

Example: A fish tank measures 80 cm × 20 cm × 25 cm. It is to be filled with water, density 1.0 g/cm^3. Calculate the mass of water in the tank when it is full.

Step 1: Calculate the volume of the tank.

$$\text{volume} = \text{length} \times \text{width} \times \text{height} = 80 \times 20 \times 25 = 40\,000\ \text{cm}^3$$

Step 2: Calculate the mass of the water.

$$\text{mass} = \text{density} \times \text{volume} = 40\,000 \times 1.0 = 40\,000\ \text{g}$$

Question

2 A half litre bottle has a mass of 80 g. It contains 500 cm^3 of liquid when full. The bottle is filled with olive oil of density = 0.90 g/cm^3.

- **a** Calculate the mass of oil in the bottle.
- **b** Calculate the mass of the full bottle.

A bottle of oil.

Calculating volume

We can rearrange the equation for density to make volume its subject, like this:

$$\text{volume} = \frac{\text{mass}}{\text{density}}$$

$$V = \frac{M}{D}$$

Example: A builder needs 20 000 kg of sand to make mortar. The sand is sold in 1 m^3 bags. How many bags will he need? (The density of sand is 2500 kg/m^3.)

We need to find the volume of the sand.

$$\text{volume} = \frac{\text{mass}}{\text{density}} = \frac{20\,000}{2500} = 8\,\text{m}^3.$$

(Notice that, because the mass is in units of kg and the density is in kg/m^3, the volume is in m^3.)

Since each bag has a volume of 1 m^3, he will need 8 bags.

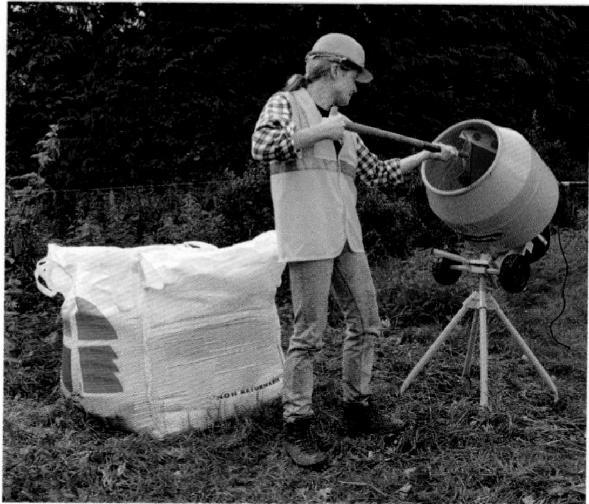

Mixing sand, cement and water to make mortar.

Question

3 A coin has a mass of 7.0 g. It is made of a metal alloy of density 5.6 g/cm^3. Calculate the volume of the coin.

Activity 9.3

Measuring the density of a gas

Air is a gas. Gases are much less dense than solids or liquids. Observe as your teacher measures the density of air.

The rigid plastic bottle once held water. We say that it is empty, but really it is full of air.

The container is weighed. This includes the mass of the air inside it.

Then the air is pumped out and the tap closed. Now the balance shows the mass of the container with no air.

Discuss the following:

- How can you calculate the mass of air in the container?
- How could you use water and a measuring cylinder to determine the volume of the container?
- How will you calculate the density of the air?

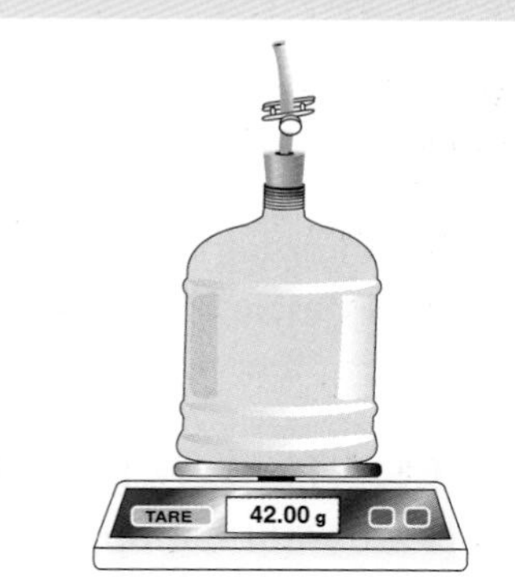

The plastic container is weighed when it is full of air, and when the air has been pumped out.

Summary

Density, mass and volume are connected by these three equations:

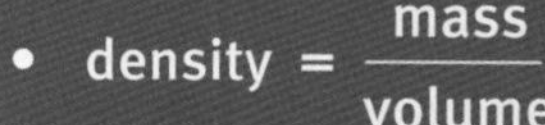

- $\text{density} = \frac{\text{mass}}{\text{volume}}$
- $\text{mass} = \text{density} \times \text{volume}$
- $\text{volume} = \frac{\text{mass}}{\text{density}}$

9.4 Pressure

A carpenter uses nails to join two pieces of wood together. The hammer hits the nail on its flat head. The nail's sharp point pushes into the wood.

Why does a nail have a sharp point? The force of the hammer is concentrated on a small area so that the nail will be able to penetrate the wood.

If a nail is blunt, the force of the hammer is spread over a bigger area and the nail will not go into the wood.

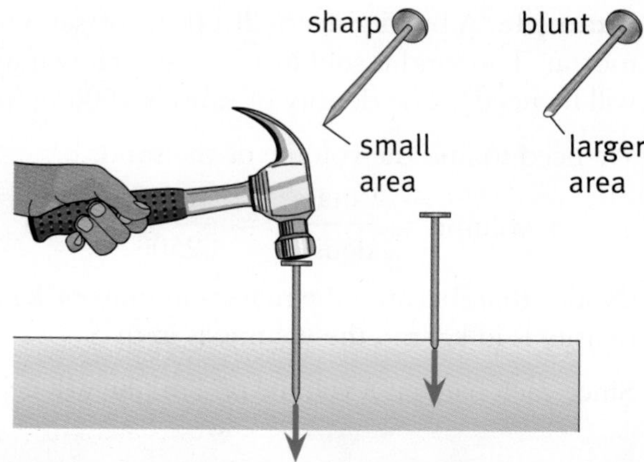

If it is sharp, a nail can be hammered further with the same force.

The idea of pressure

If a force is concentrated on a small area, we say that the force is creating a high **pressure**. If the force is spread over a bigger area, the pressure will be less.

If you lie on a bed, the force of your weight is spread over a large area. You will make a shallow dip in the mattress.

However, if you stand on the bed, your weight will be concentrated on a much smaller area. You will make a much deeper dip in the bed.

Standing makes a deeper dip in a bed.

Question

1 Who will create a greater pressure, a heavy person standing on a bed or a lighter person lying on the bed? Explain your answer.

High pressure, low pressure

Sometimes we want high pressure, sometimes we want low pressure. Here are some examples.

Sharks have sharp teeth so that, when they bite, the force of their jaws will create enough pressure to crush their prey.

A shark.

A knife is better at cutting when its blade is sharp. Then the force pushing on it will be concentrated on a small area to create a high pressure.

Camels have wide feet so that their weight is spread over a large area. Then the pressure will be low and they will not sink into the sand.

A snowboard is wide and does not sink into the snow. The Inuit people wear wide snowshoes for the same reason.

An Inuit holding his snowshoes.

Question

2 Explain the following; in your answers, use the words 'pressure', 'force' and 'area'.

- **a** A truck used in the desert has wide tyres.
- **b** A cricket stump has a sharp point at one end.
- **c** A drawing pin has a sharp point at one end and a large, flat head at the other.

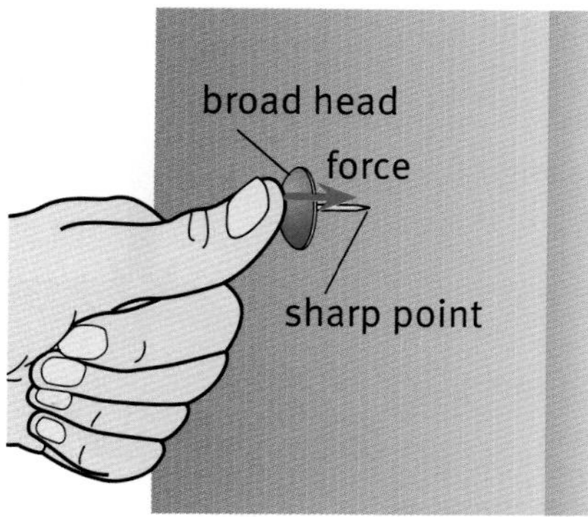

Activity 9.4

Cricket stumps

Before a game of cricket, the players must push the stumps into the ground. The picture shows four different situations – the stump may be pointed or blunt, and the force may be large or small.

Use what you know about pressure to decide which stump will go in furthest, and which will go in the least.

Be prepared to explain your ideas to the rest of the class.

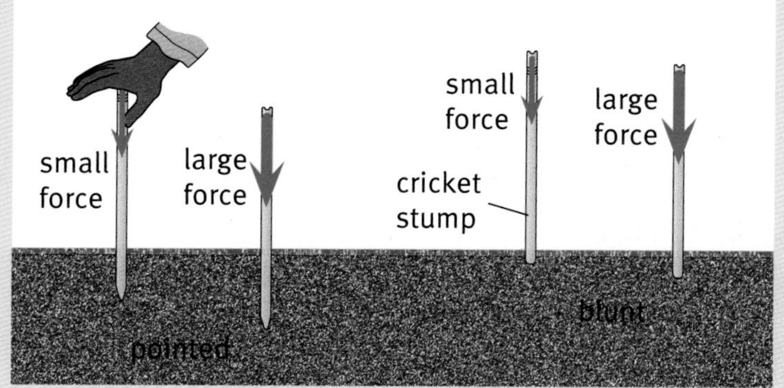

Summary

- Pressure is caused when a force acts on an area.
- A big force acting on a small area creates a high pressure.

9.5 Pressure calculations

Pressure is the quantity that tells us how concentrated a force is when it presses on an area.

Here is the equation which is used to calculate pressure, written in words and in symbols:

$$\text{pressure} = \frac{\text{force}}{\text{area}}$$

$$P = \frac{F}{A}$$

where P = pressure, F = force, A = area.

Example: The diagram shows a force of 8 N pressing on an area of $4\,m^2$.

$$\text{pressure} = \frac{\text{force}}{\text{area}} = \frac{8\,N}{4\,m^2} = 2\,N/m^2$$

So the pressure is $2\,N/m^2$. As the diagram shows, a force of 2 N is acting on each square metre of the surface.

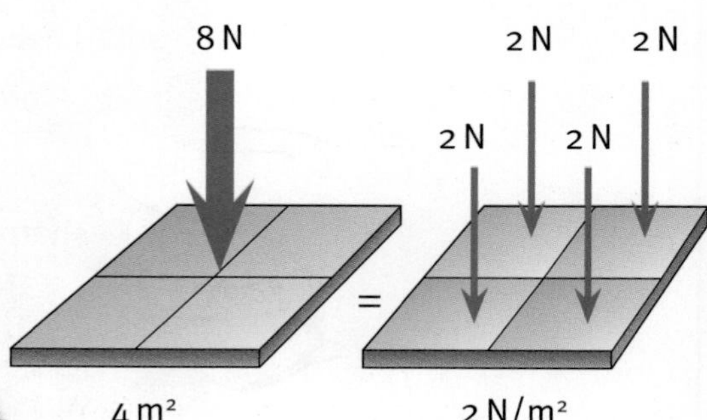

Question

1 A force of 6 N acts on an area of $2\,m^2$. What force acts on each square metre? What is the pressure on the surface?

Units of pressure

The unit of pressure is the **pascal** (Pa). 1 Pa is the same as $1\,N/m^2$. We can write the answer to the example above as:

$$\text{pressure} = 2\,\text{Pa}$$

In the next example, the area is given in square millimetres (mm^2), so the pressure is in newtons per square millimetre (N/mm^2).

Example: A hammer hits a nail with a force of 200 N. The point of the nail has an area of $0.5\,mm^2$ touching a piece of wood. Calculate the pressure on the wood.

$$\text{pressure} = \frac{\text{force}}{\text{area}} = \frac{200}{0.5} = 400\,N/mm^2$$

Hammering a nail.

Question

2 A rectangular block weighs 240 N. The area of the block in contact with the floor is $20\,cm^2$. Calculate the pressure on the floor. (Give your answer in N/cm^2.)

Calculating force

We can rearrange the equation for pressure like this:

$$\text{force} = \text{pressure} \times \text{area}$$

$$F = P \times A$$

A footbridge.

Example: A footbridge has been designed to withstand a pressure of 2000 Pa. The area of the bridge is 15 m^2. What is the greatest force the bridge can withstand (resist)?

$$\text{force} = \text{pressure} \times \text{area} = 2000 \times 15 = 30\,000\,\text{N}$$

That is the weight of about 50 people. Take care! The bridge might break if they all stand close together – that would create a greater pressure.

Question

3 When the wind blows, it creates pressure on any surface it blows against. A large window has an area of 3.5 m^2. If the wind causes a pressure of 2000 Pa on the window, what force acts on it?

Activity 9.5
Squashing foam

You can squash a piece of plastic foam by applying pressure to it. Place a stiff piece of wood on top of the foam. Place weights on top of the wood.

There are three things to measure:

- the area of the wood pressing down on the foam
- the force pressing down on the foam
- the thickness of the foam as it is squashed.

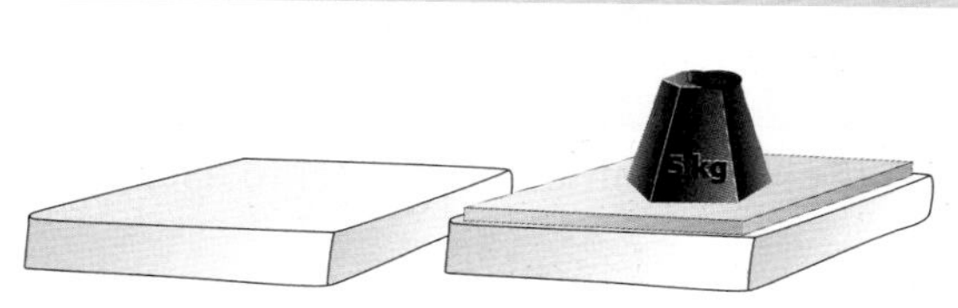

Calculate the pressure acting on the foam.

Use different weights to change the pressure. Draw a graph to show how the thickness of the foam depends on the pressure.

Summary

- $\text{pressure} = \dfrac{\text{force}}{\text{area}}$
- force = pressure × area

9.6 Pressure in gases and liquids

To inflate (blow up) a toy balloon, you must push air into it. When the balloon has been blown up, the pressure of the air inside presses outwards. This tells us that air and other gases can cause pressure.

Liquids can also cause pressure. The photograph shows a fireman using a high pressure hose to put out a fire.

A fireman at work in Mumbai, India.

Diving deep

Divers have to be careful if they want to dive to a great depth in the sea.

The weight of water above presses down on them. The greater the depth they go, the more water there is above them pressing down, and so the pressure is greater.

Pressure increases with depth in water because the weight of water pressing on the diver increases with depth.

Question

A+I

1 The photograph shows an experiment on water pressure. Water squirts out faster from the hole at the bottom of the bottle than at the top. Use the idea of pressure to explain why.

Holes in the bottle allow water to escape.

The pressure of the atmosphere

If you climb a high mountain, the air gets thinner (less dense) as you go higher. Its density decreases. Because the air is less dense at the top of a mountain, its pressure is less. We call the pressure of the air **atmospheric pressure**.

Atmospheric pressure is greatest at sea level. This is because, at sea level, we have the weight of the whole atmosphere above us, pressing down. It is as though we live at the bottom of an 'ocean' of air.

Question

2 Atmospheric pressure is about 100 000 Pa. Calculate the force of the atmosphere on a person whose surface area is $2.0\,m^2$.

9.6 Pressure in gases and liquids

Particles and pressure

We can understand the pressure of liquids and gases another way, using the **particle model** which you learnt about in Unit **5** of Stage **7**.

The diagram shows the particles of a gas in a box. The particles move around rapidly, bouncing off the walls of the box.

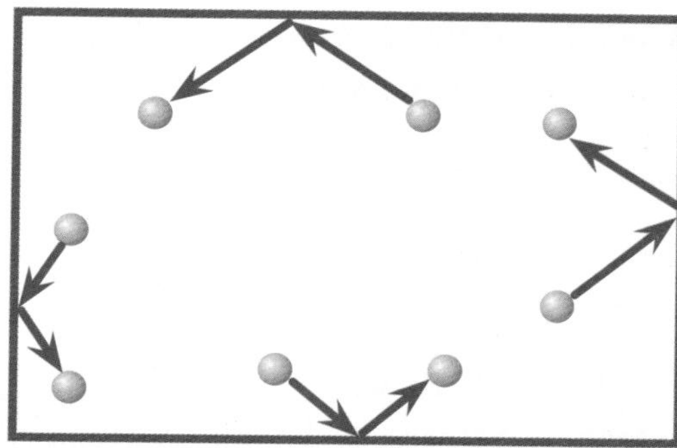

How the particles of a gas cause pressure.

Each collision of a particle with the wall causes a tiny force on the box. There are vast numbers of particles inside the box, and they are moving around very rapidly. This means that there are many, many collisions each second and all these tiny forces add up to cause the pressure on the walls of the box.

The particles of a liquid cause pressure in the same way. However, the particles are much closer together than in a gas, so they collide with the walls of their container more often, creating greater pressure.

Activity 9.6
Pressure and particles

The pictures show particles of a gas in a box. These pictures will help you to answer two questions:

- What happens to the pressure of a gas if more gas is squashed into a container?
- What happens to the pressure of a gas if it is squashed into a smaller volume?

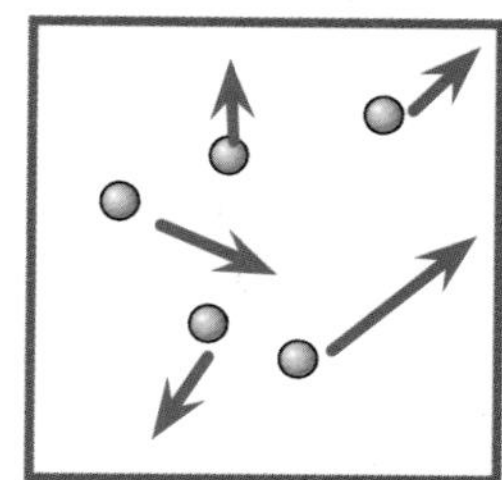

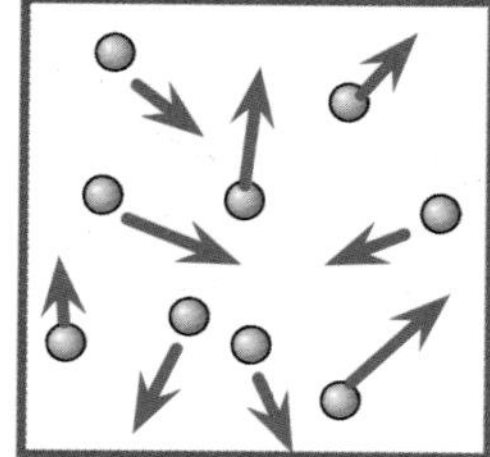

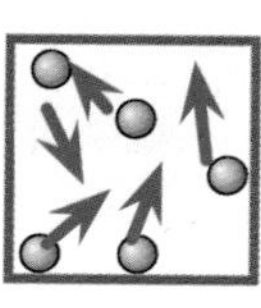

Be prepared to explain your ideas to the rest of the class.

Summary

- Liquids and gases can cause pressure.
- The pressure of a gas or liquid is caused by its weight pressing downwards.
- The particles of a gas or liquid collide with the walls of its container; this causes the pressure.

9.7 The turning effect of a force

The photograph shows how to use a spanner to turn a nut. The mechanic pushes on the long arm of the spanner.

The force of the mechanic on the spanner causes it to turn. We say that the force has a **turning effect**. To tighten the nut, the mechanic must turn it clockwise.

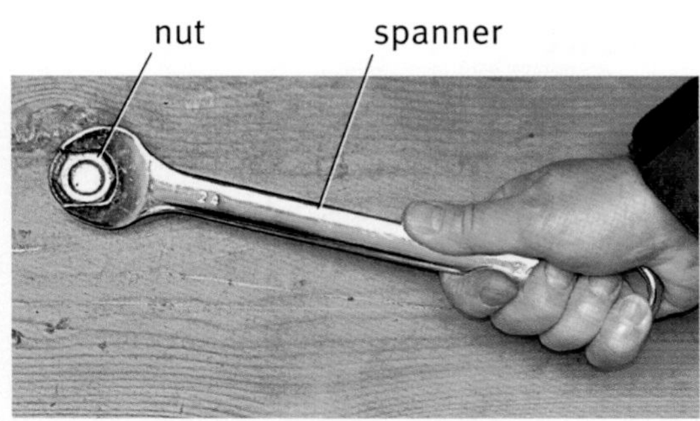

Turning a nut using a spanner.

Opening a door

It takes two forces, each with a turning effect, to open a door. First, you press down on the door handle. Then the handle turns and you can pull the door open.

The downward force of your hand on the handle makes the handle turn. The handle doesn't move straight down. This is because the handle is fixed to the door. The point where it is fixed is called the **pivot**.

Similarly, the door has hinges. When you pull on the handle, the door turns about the hinges. The hinges are the pivot about which the door turns.

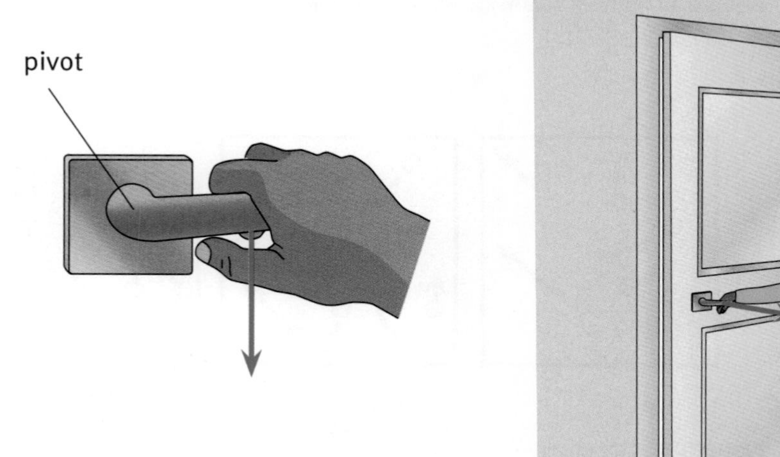

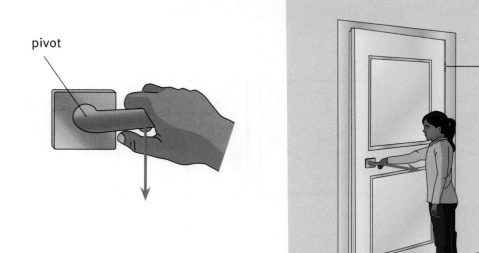

Opening a door – the forces cause the handle and the door to turn on their pivots.

Question

1 Look at the photograph of the spanner at the top of the page. Draw a diagram of the spanner and nut, viewed from above. Mark the pivot, and add an arrow to show the mechanic's pushing force.

Weighing with scales

The photograph shows a type of balance which has a pivot at the middle. A beam is balanced at the pivot.

The balance is being used to weigh apples. The apples are placed on the right. The weights on the left provide the force needed to balance the weight of the apples.

You can see that the weights are slightly heavier than the apples.

The weights cause the balance to tip downwards on the left, so that the beam turns anticlockwise.

The apples cause the balance to tip downwards on the right. This would make the beam turn clockwise, but the turning effect of the weights is greater.

Which are heavier, the apples or the weights?

Question

2 a How can you tell from the photograph that the weights are heavier than the apples?

b Draw a diagram to show the forces on the balance.

Activity 9.7

Scale maker

You can make your own simple scales using a piece of wood balanced on a pivot made from a wooden rod.

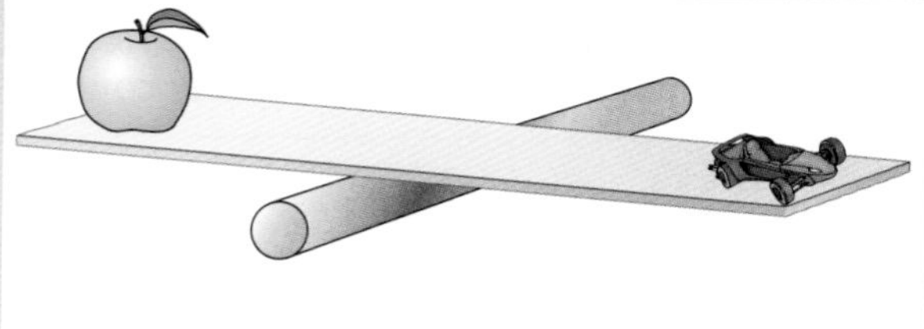

Part 1: Your teacher will give you a number of items. Use your scales to compare the different items and put them in order, from lightest to heaviest.

Part 2: Your teacher will give you a single 1 N weight. Find out which of your items are heavier than 1 N, and which are lighter.

Part 3: Can you think of a way to use your scales to find the weight of each item?

Summary

- A force has a turning effect when it causes an object to turn about a pivot.

9.8 The principle of moments

If you have ever played on a seesaw, you will have learnt about balancing the turning effects of forces.

A seesaw is a long beam balanced on a pivot. The pivot is half way along the beam.

In the photograph, you can tell that the girl (on the right) is heavier than the boy because her end of the beam is lower. Her weight has a greater turning effect than the boy's weight.

The diagram represents the seesaw. It shows the pivot and the two forces acting downwards on the beam.

These children have a seesaw in their school playground in The Gambia.

Question

1 Look at the photograph of the children on the seesaw. Does the girl's weight turn the beam clockwise or anticlockwise?

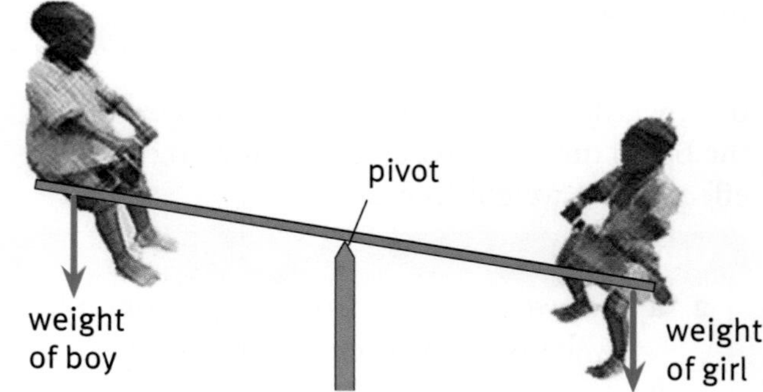

This diagram shows the forces acting on the seesaw.

Balancing up

How can the children balance the seesaw? The girl can do this by moving towards the pivot. Then her weight will have less turning effect, because it will be closer to the pivot.

Question

A+I **2** Suggest two ways in which the boy could balance the beam.

Moment of a force

The turning effect of a force depends on two things:

- The greater the force, the greater its turning effect.
- The further the force is from the pivot, the greater its turning effect.

We can calculate the **moment** of a force like this:

moment = force × distance from pivot

The bigger the moment of a force, the greater its turning effect.

Using moments

When children play on a seesaw, they balance it by changing their positions. They move along the beam until it is balanced. They are solving the balancing problem by trial-and-error.

However, if we know the children's weights, we can calculate their moments and work out how to balance the beam.

Activity 9.8
Balancing a beam

Balance a ruler on a pivot made from a wooden rod or a pencil. You are going to investigate how you can apply forces to this beam and keep it balanced.

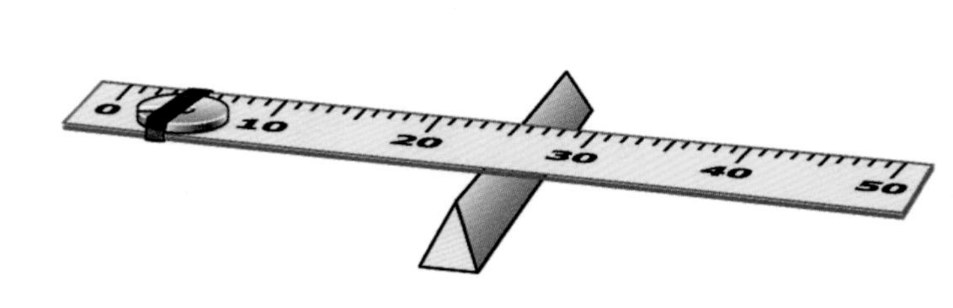

Try placing different weights on opposite sides of the pivot. Move them until the beam is balanced. Calculate the moment of each force.

Can you find the balancing rule?

The principle of moments

From the activity, you should have discovered the **principle of moments**.

For a beam to be balanced, the clockwise moment on it must equal the anticlockwise moment acting on it.

Summary

- moment of a force = force × distance from pivot
- The principle of moments states that, for a beam to be balanced, the clockwise moment acting on it must equal the anticlockwise moment acting on it.

9.9 Calculating moments

The principle of moments tells us that, when a beam is balanced, the clockwise moment acting on it is equal to the anticlockwise moment.

clockwise moment = anticlockwise moment

The diagram shows the forces acting on a beam, and their distances from the pivot. The beam is balanced because the moments of the two forces are equal.

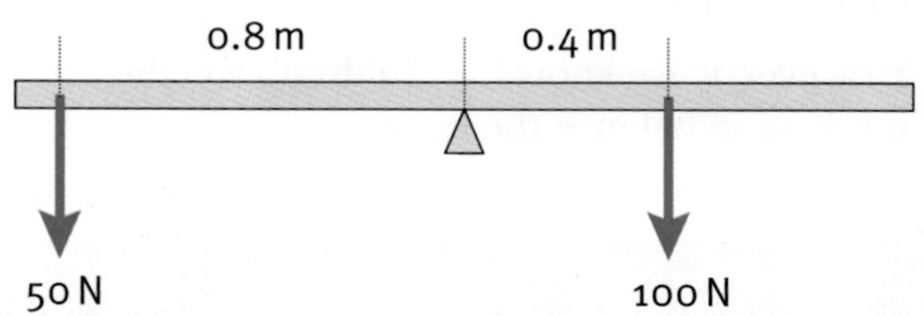

A balanced beam

Question

1 **a** In the diagram, which force has a clockwise moment (turning effect)?
b Calculate the moment of this force.
c Calculate the moment of the other force.
d Is the beam balanced? Explain how you can tell.

Calculating a distance

If we know that a beam is balanced, we can calculate the distance of a force from the pivot.

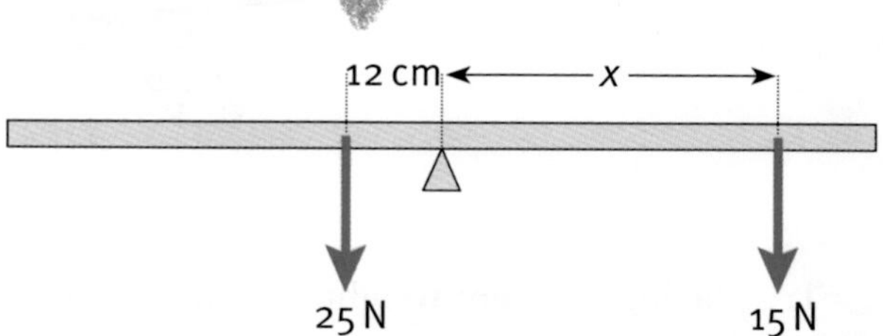

Example: In the diagram, the beam is balanced. We do not know the distance x from the pivot to the 15 N force, but we can work it out like this:

clockwise moment = anticlockwise moment

$$25\,\text{N} \times 12\,\text{cm} = 15\,\text{N} \times x$$

$$300 = 15x$$

$$x = \frac{300}{15} = 20\,\text{cm}$$

So the force must act at 20 cm from the pivot.

Question

2 A seesaw is 4.0 m long with a pivot at its midpoint. A boy who weighs 400 N sits at a distance of 1.5 m from the pivot. His sister weighs 300 N.
a Draw a diagram to show the beam, the pivot and the forces and their distances from the pivot.
b Calculate the distance at which the girl must sit if the beam is to be balanced.

Calculating a force

Similarly, we can calculate the force needed to balance a beam.

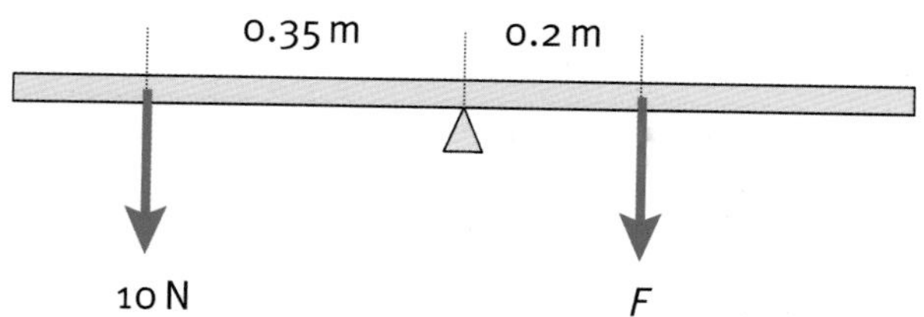

Example: In the diagram above, the beam is balanced. We do not know the force F, which is needed to keep it balanced, but we can work it out like this:

$$\text{clockwise moment} = \text{anticlockwise moment}$$

$$10\,\text{N} \times 0.35\,\text{m} = F \times 0.20\,\text{m}$$

$$3.5 = 0.20F$$

$$F = \frac{3.5}{0.20} = 17.5\,\text{N}$$

So a force of 17.5 N is needed to balance the beam.

Question

3 Calculate the force F shown in the diagram.

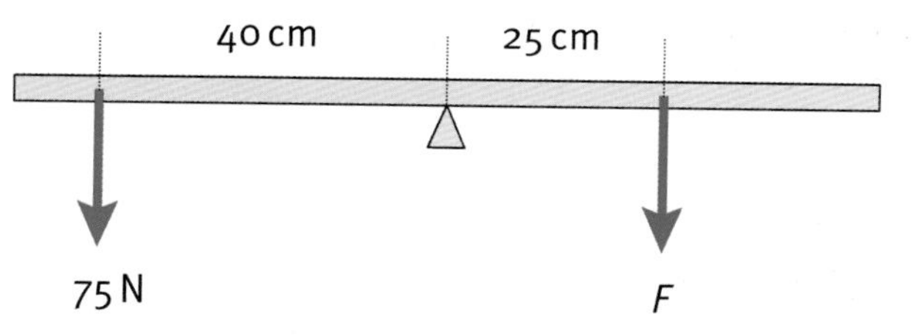

Activity 9.9
Moment challenge

Devise two 'balanced beam' problems for your partner to solve:

- one to calculate an unknown distance
- one to calculate an unknown force.

You can give each problem in words or as a diagram. Check that you agree with your partner about the answers.

Summary

- If we know that a beam is balanced, we can use the principle of moments to calculate an unknown distance or an unknown force.

Unit 9 End of unit questions

9.1 The table shows the densities of six different substances.

Substance	Density in g/cm³
water	1.0
copper	8.9
paraffin wax	0.90
steel	7.8
ice	0.92
lead	11.4

a Which **two** substances in the table would float in water? Explain how you can tell. [3]

b Which would have more volume, 1 kg of lead or 1 kg of copper? Explain how you can tell. [2]

9.2 The diagram shows a cube of marble. Each side of the cube is 2 cm in length.

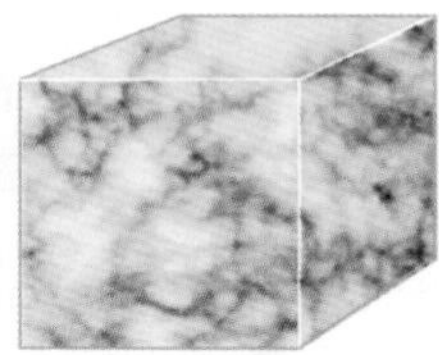

a Calculate the volume of the cube in cm^3. [2]

b The cube has a mass of 20.8 g. Calculate the density of marble. [2]

9.3 The diagram shows a brick lying on the floor. The brick has a weight of 23 N. The brick is flat and smooth on the side in contact with the floor.

a Calculate the area of the brick in contact with the floor. Give your answer in cm^2. [1]

b Calculate the pressure of the brick on the floor. [2]

c The diagram shows the molecules of a gas which is enclosed in a cylinder. The piston is pushed inwards.

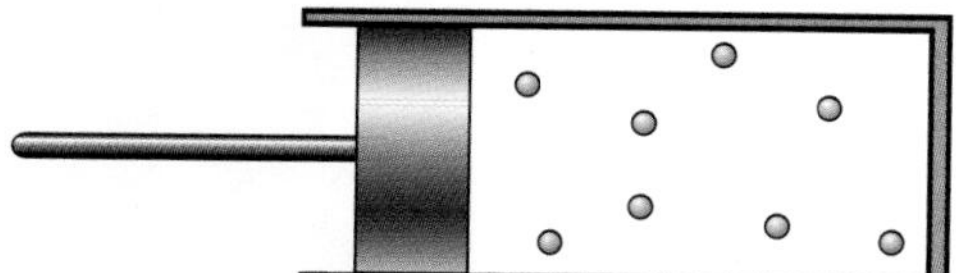

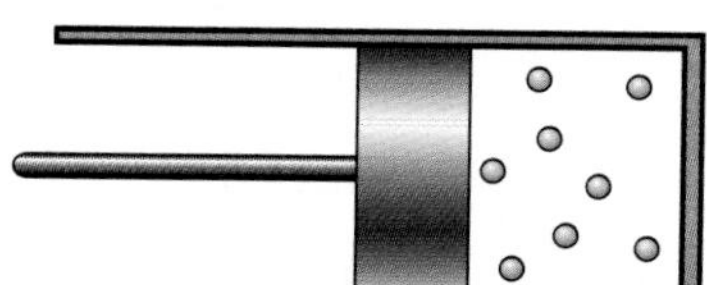

What has happened to the volume of the gas? [1]

d Explain why the pressure of the gas increases when the piston is pushed inwards. [1]

9.4 The diagram shows a force being used to make a spanner undo a nut.

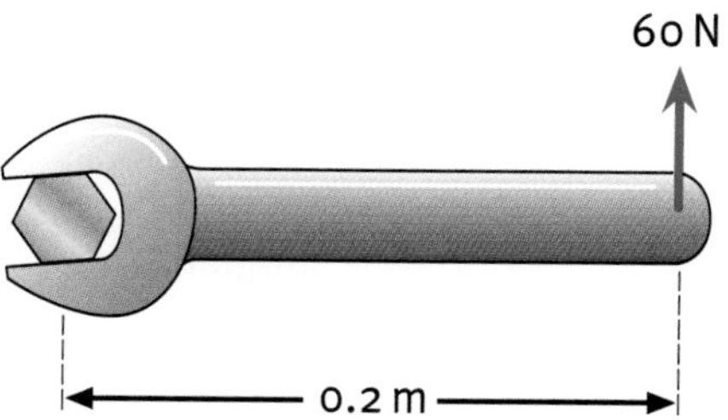

a Calculate the moment of the force about the pivot. [2]

b Does the moment of the force act clockwise or anticlockwise? [1]

c The diagram shows a beam with two forces acting on it. The beam is balanced.

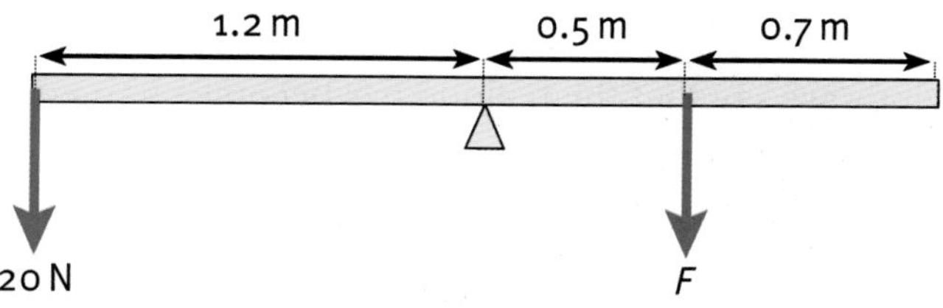

Calculate the value of the force F. [3]

10.1 Static electricity

Science begins with observations, and then we try to explain them. So, in this unit about electricity, we will start with some observations of **static electricity**.

Perhaps you have noticed the crackling of tiny sparks when you pull off a shirt or jumper as you go to bed. (This works best with clothes made from synthetic materials such as nylon, and when the air is dry.) The sparks are caused by static electricity.

Lightning is another example of static electricity, on a much larger scale. During a thunderstorm a giant spark of electricity leaps between the cloud and the ground.

A flash of lightning – natural electricity.

Question

1 What do we hear after a flash of lightning?

Activity 10.1A

Observing electrical attraction

SE

Here are some simple experiments you can try to find out about static electricity. For each experiment, record what you do and what you observe.

1. Inflate a balloon and tie the end. Rub the balloon on a woollen or cotton cloth. Hold the balloon close to your hair. Can you feel an effect?
2. Place some tiny pieces of paper, thread, plastic and aluminium foil on the bench. Rub your balloon again and bring it close to the different materials in turn. What happens?
3. Rub your balloon and touch it on the wall. Will it stick?
4. Turn on the tap so that a thin stream of water flows into the sink. Rub a plastic rod on a cloth and bring it close to the stream of water. Describe what you observe.

Describing static electricity

When you rub a balloon on a cloth, we say that the balloon has become charged with static electricity. The balloon has an electric charge.

Before it has been rubbed, we say that the balloon is uncharged.

In the activity you observed that a charged object can attract other objects. Materials such as hair, thread, paper and plastic are especially easy to attract. Metals are less easily attracted.

Electrical attraction is an example of a force. In the next activity, you will see that charged objects can also repel each other.

Activity 10.1B
Observing electrical repulsion

SE

The diagram shows one way to investigate the force of one charged object on another. A plastic rod hangs from a thread so that it is free to turn round. The rod is charged by rubbing it with a cloth.

A second rod, made of the same plastic, is also charged by rubbing it. It is brought close to one end of the hanging rod.

Try this. What do you observe?

Investigate what happens if you use two rods made of different types of plastic.

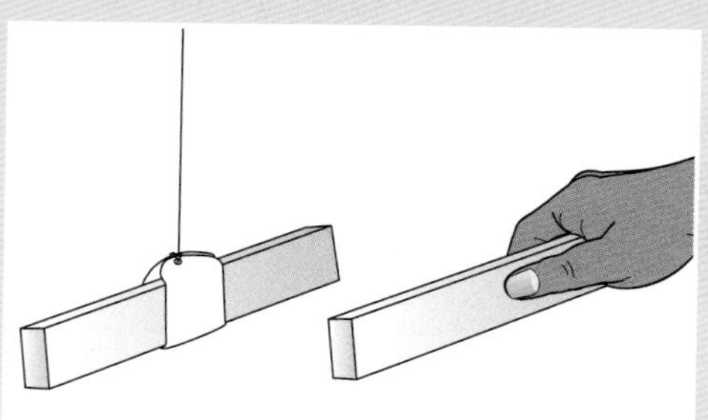

Two charged plastic rods – what happens when the end of one rod is brought close to the end of the other?

Attraction and repulsion

The experiments in this topic show that objects with an **electric charge** can attract or repel other objects. This is rather like what you learnt about magnets in Unit **13** of Stage **8**. However, it is important to realise that the electric force caused by a charged object is not the same as the magnetic force between magnets.

In the next topic, we will look at how scientists have learnt to explain static electricity.

Questions

SE

2 What are the rules of attraction and repulsion for magnetic poles?
3 How could you test whether a plastic rod that has been given an electric charge would attract or repel a magnet? Describe your method and include a diagram. What result would you expect to observe?

Summary

- Objects can be given an electric charge by rubbing them.
- Electrically charged objects can produce a force of attraction or repulsion.

10.2 Positive and negative charge

When people first began to study electricity scientifically, over 300 years ago, they had very little understanding of what was going on. They discovered different ways of charging things, and they suggested different uses for electricity.

The picture shows a German physicist, Otto van Guericke, working 350 years ago. When he turned the yellow ball of sulfur and rubbed it with a pad, he saw sparks.

Explaining electric forces

It took many years for scientists to develop a good explanation of why charged objects sometimes attract each other and sometimes repel each other.

Here is the theory they came up with.

There are two types of electric charge, which we call **positive** (+) and **negative** (–).

- Positive and negative charges attract one another.
- Positive charges repel one another.
- Negative charges repel one another.

You can remember this by remembering that 'opposites attract'. (This is the same as for magnetic poles – a north pole and a south pole attract one another.)

The diagram shows what happens when two charged balls are hung close together.

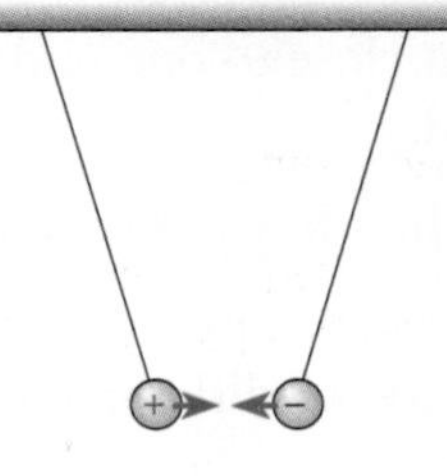

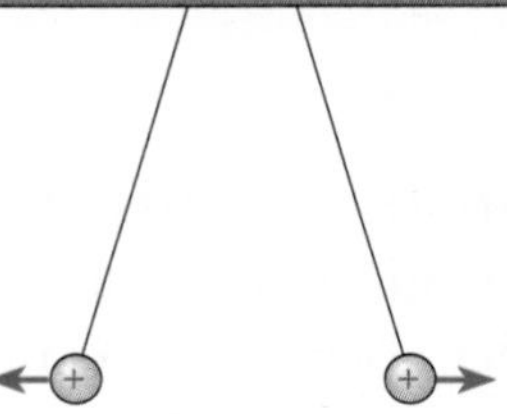

The green arrows show the forces between the electric charges.

Questions

1. Look at the picture of the charged balls. What symbols are used to represent positive and negative charge?
2. Draw a similar diagram to show what happens when two negatively charged balls are hung next to each other.

Finding the sign of an electric charge

You can use a digital meter called a coulombmeter to find out whether a charged object has positive or negative charge.

The photograph shows a polythene rod which has been charged by rubbing. The reading on the meter has a minus sign, showing that the rod has a negative charge.

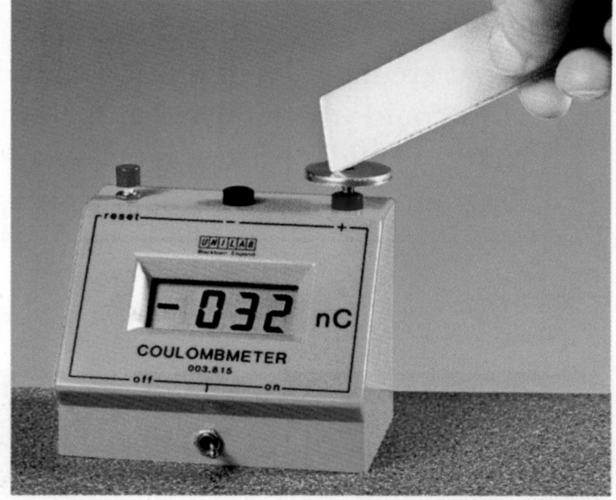

Finding the sign of an electric charge using a coulombmeter.

Charging by friction

In an experiment to investigate static electricity, you might start with a polythene rod and a woollen cloth. Neither has an electric charge. We say that they are **neutral**.

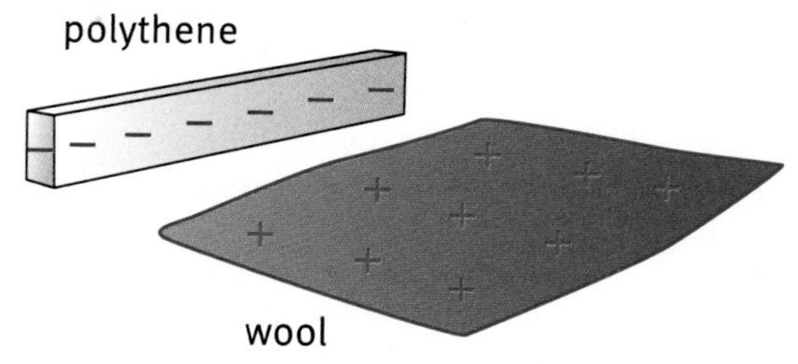

When the rod is rubbed using the cloth, the rod gains a negative electric charge. It is the force of **friction** that gives charge to the rod.

At the same time, the cloth gains a positive electric charge.

If you use a rod made of acrylic instead of polythene, you will find that the rod has a positive electric charge.

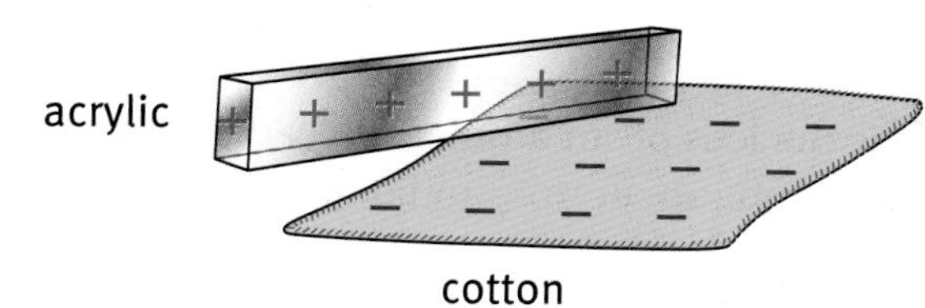

The charges that appear when two different materials are rubbed together depend which materials are used. One material gains a positive charge, the other a negative charge.

Questions

A+I

3 What force causes an object to become charged when it is rubbed?

4 What charge will the cloth have when it has been used to rub an acrylic rod?

Activity 10.2
Testing ideas about charge

SE

When a plastic rod and a cloth are rubbed together, they gain opposite electric charges. Your task is to test this idea in two ways:

- Use a coulombmeter to find out about the charges on the rod and the cloth.
- Show that the charged rod and the charged cloth attract each other.

Write a step-by-step description of how you will go about each of these tasks. Check with your teacher before you carry out your plans.

Summary

- There are two types of electric charge, positive (+) and negative (–).
- Opposite charges attract, like charges repel.
- A digital meter (coulombmeter) can be used to show whether an object has positive or negative charge.

10.3 Electrons on the move

It is easier to understand how something becomes electrically charged if we can picture the particles of which it is made.

All substances are made of atoms. If you have studied Unit **4**, you will know that every atom has a tiny nucleus at its centre. Electrons orbit around the nucleus.

The nucleus has a positive electric charge. The electrons have negative electric charge.

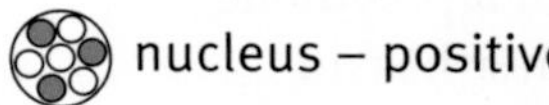

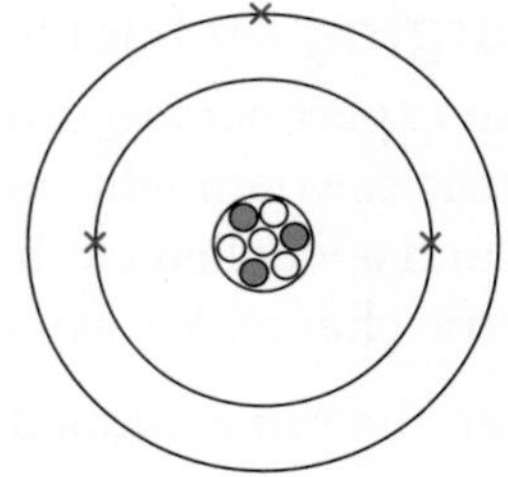

Atoms are made up of charged particles. This shows the positive and negative particles in an atom of lithium.

Questions

1 An atom is usually described as 'neutral'. What does this tell you about the amounts of positive and negative charge in an atom?

A+I **2** The nucleus of an atom attracts the electrons which orbit around it. This is what stops an atom from falling apart. Explain why the nucleus and electrons attract each other.

Explaining static electricity

When an acrylic rod is rubbed with a cloth, it becomes positively charged. What is going on?

The cloth rubs against the atoms which make up the surface of the rod. The force of friction rubs electrons from these atoms onto the cloth.

Because the cloth has gained negatively charged electrons, it now has a negative charge.

The rod is no longer neutral. It has lost electrons, so it has a positive charge.

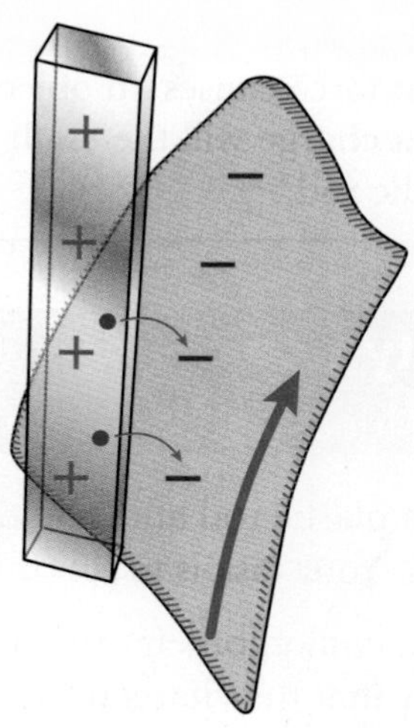

Rubbing transfers electrons from the rod to the cloth.

Why do electrons move from the rod to the cloth? The reason is that the electrons are on the outside of the atoms, so they are easily transferred from one material to the other.

Some materials hold on to their electrons more strongly than others. Acrylic holds its electrons weakly, so it easily loses them and becomes positively charged. Polythene holds its electrons more strongly.

Question

A+I **3** Use the same ideas to explain why a polythene rod gains a negative charge when it is rubbed with a cloth.

Explaining why neutral objects are attracted by charged objects

If you rub a balloon on a cloth, it will become charged. If you hold the charged balloon near a scrap of paper, it will attract the paper.

The paper is not charged. So why is it attracted?

The reason is that the paper contains electrons. (Everything that is made of atoms contains electrons.) If the balloon has a positive charge, it attracts the electrons in the paper and so the paper feels a force towards the balloon.

Understanding how electrons behave is the key to understanding electricity. J. J. Thomson discovered electrons in 1897, so it is not surprising that scientists did not really understand what was going on before then.

Question

4 If you put two electrons next to each other, would they attract or repel each other? Explain your answer.

Activity 10.3
Everything's electric!

It is important to understand that everything is made of atoms. Atoms have electrons and so everything is electric.

Use thread to hang different items, so that they are free to turn. Make sure that they are not moving.

Charge a plastic rod by rubbing it with a cloth. Bring the charged rod close to one end of the hanging item. Can you observe attraction?

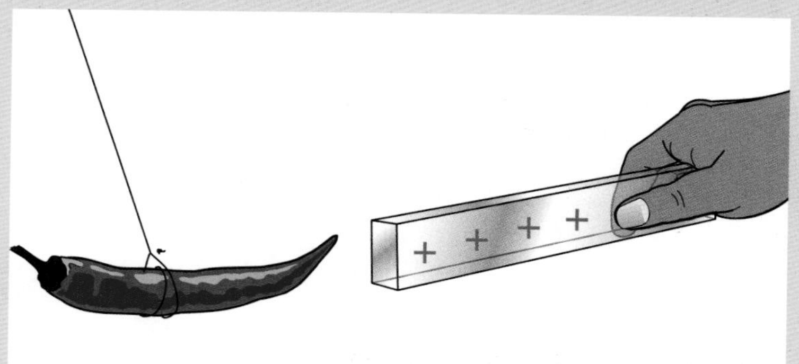

Even a pepper (capsicum) contains electrons and can be attracted by a charged rod.

Summary

- Objects become charged when electrons are rubbed from one object to another.
- The object which gains electrons has a negative charge; the object that loses electrons has a positive charge.

10.4 Conductors and insulators

Most houses and other buildings have electricity. There are wires hidden in the walls and under the floors which carry electricity to where it is needed.

These wires are made of a metal, copper – that is the part that carries the electricity. The metal is covered with plastic – this makes sure you do not get a shock if you touch the wire.

Metals are described as **conductors** because they allow electricity to pass through them. Plastic and other non-metals are described as **insulators** – they do not allow electricity to pass through them.

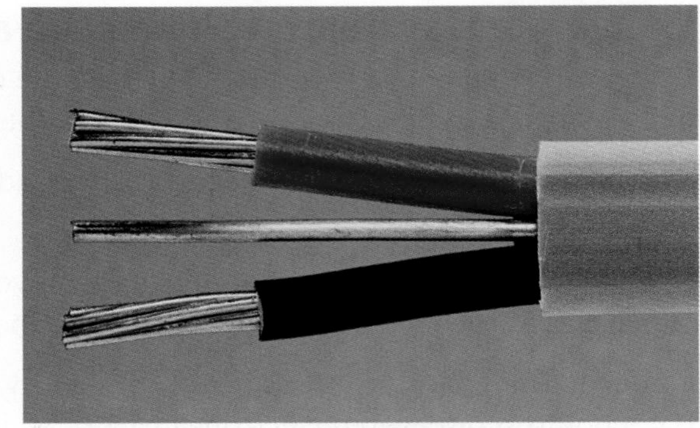

Wires like these are used to carry electricity around a building.

Activity 10.4

Metals and non-metals

SE

You can use the circuit shown to test whether materials are conductors or insulators.

Use the clips to connect onto the ends of a piece of metal, plastic or other material.

If the lamp (bulb) lights up, the material is a conductor.

1 Test some different materials. Divide them into conductors and insulators. Can you find a non-metal that conducts electricity?

2 Some metals are better conductors than others. Use the circuit to put your metal samples in order, from best conductor to worst conductor.

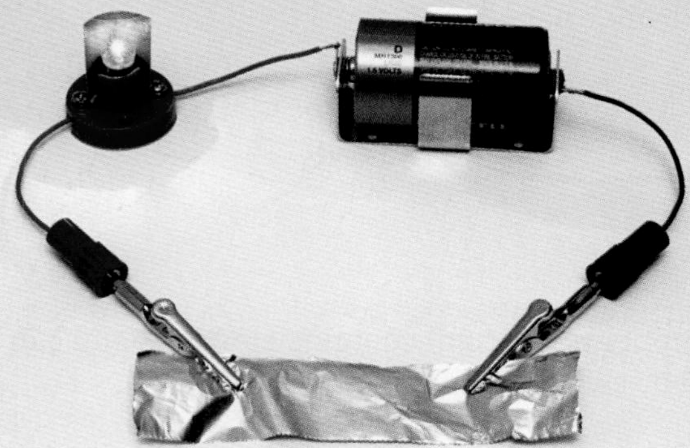

Testing a piece of aluminium foil.

Question

A1 In the photograph, a piece of aluminium foil is being tested. Is aluminium a conductor? Explain how you can tell.

Electric current

Electricity makes a lamp light up. 'Electricity' is a vague word. It is better to talk about electric current. We say:

The lamp lights up because there is an **electric current** in the circuit.

Two things are needed for there to be an electric current:

- a complete circuit of metal around which the current can flow
- a **cell** (a battery) to make the current flow.

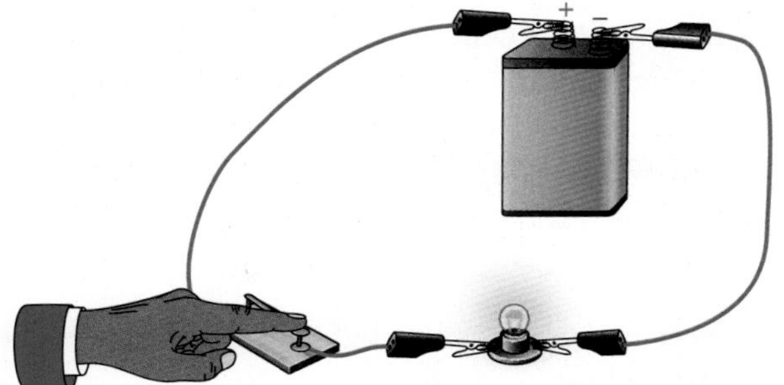

A switch breaks a circuit to stop the current flowing. The picture shows three components connected up to make a circuit.

Question

1 Study the picture of the circuit. The electric current flows from the positive (+) end of the cell. Which component does it reach first, the switch or the lamp?

Circuit symbols

Scientists and engineers draw **circuit diagrams** to show how different components are connected together in an electric circuit. They use a **circuit symbol** for each type of component. Because everyone uses the same symbols, they can understand each other's diagrams. Computers can understand the diagrams, too.

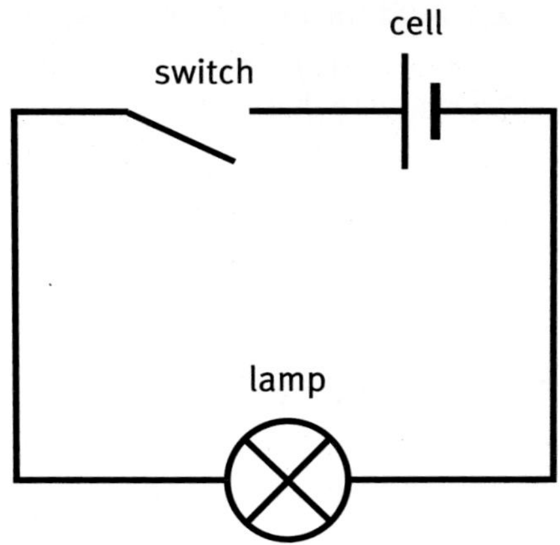

The diagram shows the same circuit as in the picture above.

- Each symbol is labelled with the name of the component it represents.
- The wires joining the components are shown as lines.

Question

2 Study the circuit diagram. Draw the circuit symbols for a cell, a switch and a lamp.

3 Which part of the symbol for a cell represents the positive end, the long line or the short line?

Summary

- Metals are good conductors of electricity. Non-metals are usually insulators.
- A complete circuit is needed for a current to flow.

10.5 Electric current in a circuit

A lamp can show us when there is an electric current in a circuit.

- If the lamp lights up, there is a current.
- A brighter lamp shows a bigger current.

The photograph shows a very simple circuit. A lamp is connected to a cell. You can see that the lamp is shining, showing that an electric current is flowing through it.

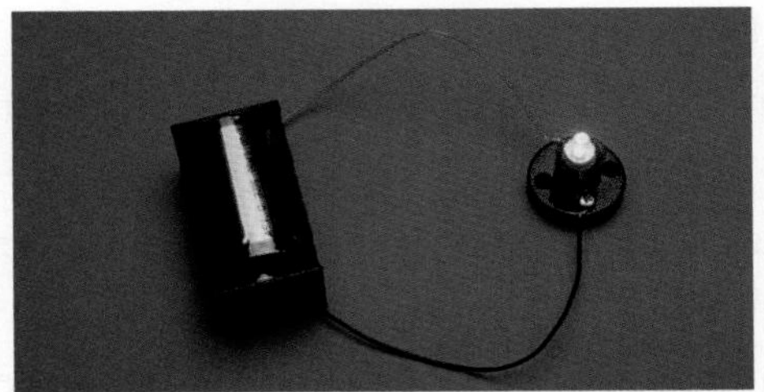

An electric current makes the lamp light up.

Activity 10.5A

Connecting lamps in series

SE

You can use a cell to light up two lamps. The circuit diagram shows how to do this.

1. Before you try this, make a prediction. How bright will the lamps be? Will they both be equally bright, or will one be brighter than the other?
   Try to give an explanation for your prediction. Discuss your ideas with a partner, and then present them to the rest of the class.
2. Build the circuit and test your ideas. Do you need to change your ideas?
3. Predict what you will observe if you make a circuit with three lamps, all in a row. Test your prediction.

When you have learnt more about electric currents, you will have a better understanding of this experiment.

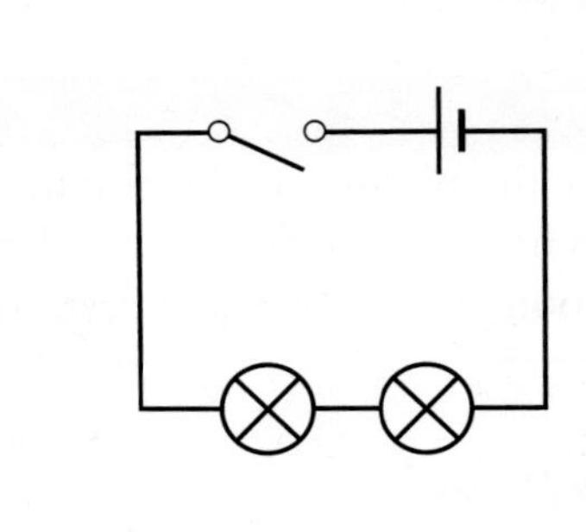

A circuit with a cell, a switch and two lamps.

Measuring electric current

We can measure the current in a circuit using an instrument called an **ammeter**.

The unit of electric current is the **amp** (symbol A).

To connect an ammeter in a circuit, it is necessary to make a break in the circuit. Then the current can flow through the ammeter.

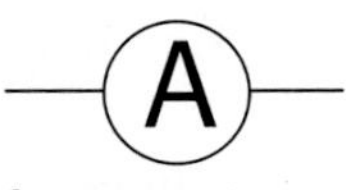

An ammeter circuit symbol.

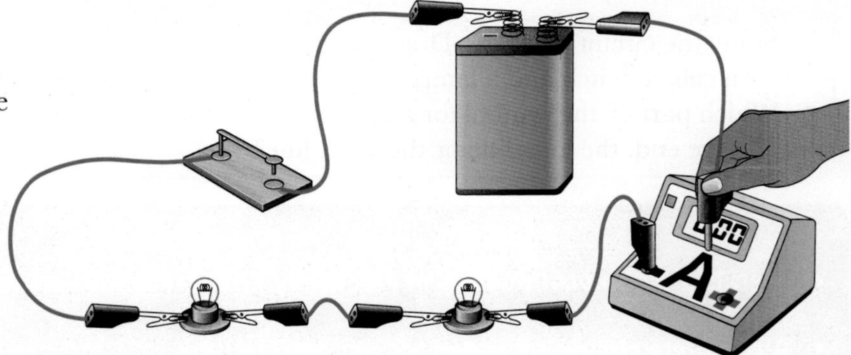

Adding an ammeter to a circuit.

Activity 10.5B

Measuring current around a circuit

SE

Now you can find out more about the current in a circuit.

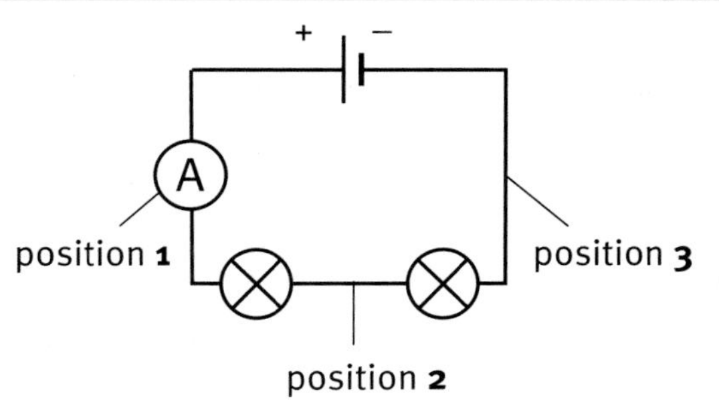

1. Set up a circuit with a cell and two lamps, as before. You should find that the two lamps are equally bright.
2. Connect an ammeter as shown at position **1** in the circuit. Note the value of the current.
3. Repeat with the ammeter at position **2**, and then at position **3**.
4. Discuss whether your results agree with what you found when you used lamps instead of an ammeter.

Current in a series circuit

In the experiments in this topic, you should have found that the current is the same all the way round each circuit.

We picture the current coming from the positive end of the cell. It flows round the circuit, through the ammeter, one lamp and then through the next.

It then flows back to the negative end of the cell. It doesn't get used up as it goes through the lamps.

A circuit like this, where the components are connected end-to-end, is called a **series circuit**. The current flows through the components one after another. The current is the same all the way round a series circuit.

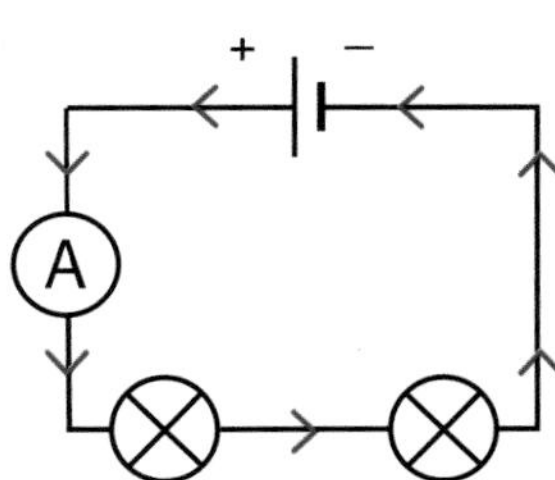

The current, shown by the blue arrows, is the same all the way round a series circuit like this.

Questions

1. Does the electric current get used up as it goes round an electric circuit?
2. In a series circuit, an ammeter shows that the current leaving the positive end of a cell is 0.5 A. What current flows into the negative end of the cell?

Summary

- A circuit with all the components connected end-to-end is called a series circuit.
- The current is the same all the way round a series circuit.

10.6 Understanding electric current

Here are some things you have learnt about electric current.

- An electric current can flow through a metal but not through plastic.
- A cell can make a current flow round a circuit.
- The current is the same all round a series circuit.
- An electric current can light up a lamp.

We can understand this if we think about electrons, the tiny particles which helped to explain static electricity (topic **10.3**).

Question

1 Test what you remember about electrons.

a Which is bigger, an atom or an electron?

b What charge do electrons have, positive or negative?

c What charge would attract an electron, positive or negative?

Why metals conduct electricity

Metals are useful materials because they contain lots of electrons which can move about inside the metal. These electrons are not tightly attached to their atoms. That is what makes metals different from other materials.

A cell can make a current flow in a metal wire. If you could look into the wire, you would see the electrons moving along. Electrons have an electric charge, so charge is moving through the metal. This is what we call an electric current.

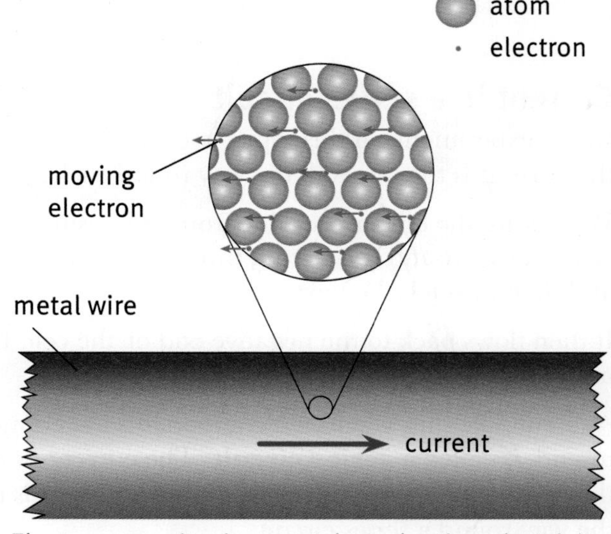

Electrons moving in a metal conducting electricity.

How a cell makes a current flow

Think about a cell. One end is positive (marked +), the other negative (marked –). The positive end attracts electrons (because electrons have negative charge). The negative end repels electrons.

So, when a circuit is complete, the electrons in the metal of the circuit start moving around it. They are pushed from the negative end of the cell, and attracted towards the positive end.

Now you can see why we need a complete circuit. The electrons need to be able to travel all the way round, from one end of the cell to the other.

That is why the current is the same all the way round the circuit. The electrons don't disappear or get used up.

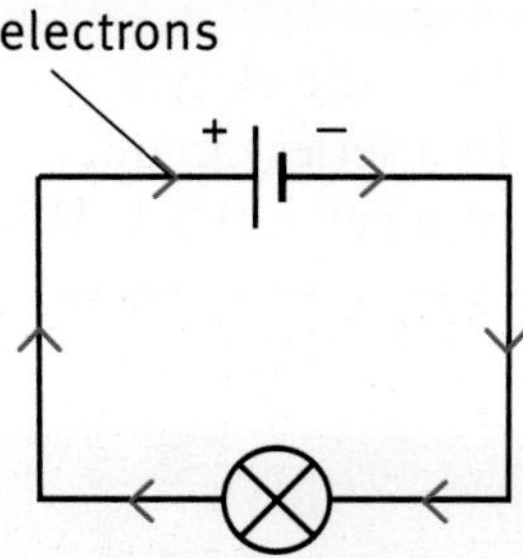

Electrons move in the opposite direction to conventional current.

Activity 10.6

Long wires

SE

Your teacher will set up a circuit with a cell, a switch and a lamp. When the switch is closed, the lamp lights up.

But what will happen if the connecting wires are very, very long? Will it take a while for the current to reach the lamp? Will the lamp light up sooner if it is closer to the cell?

Use what you have learnt about electrons to decide what you think will happen. Then test your ideas.

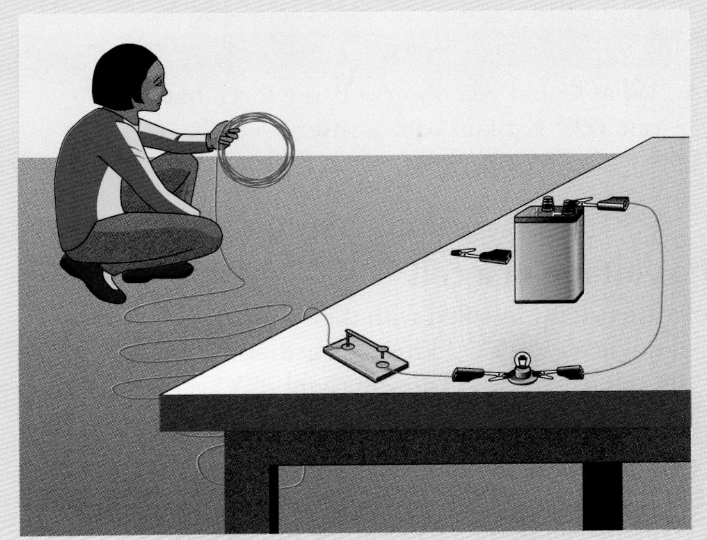

Lighting a lamp – current and energy

When you push a switch, a current starts immediately. The electrons are waiting in the wire. They start to move all round the circuit as soon as the switch is closed.

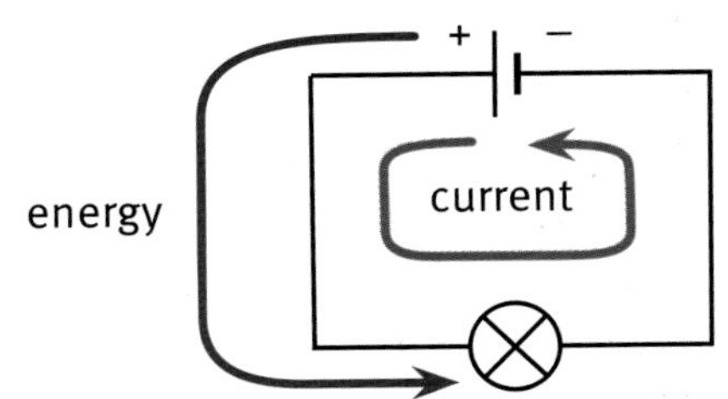

- The cell is the energy source for the circuit. It is a store of chemical energy.
- The current transfers energy from the cell to the lamp.
- The lamp gets hot and shines. It is a source of light energy and heat energy.

Question

A+I

2 A cell can make a buzzer buzz.

a Explain why the buzzer starts to buzz as soon as the circuit is complete.

b What energy changes are happening in this circuit?

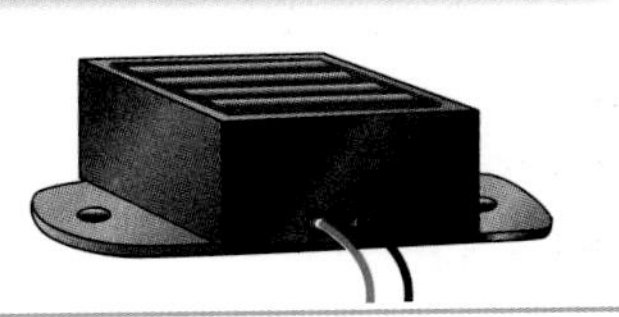

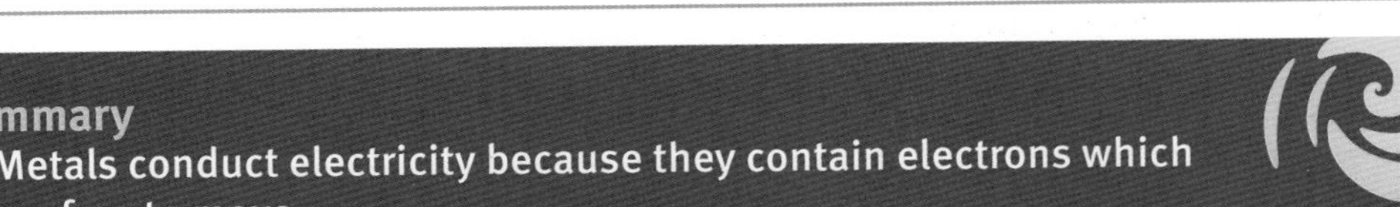

Summary

- Metals conduct electricity because they contain electrons which are free to move.
- An electric current is a flow of charge.
- A cell pushes electrons round a circuit, transferring energy to the components in the circuit.

10.7 Changing circuits 1

Many electrical appliances use cells (batteries). The X-ray photograph shows a torch with two batteries inside it. You can see that the batteries are connected end-to-end – they are in series.

A torch like this needs two cells to give enough current to light the lamp brightly.

Question

A+I **1** What would you observe if the torch had only one cell? Explain your answer.

The voltage of a cell

Cells are usually labelled with their **voltage**. The label might say '1.5 V'. This means that the voltage of the cell is 1.5 volts. The volt (symbol V) is the unit of voltage.

A **voltmeter** is used to measure voltage. To measure the voltage of a cell, wires are connected from the ends of the cell to the terminals of the voltmeter. The positive (red) terminal of the voltmeter should be connected to the positive terminal of the cell.

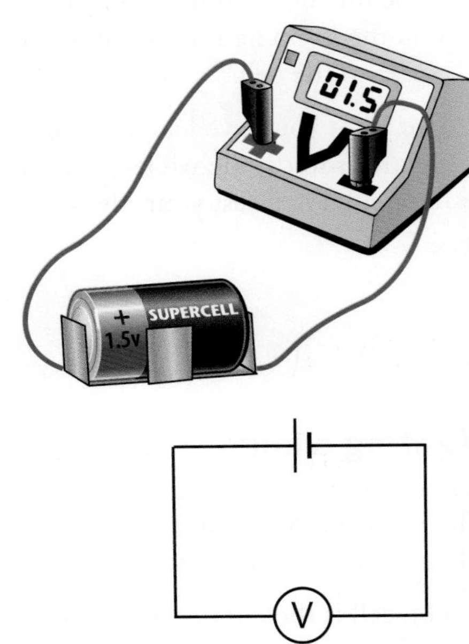

More cells

If two or more cells are connected together in series, their voltages add up. The diagram shows how to represent two or more cells connected in series, and the value of their combined voltages. In this diagram, each cell is 1.5 V.

Take care! If you connect two cells back-to-front (positive to positive or negative to negative), their voltages will cancel out.

1.5 V   3.0 V   4.5 V   0 V

Questions

2 Draw the circuit symbol for a voltmeter.

3 If the torch in the photograph above had two cells, each labelled '1.2 V', what would the total voltage be?

SE

Activity 10.7
Combining cells

Your task is to find out how the voltage of the cells in a circuit affects the current in the circuit.

1 Set up a circuit with a cell, a switch and a lamp. Add an ammeter to measure the current. Add a voltmeter to measure the voltage of the cell.
2 Ask your teacher to check your circuit before you close the switch.
3 Close the switch to complete the circuit. Record the values of the current and the voltage.
4 Repeat the experiment using two cells, and then three cells. What pattern can you see?
5 Repeat the whole experiment with a resistor in the circuit instead of the lamp. Do you find the same pattern?

More volts, more amps

The activity shows that, if the cells in a circuit are providing a bigger voltage, the current will also be bigger. This is because, if there are two cells connected in series, they give a bigger push to the electrons in the wires, so there is a bigger current.

If there is a bigger current, the lamp will shine more brightly. The current is transferring energy more quickly from the cells to the lamp.

Question

A+I

4 Study the circuits in the diagram. Each circuit will have a different current flowing in it. Put them in order, starting with the one with the biggest current. (All the cells have the same voltage.)

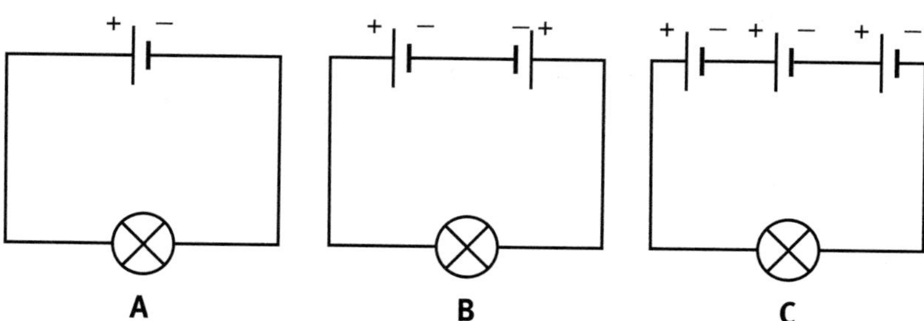

Summary

- A voltmeter is used to measure the voltage of a cell.
- When two or more cells are connected positive to negative in series, their voltages add up.
- A bigger voltage in a circuit makes a bigger current flow.

10.8 Changing circuits 2

Adding more cells to a series circuit increases the voltage and so the current is bigger. What happens if we add other components to a series circuit?

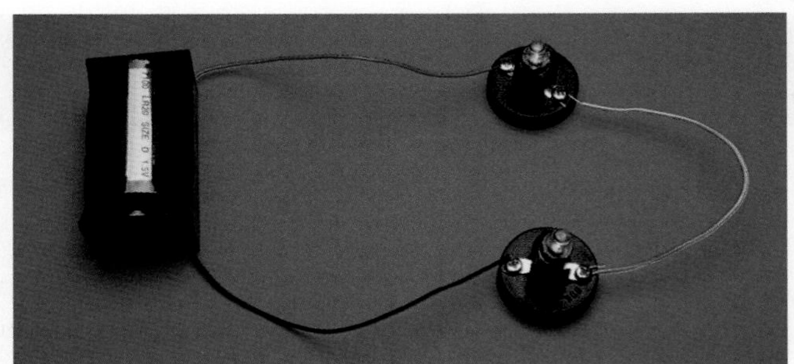

In topic **10.5** you saw what happens if two lamps are used in series instead of one. The lamps are both dim (not bright). The photograph shows this.

Question

A+I

1 How could you change the circuit to make the lamps brighter? Explain your answer.

One after another

By thinking about the electrons in the circuit, we can understand why the current is smaller when there are two lamps in the series circuit.

The electrons are being pushed by the cell. It has to push them through one lamp and then through the next.

It is easier for the cell to push the electrons through one lamp than through two, and so the current is bigger when there is only one lamp in the circuit.

Electrical resistance

We say that a lamp has **resistance**. The more resistance there is in the circuit, the harder it is for the cells to push the electrons round, and so the current is smaller.

The pictures show some other components which have resistance.

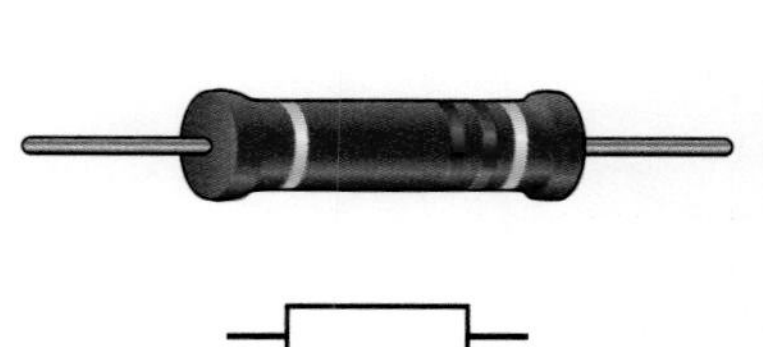

A **resistor** is used to make the current smaller in a circuit.

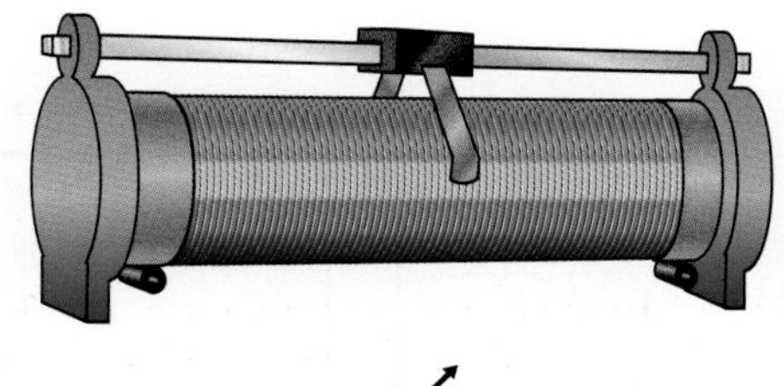

A **variable resistor** allows you to control the amount of current in a circuit.

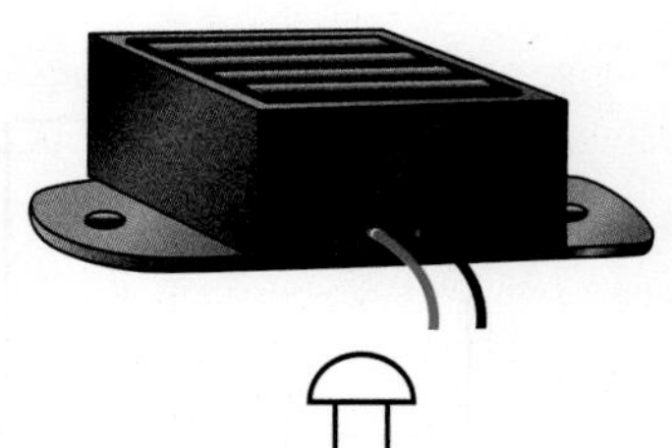

A buzzer makes a sound when the current flows through it.

Activity 10.8A
Variable resistors

SE

Your teacher will show you how a variable resistor can be used to change the current in a circuit.

1 Draw a circuit diagram to represent this circuit.
2 Write a sentence to describe what you observe as the variable resistor is altered.
3 Write another sentence to explain what you observe.

Moving the slider along changes the resistance in the circuit.

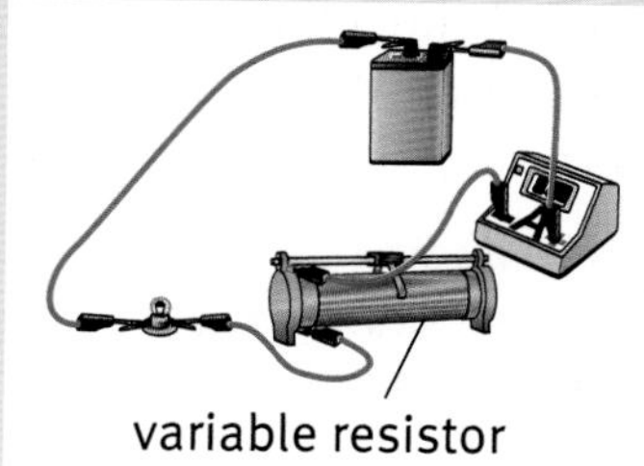

Activity 10.8B
Make your own variable resistor

SE

In the circuit shown, two clips connect to a length of resistance wire.

Construct the circuit and observe what happens when you slide the clips along the wire so that they are closer together or farther apart.

Try to explain what you observe.

Resistance wire has more resistance than normal wire.

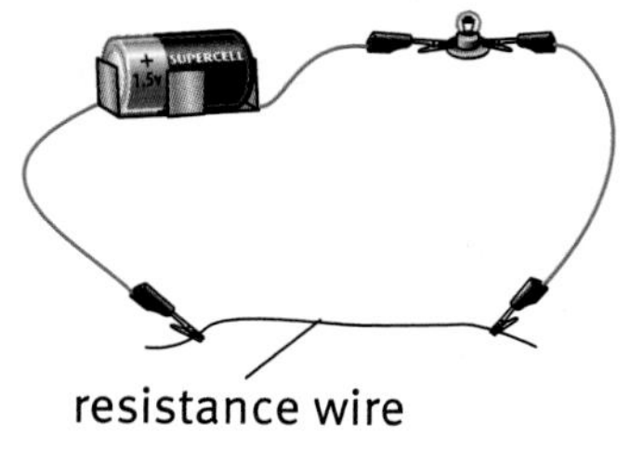

Losing energy

When two components are connected in series in a circuit, it is harder for the current to flow. There is more resistance, and so the current is smaller.

It requires energy for the electrons to flow through any component which has resistance. That's not a bad thing! We want the current to transfer energy to a buzzer so that it will make a sound or a lamp so that it will give out light.

Question

2 a Draw a circuit diagram to show a circuit with two cells and two resistors connected in series. Include an ammeter to measure the current in the circuit.
b Add arrows to show how the electric current flows around the circuit.
c Explain why the current in the circuit would be bigger if there was only one resistor in the circuit.

Summary

- Components with resistance make the current in a circuit smaller.
- When components are connected in series, the resistance in the circuit is greater and so the current is smaller.

10.9 Components in parallel

We have seen that, when two lamps are connected in series to a single cell, they are dim. This is because the current in the circuit is small.

It is more difficult for the electrons to flow round the circuit than if there was only one lamp. Two lamps have more resistance than one lamp.

There is another way to connect two lamps to a cell. Place them side by side, as shown in the photograph. You can see that both lamps shine brightly.

When components are connected side by side in this way, we say they are **in parallel** with each other.

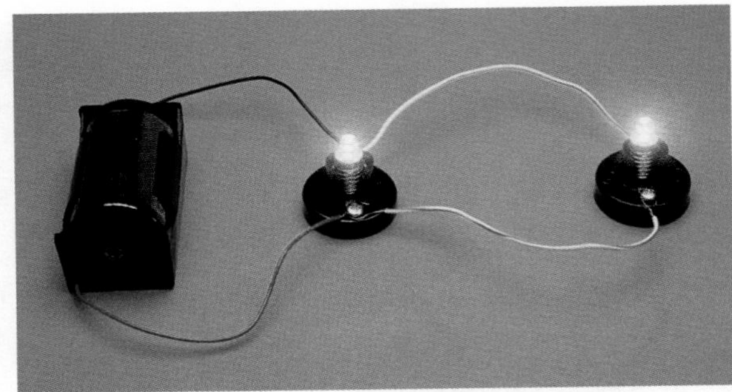

These two lamps are connected in parallel.

Parallel diagrams

The circuit diagram shows how we represent the circuit with two lamps connected in parallel.

If you look closely, you will see that each of the two lamps has one end connected directly to the positive end of the cell, and the other end connected directly to the negative end.

Each lamp feels the full push of the cell and so it lights up brightly.

To remember the difference between series and parallel:

- 'in series' means 'connected end-to-end'
- 'in parallel' means 'connected side by side'.

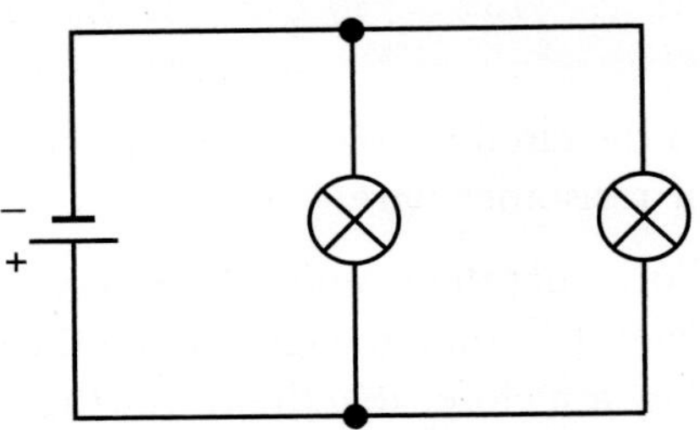

Circuit diagram to show two lamps connected in parallel.

Activity 10.9

Parallel connections

SE

1 Set up a circuit with a single cell and a single lamp.
2 Connect a second lamp in parallel with the first.
3 Draw a circuit diagram to show your parallel circuit. Make a note of how bright your lamps are. Does the brightness of the first lamp change when you add the second?
4 Now repeat steps **1** and **2**, this time including an ammeter in the circuit next to the cell to measure the current flowing from the cell. Make a prediction: how will the current change when you add the second lamp?
5 Draw a diagram to represent the circuit with the ammeter. Make a note of the value of the current in the circuit when there is one lamp, and when there are two.

Current in parallel circuits

The circuit diagram shows the same circuit as before, but drawn slightly differently to make it easier to understand how the current flows when two identical components are connected in parallel.

The current flows from the positive end of the cell. When it reaches point **A**, it divides. Half of the current flows through one lamp, and half flows through the other. When the two currents reach point **B**, they join together again. Then they flow back to the cell.

This means that, when there are two identical lamps in parallel, there is twice as much current as when there is only one lamp. Each lamp gets its own share of the current.

This shows that it is easier for the current to flow when two components are connected in parallel in a circuit. There is less resistance, and so the current is bigger.

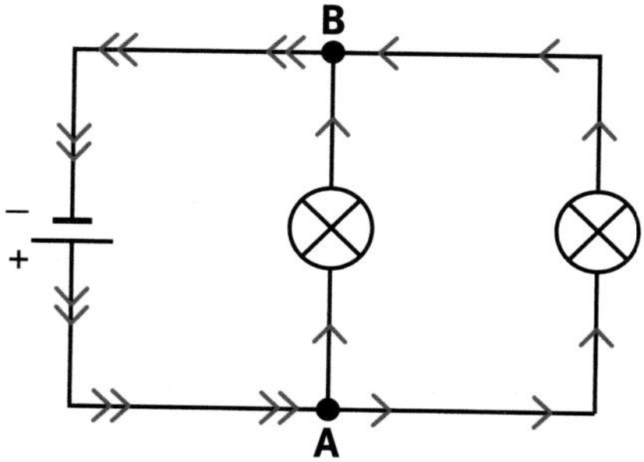

The blue arrows show how the current flows in this parallel circuit.

Question

1 a Draw a circuit diagram to show a circuit with one cell and two resistors connected in parallel. Include an ammeter to measure the current flowing from the cells.

b Add arrows to show how the electric current flows round the circuit.

c Mark with an X the point where the current divides.

d If each resistor has a current of 0.5 A flowing through it, what current would the ammeter show?

Summary

- Components connected side by side are in parallel.
- The current in a circuit divides as it passes through the components connected in parallel.

10.1 Two plastic balls, **A** and **B**, are hung side by side on threads, as shown.
The balls are given an electrical charge.

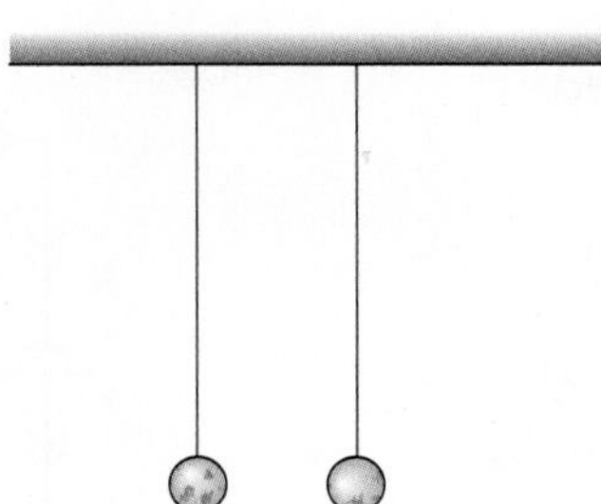

The table shows the charges given to each ball in two separate experiments.

	Charge of ball A	Charge of ball B	Attract/repel?
Experiment 1	positive	negative	
Experiment 2	negative	negative	

a Copy the table and complete the last column to show whether you would expect the balls to attract or repel one another. [2]
In a third experiment, ball **A** is given a negative charge. A polythene rod is charged by rubbing it with a cloth. It repels ball **A**.

b What force causes the rod to become charged? [1]

c What charge does the rod have, positive or negative? [1]

d What particles are transferred from the cloth to the rod when it becomes charged? [1]

10.2 The table shows the circuit symbols for four different components **A**–**D**.

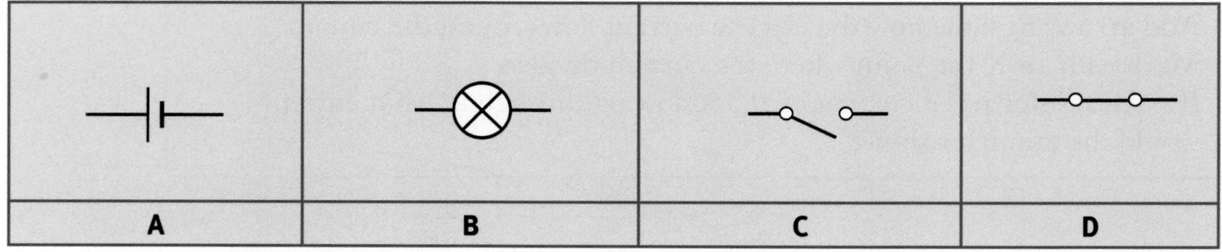

a Name each of the components **A**–**D**. [4]

b Draw a diagram to represent a circuit in which two 1.5 V cells are connected in series with a single resistor. [2]

c Draw arrows on your circuit diagram to show the direction of the current in the circuit. [1]

d What will be the combined voltage of the two cells? [1]

10.3 The diagram shows a simple circuit in which a cell is connected to a buzzer and an ammeter.

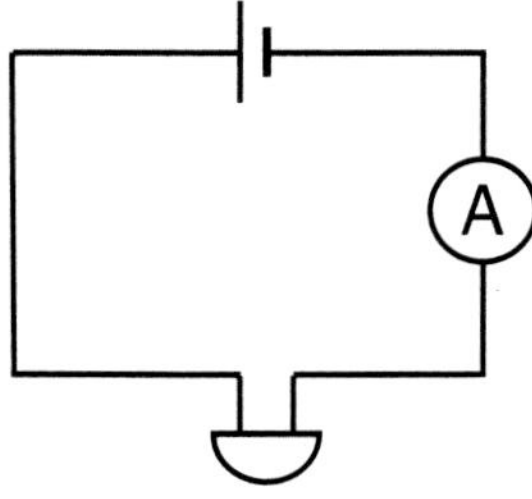

- **a** Copy the diagram. Add a voltmeter to show how you would measure the voltage of the cell. [1]
- **b** What is measured by the ammeter? [1]
- **c** The reading on the ammeter is 0.4 A. What unit does 'A' represent? [1]

10.4 What type of circuit is described by each of the following statements? Answer 'series' or 'parallel'.

- **a** All components are connected end-to-end. [1]
- **b** The current in the circuit divides so that some flows through one component and the rest through another component. [1]
- **c** Two lamps are connected side by side so that each lights brightly. [1]
- **d** The current has the same value everywhere in the circuit. [1]

11.1 How we use energy

Energy is important to us. Whatever we do, we need a supply of energy.

Our bodies use the energy that we get from our food. This enables us to move around, to think, to stay warm and so on.

Maize, an important food crop, supplies energy to millions of people around the world.

Questions

1. You learnt about food and digestion in Stage **8** Unit **2**. What two types of nutrient are our main sources of energy?
2. What is the original source of the energy we get from our food?

More and more energy

It is useful if we can find other ways of using energy. For example, many people work on farms. Farmers can also make use of animals to do some of the heavy work, such as pulling loads.

Machines can also do work for us. Like people and animals, machines need a supply of energy. Some work using electricity. Others use fuels, such as coal or oil.

Over many centuries, people have discovered how to make use of many different sources of energy.

Cars are machines. They usually use diesel or petrol (gasoline) as their energy supply.

What we use energy for

The pie chart shows the three main types of energy we use.

In our homes, schools, factories and offices, we use energy for heating and cooling, for cooking, for lighting and so on.

We need energy to travel around, so we use energy for transport.

Industry uses energy for making things. Everyone uses things that are manufactured.

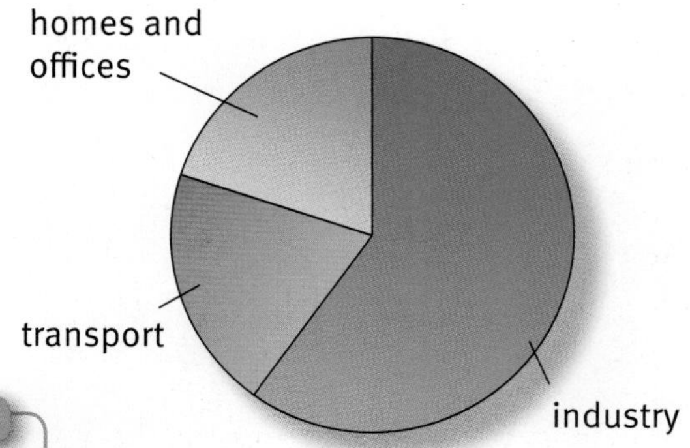

The three main sectors where energy is used. These data are for the whole world.

Question

3. Look at the pie chart. Which sector uses the most energy?

Energy and development

As countries become richer, people have more money to spend. They buy cars and use more fuel. They live in bigger houses, use more clean water and consume more goods.

All of these things require more supplies of energy. The bar chart shows how much energy each person uses per year in different regions of the world. (These are average figures. Some people use more, some people use less.)

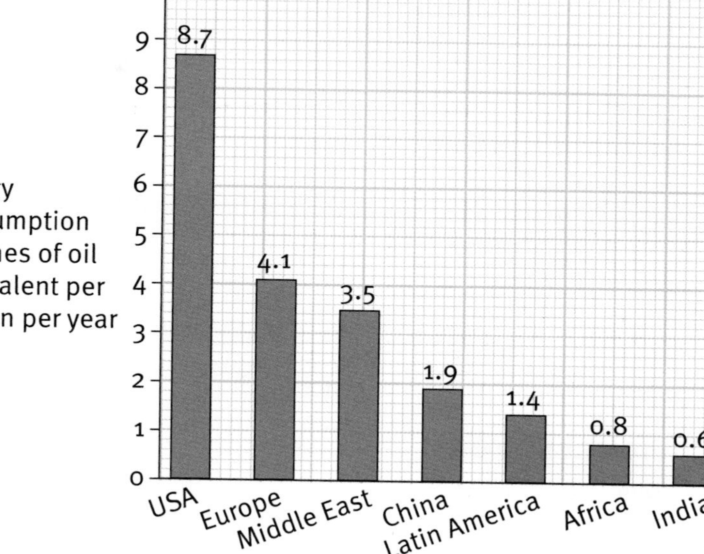

Annual energy consumption per person around the world.

Question

4 Study the bar chart. The average energy consumption per person around the world is 2.2 units. In which regions or countries do people use more than this?

Activity 11.1

Energy in China and the USA

The pie charts show how energy is used in China and the USA.

With a partner, discuss what these charts tell you about the differences between people's lives in China and the USA. (You may be able to make use of data in the other diagrams on these pages.)

Use the internet or other sources to find out how energy use varies from one country to another. Make a poster to present your findings to the class.

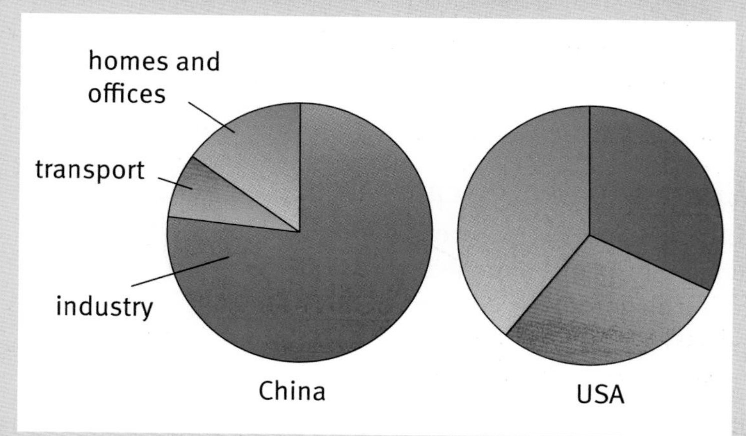

Summary

- Many human activities require a supply of energy.
- Energy consumption varies greatly around the world.

11.2 Fossil fuels

An **energy resource** is anything from which we can obtain energy. The pie chart shows the energy resources we use, and the fraction of our total needs each type contributes.

You can see that most of the energy we use comes from **fossil fuels**. These are coal, oil and natural gas.

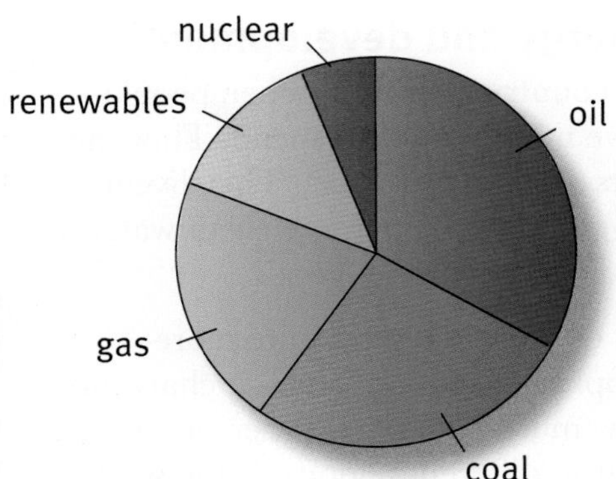

The energy resources we use around the world.

Question

1 **a** Which fossil fuel is used the most as an energy resource?
b Use the pie chart to estimate the fraction of our energy which comes from fossil fuels.

Chemical stores

In Stage **7** Unit **10** you learnt about how energy changes from one form to another. Fossil fuels are stores of **chemical energy**. The energy is released when the fuel is burnt.

For example, in a car engine, petrol and air are mixed together. A spark ignites the mixture and it burns. The energy released makes the car move forward.

Fossil fuels are useful because they are very concentrated stores of energy. It takes only a minute or two for a driver to put 50 litres of petrol into the car's tank. Then it is ready to travel 1000 km or more.

Refuelling a taxi with petrol at a filling station in Borneo.

Questions

2 What name is given to the energy of a moving car?
3 Many people use oil to heat their homes. Draw a diagram to show this energy change.

Where the energy came from

Fossil fuels are found underground. Coal formed from the remains of plants that died millions of years ago. Oil and gas formed from the remains of sea creatures.

Those living organisms gained their energy originally from sunlight. So, when we burn fossil fuels, we are making use of the energy of sunlight which fell on the Earth a very long time ago.

In some parts of the world, oil and gas are extracted from under the seabed.

Question

4 Why is it wrong to say that fossil fuels are stores of light energy?

Generating electricity

Electricity is a convenient way of sending energy from place to place. Most electricity is generated in power stations which burn fossil fuels, especially coal and gas.

A coal fired power station in China.

Activity 11.2

Energy changes

A nuclear power station is supplied with nuclear fuel. It produces electricity. Some energy is wasted – it escapes as heat energy.

The diagram shows the inputs and outputs with red arrows. The blue energy arrow shows the energy change which takes place within the power station.

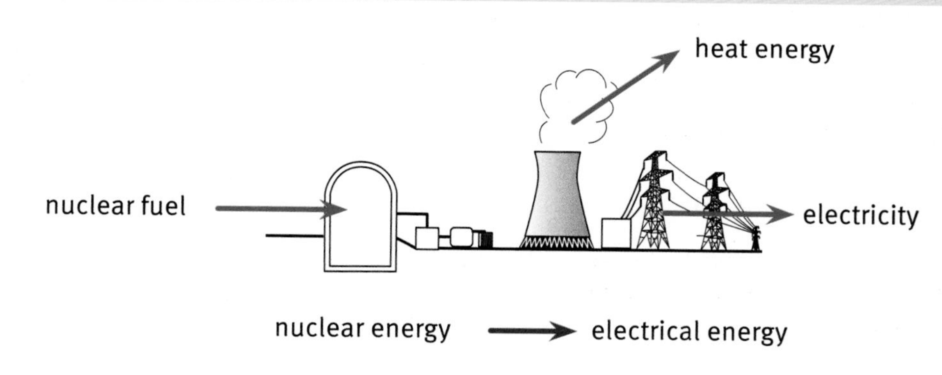

Your task is to draw similar diagrams for the situations described below. You may need to revise the different forms that energy can take. Look at Stage **7** Unit **10** again.

1. Coal is burned in a power station to generate electricity.
2. When a car starts moving, it uses petrol stored in its fuel tank.
3. A stove uses gas to heat water for cooking.
4. An aircraft burns kerosene to fly fast and high.

Summary

- Fossil fuels are stores of chemical energy.
- Fossil fuels are burnt to release their energy.
- Most of our electricity is generated in fossil fuel power stations.

11.3 Renewables and non-renewables

About one-eighth of our energy comes from **renewable energy resources**. These include wind and water power, solar energy and biofuels.

A renewable energy resource is one which we cannot use up. The energy we use today will be replaced naturally in the future.

The three blades of the turbine are turned by the wind. The generator is behind the turbine.

Wind power

The wind can turn a windmill. Nowadays, wind turbines are used to generate electricity.

Water power

A river can turn a mill wheel. If the river is dammed, the water can be used to turn turbines connected to generators – this is hydroelectricity. Waves and tidal currents can also be used to generate electricity.

Solar energy

The Sun's rays can be used to heat water. They can also be used to generate electricity using photovoltaic cells (solar cells).

These are photovoltaic cells generating electricity from sunlight.

Biofuels

Wood is a biofuel that many people around the world rely on. Crops, such as maize and sugar cane, can be harvested and fermented to produce liquid fuel for cars and trucks.

Questions

1. List the **four** ways of generating electricity mentioned above.
2. Draw energy arrow diagrams to show the energy changes that happen in a solar cell and in a wind turbine.

Fossil fuels are described as **non-renewable energy resources**. This is because, once they have been burnt, they are gone forever. Because they take millions of years to form, we would have to wait a very long time for new fossil fuels to form to replace the ones we use.

Solar energy is described as renewable. This is because, if we use the energy of sunlight to heat water or to generate electricity today, there will be more sunlight tomorrow.

Question

3. Explain why wind energy, used to turn a wind turbine, is a renewable energy resource.

Nuclear power

Most power stations generate electricity using fossil fuels. However, some power stations use a different type of fuel – they use nuclear fuels such as uranium. These are stores of **nuclear energy**. Nuclear fuels are not burnt. Their energy is released in a nuclear reactor.

A nuclear power station in India.

Question

A+I

4 Uranium is a nuclear fuel. It is mined from under the ground. Is uranium a renewable energy resource? Explain your answer.

Activity 11.3

Energy futures

The graph shows that we are using more renewable energy resources.

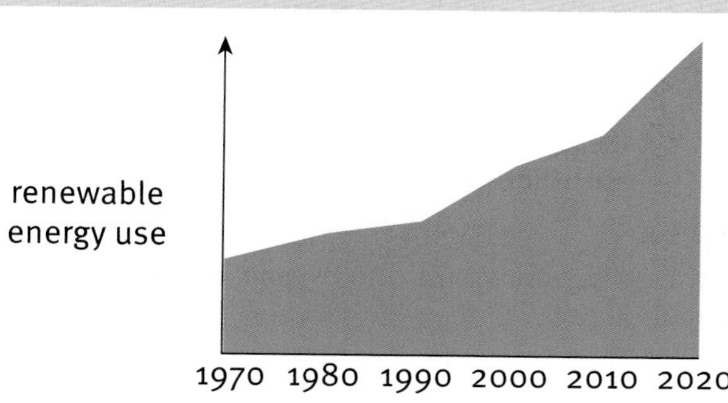

Your task is to find out more about one of the different renewable energy resources and prepare a report or presentation to share with the rest of the class.

You should answer these questions:

- How is the energy resource used?
- Is it used in your country?
- What energy changes are involved?
- Why is it described as renewable?
- What are its benefits and problems?

Summary

- Renewable energy resources include wind, water, solar and biofuels.
- Renewable resources cannot be used up – they are replaced naturally.

11.4 Conduction of heat

Sarina is stirring a hot drink. She is using a metal spoon.

Soon the handle of the spoon is too hot to hold.

The drink is hot. It is a store of thermal energy. Some of the energy goes into the spoon and travels up the handle. When Sarina touches the handle, it feels hot.

Why does the spoon get hot?

Question

1 If Sarina used a plastic spoon, would she notice the same thing?

Conduction

Sarina has observed the process of **thermal conduction** (or heat conduction). Energy is travelling from a hot place to a cooler one through the solid metal of the spoon.

We use the term 'conduction' because this is similar to electrical conduction which you studied in Unit **10**. But remember that here we are thinking about energy travelling through a material from a hot place to a cooler place.

The picture below shows one way to observe thermal conduction in a metal rod.

The rod has several drawing pins (thumb tacks) attached to it using wax. One end of the rod is heated using a Bunsen burner.

Gradually, energy spreads along the rod. The drawing pins drop off one by one, as the rod gets hot and the wax melts.

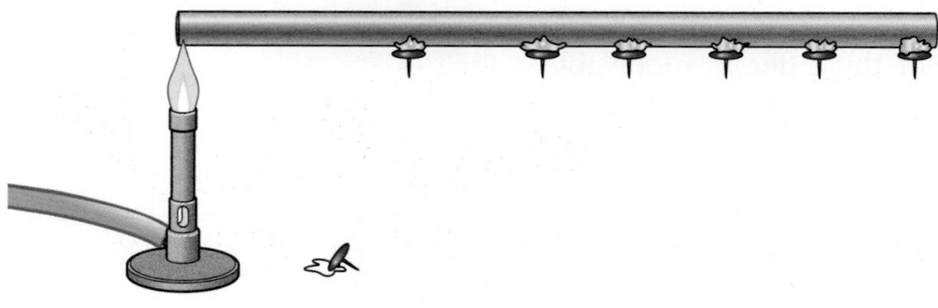

Observing energy conducting along a metal rod.

Activity 11.4A
Comparing metals

Your teacher will show you rods made of several different metals.

Discuss how you could adapt the experiment shown above in order to compare these metals. How will you decide which metal is the best thermal conductor?

Conductors and insulators

Metals such as copper, aluminium and steel are good **thermal conductors**. Most non-metals such as wood and plastic are poor thermal conductors. A poor thermal conductor is called a **thermal insulator**.

The picture shows how energy conducts through solids.

At the hot end, the particles are vibrating a lot because they have a lot of energy. They bump into their neighbours, giving them some of their energy. Then these atoms vibrate more and give some energy to their neighbours, and so on. In this way, energy travels through the solid from the hot end to the cold end.

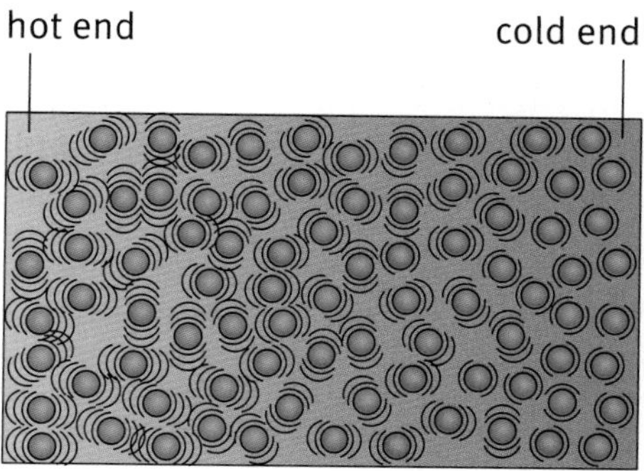

In a solid, the particles vibrate more at the hot end than the cold end.

Questions

A+I **2** Hot drinks are often served in plastic (Styrofoam) cups. Why are these easier to hold than a paper cup?

A+I **3** Suggest **two** reasons why cooking pots are made of metal, not plastic.

Activity 11.4B

Melting ice

In this activity, you will have two blocks, one made of metal and the other of plastic.

An ice cube is placed on each block. Which will melt first?

Before you carry out the experiment, think about these questions:

- Why will the ice melt?
- How can energy get into the ice?

Explain your thoughts. Write a description of what you observe, together with an explanation.

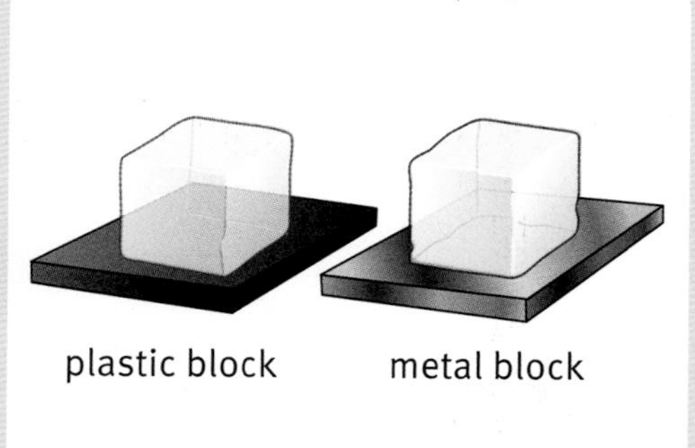

Summary

- Energy can be conducted through a solid or liquid from a hotter place to a cooler place.
- When energy is conducted through a material, the material itself does not move.
- In conduction, energy is transferred from one vibrating particle to the next.

11.5 Convection

Conduction is just one way in which energy can be transferred from a hotter place to a colder place. Here is another.

The eagle in the photograph does not have to flap its wings to stay up in the air. It has found a place where warm air is rising. The rising air supports the eagle.

Warm air rising like this is called a **convection current**. The rising air carries energy from the warm ground up into the cold atmosphere.

The eagle is soaring on warm, rising air.

Convection at home

When it is cold, you may use a heater to warm the room you are in.

- The heater transfers energy to the air next to it.
- This warm air rises.
- Cold air flows in to replace the warm air.

In this way, a convection current is set up in the room, and this spreads the energy from the heater all round the room.

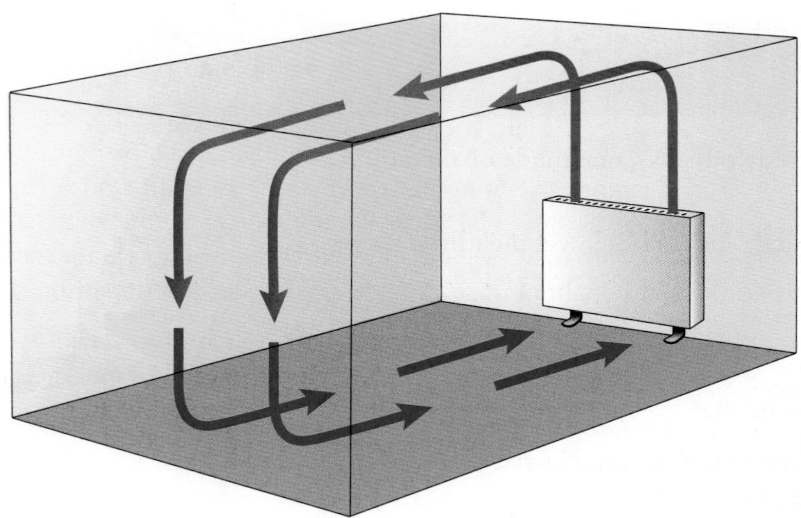

A convection current transfers energy from the heater to the rest of the room.

Question

A+I

1 If you go to the beach on a hot day, you may notice that a cool breeze blows from the sea onto the land. Explain why this breeze happens.

Activity 11.5
Observing convection

SE

Your teacher will demonstrate a convection current rising above a heater using a paper circle cut into a spiral.

You will also see how a convection current spreads energy through water. Coloured water is needed to show how it flows.

Write an explanation of how the convection current transfers energy through the water.

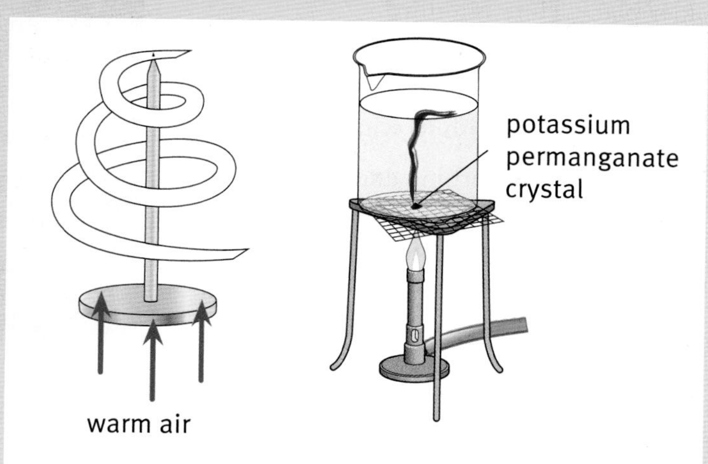

How convection works

Convection can happen in gases or liquids (fluids) – any material which can flow.

Think about air. It is a gas. Its particles are quite far apart and can move about freely.

When air is heated, its particles move faster and they move farther apart. The air expands.

Now the air is less dense than the surrounding air and it floats upwards. It carries energy with it.

At the same time, cooler, denser air flows in to replace it.

So convection is the transfer of energy through a fluid when the fluid itself moves.

Questions

2 Explain why convection cannot transfer energy through a solid.

A+I **3** Why does the wind blow? In the past, some people thought it was the trees moving their leaves that created the wind. How could you convince someone that this idea is wrong?

A+I **4** Ocean currents help to transfer energy from the tropics to polar regions. Explain why warm water currents flow near the ocean surface but cold water currents flow at greater depths.

Summary

- Convection is the transfer of energy through a fluid when the fluid itself moves.
- Warmer fluid is less dense and so floats upwards through cooler fluid.

11.6 Radiation

You have learnt about conduction and convection, two ways in which energy can be transferred from a hotter place to a colder place. Here is a third.

A butterfly cannot fly until its temperature reaches 16 °C. On a cold day, it will find a sunny spot and sit with its wings open.

The butterfly is absorbing energy from the Sun's rays. If you sit in a sunny spot, you may get too hot as you, too, will absorb energy from sunlight.

This butterfly is basking in the sunlight in the Ghanaian rainforest.

Energy from the Sun

The Earth receives a lot of energy from the Sun. How does it get here?

It cannot travel by conduction or convection because it has to pass through a vacuum (empty space) to get here. There is no matter in space.

Instead, it travels as **infra-red radiation**. Infra-red radiation is similar to light, except that it is invisible to our eyes.

Anything which is warm gives out infra-red radiation. The hotter it is, the more energy it radiates. Anything which absorbs radiation gets warm.

Infra-red radiation can travel through empty space and through any transparent material such as air or glass.

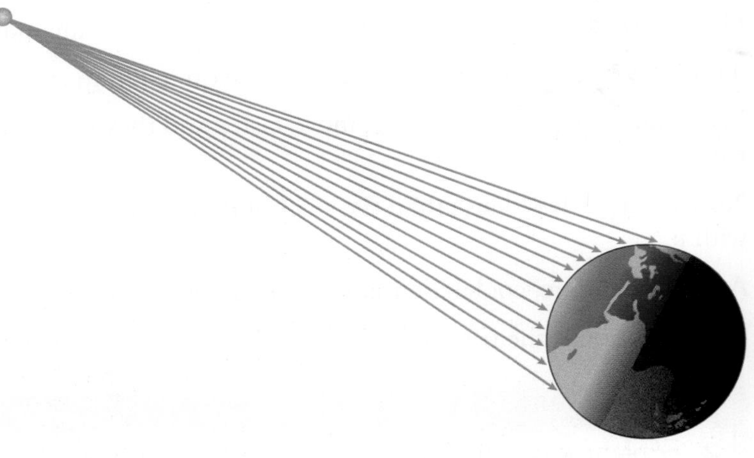

Infra-red radiation brings us energy from the Sun. At night, the Earth cools down.

Questions

A+I

1 If you stand in front of a hot oven, you will get warm. Is its energy reaching you by conduction, convection or radiation? Explain your answer.

A+I

2 It is easy to understand why it gets warmer during the day – the Earth is absorbing radiation from the Sun. But why does it cool down at night? Where is the Earth's energy going?

Good and bad radiators

Matt (not shiny) black surfaces are good at radiating heat energy. That is why the inside of an oven is often painted black – then, as it heats up, it radiates energy at the food.

Shiny white or silver surfaces reflect radiation, just as they reflect light. This shows that it is difficult for radiation to pass through a shiny surface.

This means that shiny surfaces are poor absorbers of radiation – it reflects off them. It also means that shiny surfaces are poor emitters of radiation – energy escapes only slowly from a hot, shiny object.

The seats in this car are black. The driver has fitted a sunshield inside the windscreen.

A+I

Question

3 Explain why the car in the photograph would get hot on a sunny day. How will the sunshield help to keep the car cool?

Activity 11.6

Conduction, convection and radiation

SE

If you put hot water in a container, it will gradually cool down.

Set up a number of different containers, similar to those shown in the picture. They could be made of metal, glass, plastic or cardboard. The outer surface may be black, white or silver. Some should have a lid.

Pour boiling water into each and add a thermometer. Record each temperature as the water cools.

Analyse your results. Can you say whether the energy is escaping from the water by conduction, convection or radiation?

Summary

- Energy can be transferred through a vacuum or transparent substance by infra-red radiation.
- Matt black surfaces are good at absorbing radiation.
- Shiny surfaces are good at reflecting radiation.

11.7 Evaporation

The sea is a bit of a puzzle. Rivers flow into the sea, but it never seems to get any fuller. Why not?

The answer can be found by looking at puddles. When the rain stops, puddles gradually disappear. The water has evaporated.

Evaporation is a bit different from boiling. The temperature of the water doesn't have to reach 100 °C. Even when the temperature is quite low, the water gradually turns into **water vapour** in the air.

The cyclist gets wet but his clothes will soon dry out, thanks to evaporation.

Questions

A+I **1** Use these ideas to explain why the sea does not get any fuller.

Evaporation cools you down

On a very sunny day, you may get too hot. One way to cool down is to get wet – to have a swim in a river or the sea. When you get out, water evaporates off your skin, and this cools you down. If there is a breeze blowing, the water will evaporate more quickly and you will cool down more rapidly.

This boy got wet at the beach and now he is feeling cold.

Now think about getting wet on a cold, windy day. The wind makes the water evaporate from your body and you get very cold. This is the 'wind chill factor' which is sometimes mentioned on the weather forecast.

Desert foxes cool themselves by panting. They breathe over their tongues, and water evaporates, cooling them down.

Questions

A+I **2** Look at the photograph of the cyclist at the top of the page. Explain why he may start to feel cold as he continues cycling.

A cape fox from southern Africa, panting to keep itself cool.

11.7 Evaporation

Evaporation and energy

When water evaporates from your body, it carries energy away. That is why you feel cooler.

Why does evaporation have a cooling effect? We need to think about the particles of the water.

The particles in water are moving around. Some have enough energy to escape from the surface. They become water vapour in the air.

The particles with the most energy are the ones that escape. The ones with less energy are left behind, so the water is colder than before. Its temperature decreases.

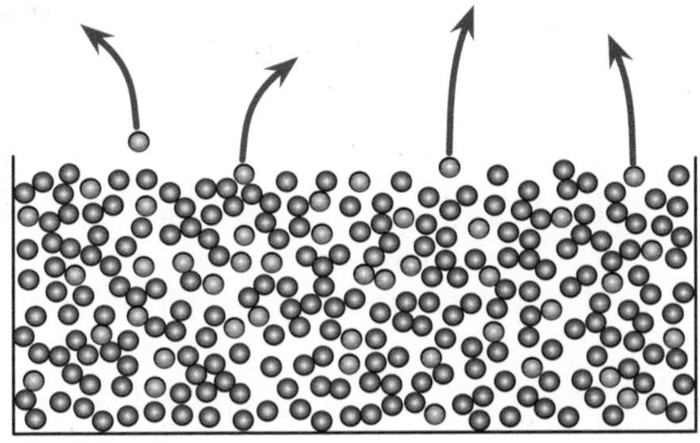

Some particles in the water are moving around faster than others. The fastest ones (shown in red) can escape into the air.

Questions

3 Explain why hot water evaporates more quickly than cold water.

4 If you hang washing on a line to dry, it dries more quickly on some days than others. What is the best sort of weather for drying washing quickly? Explain your answer.

5 The drawing shows two containers of water. Explain why the water in the wide container will evaporate more quickly than the water in the narrow container.

Activity 11.7
Observing and explaining evaporation

Your teacher will demonstrate two simple experiments which involve evaporation.

Experiment 1: A drop of alcohol (ethanol) is placed on a cold metal plate, on the back of someone's hand, and on a warm metal plate.

Experiment 2: Two drops of water are placed on a warm metal plate. One is spread out, the other is not.

For each experiment, note down what is done and what is observed. Then write an explanation using the ideas you have learnt in this topic.

Summary

- When water evaporates, its temperature decreases.
- This is because faster particles escape from the water's surface to become water vapour in the air.
- When water evaporates, it takes energy and therefore has a cooling effect.

Unit 11 End of unit questions

11.1 Here is a list of four different fuels:

wood **coal** **uranium** **natural gas**

a Which **one** is an example of a nuclear fuel? [1]
b Which **one** is an example of a biofuel? [1]
c Which **two** are examples of fossil fuels? [1]
d Which **one** is an example of a renewable resource? Explain your answer. [2]

11.2 The diagram shows a photovoltaic cell (a solar cell).

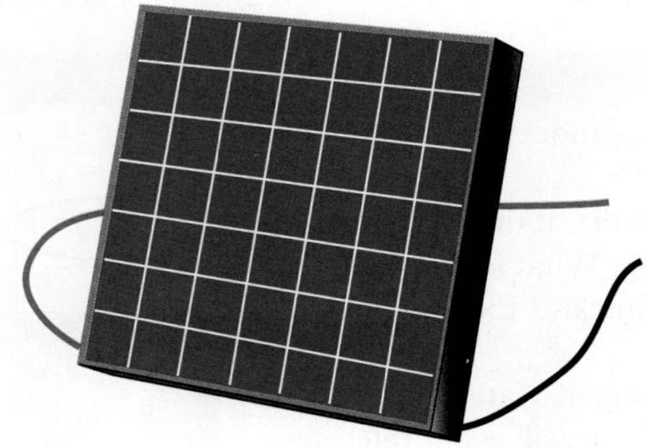

a What energy change takes place when the cell absorbs sunlight? [2]
b State **one** other way in which sunlight can be used as an energy resource. [1]
c Explain why sunlight is described as a renewable energy resource. [1]

11.3 Here are three ways in which energy may be transferred from a hotter place to a colder place:

conduction **convection** **radiation**

For each of the statements below, decide which method of transfer it describes.
a Warm air rises above a hot road surface. [1]
b The planet Venus is warmed by energy from the Sun. [1]
c Energy travels quickly along a steel rod but more slowly along a glass rod. [1]
d When a fluid is heated, its density decreases and it floats upwards. [1]
e Energy is passed from one vibrating particle to the next. [1]
f Energy is transferred through a vacuum (empty space). [1]

11.4 The diagram shows a dish of water which has been left on a table on a warm day. After a few hours, most of the water has disappeared from the dish.

a Name the process by which water leaves the dish. [1]

b The water has become water vapour. Is this a solid, liquid or gas? [1]

c The temperature of the water is less than the temperature of its surroundings. Explain, in terms of the particles of the water, why this is so. [3]

Reference

Working with equations

In science, we often use equations to show how two or more quantities are related to each other. You need to be able to use equations. Sometimes you will have to rearrange an equation before you can calculate the quantity you are interested in.

Here is an equation from Unit **9**:

$$\text{density} = \frac{\text{mass}}{\text{volume}}$$

This equation tells us how we can calculate the density of a substance. We need to know two quantities:

- the mass of a sample of the substance
- the volume of the sample.

Then we calculate the density of the substance by dividing mass by volume.

Remembering an equation

You may be able to memorise an equation simply by repeating it to yourself. It may be easier if you change the names of the quantities into letters or other symbols, like this:

$$\text{density} = \frac{\text{mass}}{\text{volume}}$$

$$D = \frac{M}{V}$$

Another way is to think about the meaning of the quantity. Density tells us how to compare two materials – which is heavier? To make it a fair test, we have to compare equal volumes. So we compare the masses of $1\,cm^3$ or $1\,m^3$.

An alternative is to think about units. The unit of density is g/cm^3, or kg/m^3. This should remind you to divide the mass (in g or kg) by the volume (in cm^3 or m^3).

Rearranging an equation

The equation for density has density as its subject (the quantity on its own, on the left). But sometimes, we might want to calculate one of the other quantities. For example:

What is the mass of $4\,cm^3$ of mercury? The density of mercury = $13.5\,g/cm^3$.

We need to rearrange the equation to make mass M its subject. To do this, multiply both sides by volume V:

$$D \times V = M$$

So

$$M = D \times V = 13.5 \times 4 = 54\,g$$

It can help if you think about units. We want to know the mass (in g). We can find this if we multiply the density (in g/cm^3) by the volume (in cm^3).

$$M = 13.5\,g/cm^3 \times 4\,cm^3 = 54.0\,g$$

(The cm^3 units cancel out.)

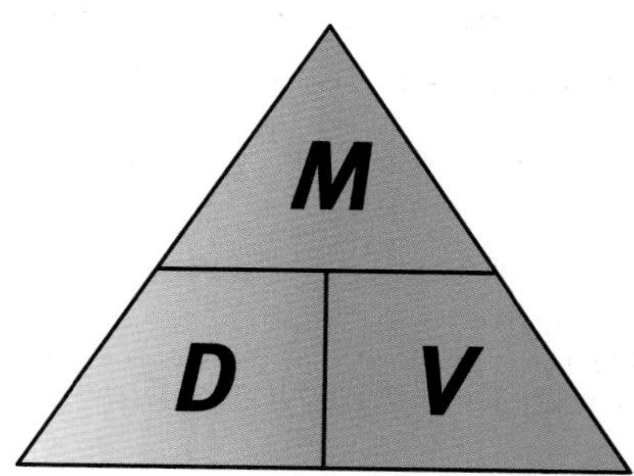

Another method is to use a 'formula triangle'. The three quantities in the equation are put into a triangle, as shown. Mass M is at the top.

To find the equation which has volume V as its subject, cover the V in the triangle.

You will see that this leaves $\frac{M}{D}$.

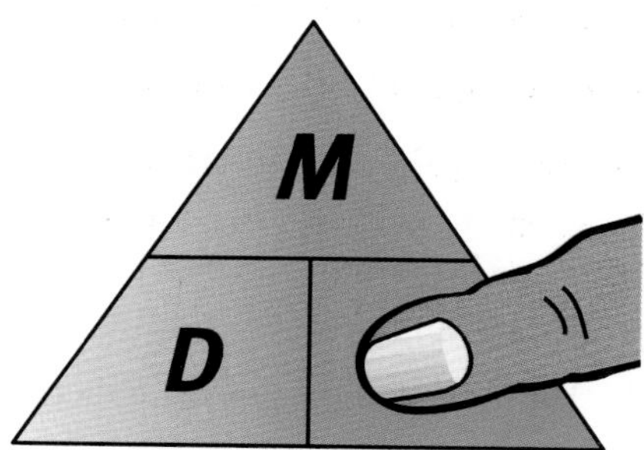

$$\text{volume} = \frac{\text{mass}}{\text{density}}$$

$$V = \frac{M}{D}$$

Question

1 Use the density formula triangle to find the equation with mass M as its subject.

2 The diagram below shows the formula triangle for pressure.

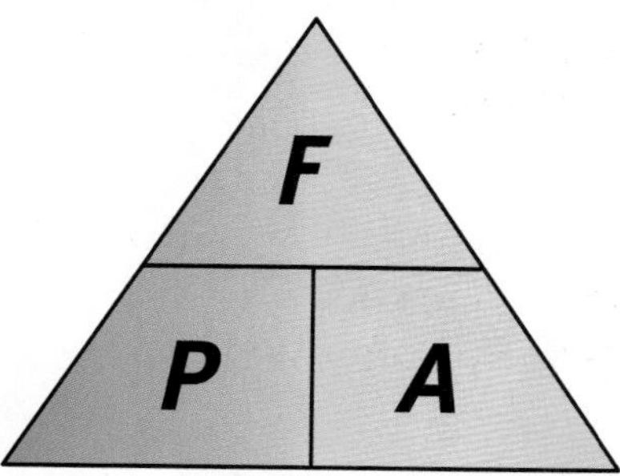

a Use the pressure formula triangle to find the equation with area A as its subject.

b Calculate the force on an area of $3\,m^2$ when a pressure of $50\,N/m^2$ acts on it.

3 Here is the equation for the moment of a force:

moment = force × distance from pivot

a Rearrange the equation to make force the subject.

b Calculate the force which must be applied at a distance of 10 m from a pivot to give a moment of 500 N m.

Ideas and evidence

During your Cambridge Secondary Science course, you have learnt how to plan experiments to try to find the answers to questions. You have learnt how to collect results and use them to make conclusions.

In this section, you can read about some examples of how scientists have investigated some 'big' questions. You will see that not every question can be answered yet. You will also see that some experiments have not been very well planned!

Question: Is there intelligent life beyond Earth?

Many people have wondered: Are there people like us walking around on a planet orbiting a distant star? In other words, is there extra-terrestrial intelligence? ('Extra-terrestrial' means beyond the Earth.)

We can be fairly sure that there are not intelligent creatures living on another planet or moon in our solar system. However, there are billions of stars in our galaxy and billions of galaxies in the universe, so many scientists think that there must be large numbers of planets similar to Earth. Life may have appeared on them, and intelligent creatures like us may have evolved.

In 1960, a young scientist called Frank Drake decided to find out if he could detect any radio signals coming from space which might be from a distant civilisation. He used a radio telescope to collect radio waves from space. Then he analysed them to see if there were any patterns that looked like messages from intelligent beings.

He had no luck. Since then, scientists have used bigger and better radio telescopes to hunt for signals. They set up a project called the Search for Extra-Terrestrial Intelligence (SETI).

Today, the SETI project has even bigger and better telescopes. They collect lots of data which must be checked to see if it contains extra-terrestrial signals. Anyone can join the project and use their computer to help check the scientists' data to see if there is any sign of messages from space.

So far, no signs of alien intelligence have been detected. However, because astronomers now have better telescopes, they have been able to detect planets going around other stars in our galaxy. They can analyse the atmospheres of these planets. This may show if any of them are home to life.

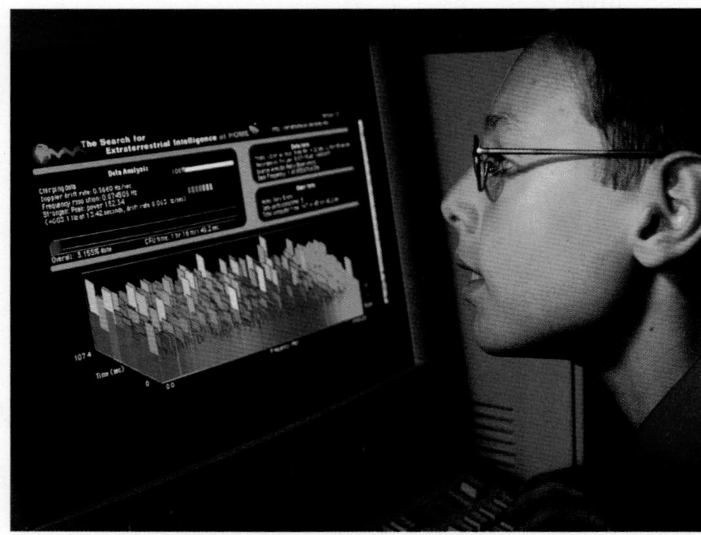

If someone signs up to help with the SETI project, their home computer can help to analyse the radio signals from space.

Question

1 **a** What question was Frank Drake trying to answer?
  b How did he try to answer it?

2 How has new technology helped the SETI project to collect and analyse more data?

3 So far, the SETI project has not found signs of extra-terrestrial intelligence.
  a Does this mean that we are the only intelligent creatures in the universe? Explain your answer.
  b Give at least two reasons why it might be difficult to detect intelligent extra-terrestrial life.

4 Suggest an alternative way to look for alien life.

Question: Does fish oil improve exam performance?

In 2006, a county council (local government institution) in the United Kingdom announced that they were going to run a trial to find out if taking tablets containing fish oil could improve students' performance in their GCSE exams.

This is what they did:

- They gave fish oil tablets to 3000 children in Year 11 (the start of the year in which they would take their GCSE exams). The students were supposed to take their tablets regularly.
- By the time the students took their exams, only 832 of them were still taking the tablets on at least 80% of the times that they should.
- The researchers 'matched' 629 of these students against similar students out of the original 3000 who had stopped taking their fish oil tablets. They did this by finding students who went to the same school, were the same sex, had similar marks in school and had a similar social background.
- They found that, on average, the student in each pair who had taken fish oil did better than the one who had not.

The Activity on page 180 will help you to think about the design of this investigation.

Activity
Designing a better experiment

Scientists think that the fish oil experiment was not well designed.

In your group, discuss these questions:

1. If the researchers wanted to find out whether students who took fish oil tablets did better in their exams than students who didn't, what should they have done right at the start of their experiment?
2. How many students stopped taking the fish oil tablets before they took their exams? Think of reasons why some students might have stopped taking the tablets, while others carried on (continued) taking them.
3. What do you think of the 'matched pairs' idea, for comparing students who took tablets with those who did not?
4. The results did show that the students who had taken fish oil did better in their exams that the students who did not. But does this really mean that it was taking the fish oil that made the difference? Can you think of any other explanations?
5. Imagine you were given the task of designing an experiment to find out if taking fish oil tablets for one year improves performance in exams. Write down exactly what you would do.

Electric circuit symbols

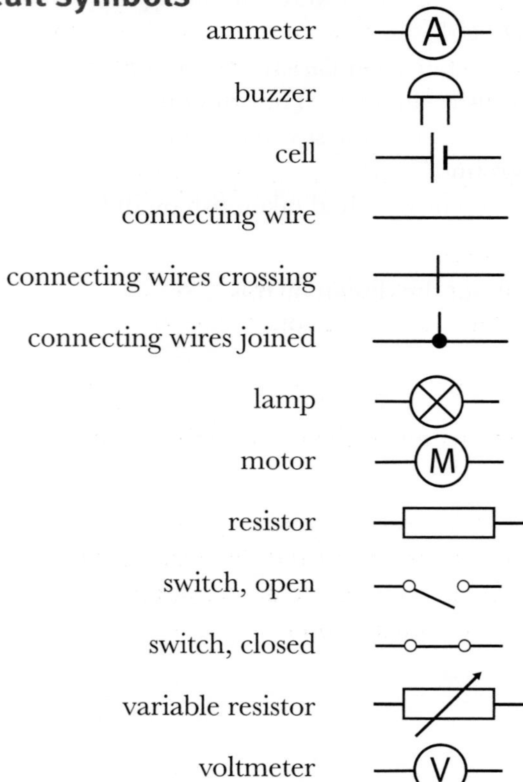

Anomalous results

Sarah did an experiment to find out how temperature affects the rate of reaction between magnesium and hydrochloric acid. She used acid at different temperatures and measured the volume of gas produced.

Sarah made three measurements for temperature. This table shows her results.

Temperature of acid / °C	Volume of gas produced in one minute / cm^3			
	1st try	2nd try	3rd try	Mean
10	4.5	4.2	4.6	
20	9.1	9.3	8.9	
30	18.0	17.9	18.1	
40	31.1	36.0	36.2	

Sarah thought that one of her results didn't look right. Can you spot which one it is?

A result like this, that does not fit the pattern of all the other results, is called an **anomalous result**.

If you get something that looks like an anomalous result, there are two things that you can do.

1 The best thing to do is to try to measure it again.
2 If you can't do that, then you should ignore the result. So Sarah should not use this result when she is calculating the mean. She should use only the other two results for that temperature, add them up and divide them by two.

Questions

1 Which is the anomalous result in Sarah's table?
2 Explain how you picked out the anomalous result.
3 Calculate the mean volume of gas produced in one minute for each temperature of acid. Remember – don't include the anomalous result in your calculation!

Spotting an anomalous result in a results table can be quite difficult. It is often much easier if you have drawn a graph.

Rajesh did an experiment to investigate how adding ice to water changed its temperature. He added a cube of ice to 500 cm^3 of water and stirred the water until the ice had completely melted. Then he measured the temperature of the water before adding another ice cube. The graph on the next page shows his results.

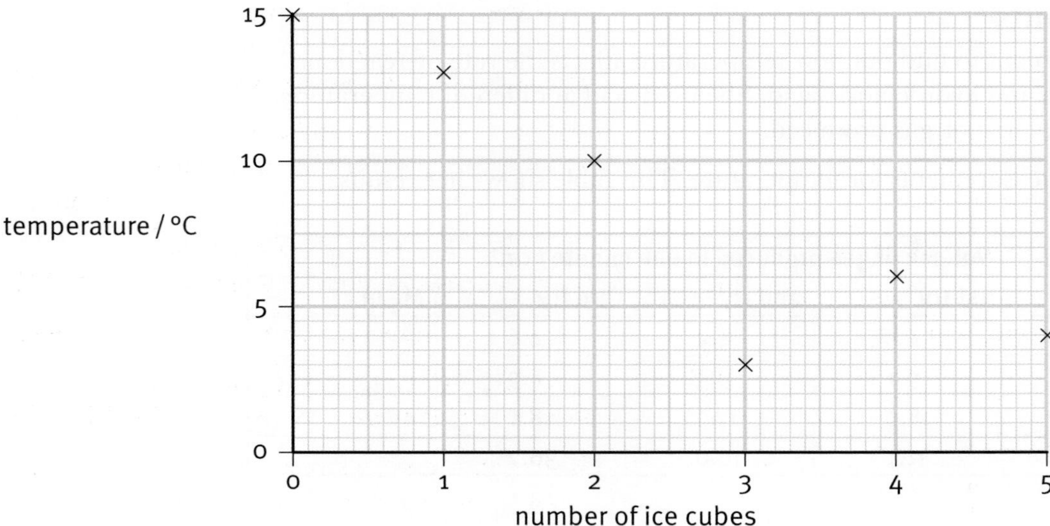

It's easy to see that the point at (3, 3) doesn't fit the pattern of all the other results. Something must have gone wrong when Rajesh was making that measurement.

When Rajesh draws the line on his graph, he should ignore this result. He should also think about why it might have gone wrong. Perhaps he misread the thermometer – was the correct reading 8 °C? Or perhaps he forgot to stir the water and measured the temperature where the cold ice had just melted. If you think about why an anomalous result has occurred, it can help you to improve your technique and avoid such problems in the future.

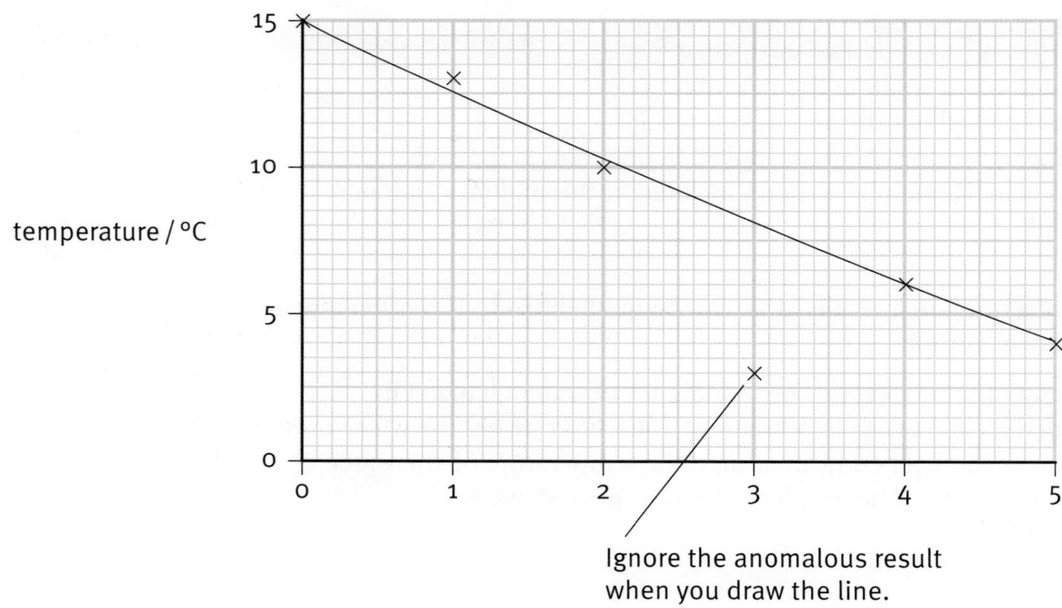

Glossary and index

algal bloom a big population of algae in a lake, river or sea, often caused by fertiliser 34

alkali metals metals in Group 1 of the Periodic Table that produce alkalis when they react with water 64

ammeter a meter used to measure electric current 148

amp the unit of electric current; symbol A 148

annual plants plants that germinate, grow, flower, produce seeds and die in less than a year 23

anthers the parts of a flower in which pollen is made 12

aquatic living in water 23

atmospheric pressure the pressure of the atmosphere 130

atom a very small particle of an element 60, 61

atomic number the number of protons in an atom; each type of atom has a unique atomic number 62

base a metal oxide; soluble bases dissolve in water to form alkalis 101

biodiversity the number of different species in a particular area 36

biological catalyst another term for an enzyme 117

blast furnace a structure used for the large-scale production of iron from iron ore 90

carbohydrate a group of chemicals found in living organisms, which includes sugar, starch and cellulose 6

carnivore an animal that eats other animals 29

catalase an enzyme found in living cells that speeds up the breakdown of hydrogen peroxide 117

catalyst a substance that speeds up a reaction but remains unchanged by the reaction 116, 117

cell (electrical) a battery, a device that produces a voltage in a circuit 147

charge **see electric charge** 60–62

chemical energy energy stored in chemical substances 70, 71, 74, 151, 162, 163

choice chamber a piece of apparatus in which small animals are given a choice of places to go with different conditions, for example dark or light 25

chromosomes threads of DNA, found in the nucleus of a cell, which are made up of thousands of genes 48, 49

circuit diagram a representation of an electric circuit using standard symbols 147, 148

circuit symbol a symbol representing any component in an electric circuit 147, 148, 176

collision bumping into something 107

combustion burning 70, 71

conductor an object or material through which electric current can pass 146, 167

convection the transfer of heat energy from one place to another, carried by the material as it moves 168, 169

convection current the flow of a hot gas or liquid, carrying heat energy with it 168

cotyledons structures found inside some kinds of seeds, for example beans, which store food for the young embryo 17

decomposers organisms that break down organic matter, for example earthworms and fungi 30, 31

density property of an object or material, calculated by density = mass/volume 120–125

dispersed spread over a wide area 18, 23

displacement reaction a reaction in which a more reactive metal 'pushes out' a less reactive one from a compound 88, 90

DNA the chemical from which genes and chromosomes are made; DNA carries a code of instructions that determines how cells and organisms develop 48

ecologists people who study the relationships between living organisms and their environment 26, 27

ecology the study of living organisms in their environment 26, 27

electric charge a property of an object which causes it to attract or repel other objects with charge 140–145, 150

electric current the movement of electric charge 147–151

electron a negatively charged particle found surrounding the nucleus of an atom 60, 62

electronic structure the arrangement of electrons in the shells around the nucleus of an atom 62, 65

embryo a very young, new organism, which has developed from a zygote 17, 18

endangered at risk of becoming extinct 36

endothermic process a process (such as a change of state) in which energy is taken in from the environment 75, 77

endothermic reaction a chemical reaction in which energy is taken in from the environment 74–77

energy resource anything which is a source of energy 162–165

environment anything in the surroundings of an organism that affects it in any way 45, 47

enzyme a biological catalyst that speeds up a reaction in a living system 30, 117

evaporation when a liquid changes to a gas (a vapour) at a temperature below its boiling point 172, 173

exothermic process a process (such as a change of state) in which energy is given out into the environment 76

exothermic reaction a chemical reaction in which energy is given out into the environment 70, 72, 73, 76, 90

extinct disappeared from the Earth; an extinct species is gone forever 36, 37

fertilisation the joining together of the nucleus of a male gamete and the nucleus of a female gamete 16, 49

fertilisers mineral ions that plants need for healthy growth, and that are added to the soil to help crops grow better 8, 9, 34, 35

fossil fuels coal, oil and natural gas 162

friction the force that appears when two objects try to slide over each other 143

fruit a structure that contains seeds; fruits develop from ovaries after fertilisation, and often help the seeds to be spread away from the parent plant 18, 19

genes instructions, in the form of a DNA code, in the nucleus of a cell; genes affect many of the characteristics of an organism 45–49

global warming the gradual increase of the Earth's temperature 39, 53

group (in the Periodic Table) the elements in a column of the Periodic Table 64, 81

habitat the place where an organism lives 22, 29

halogens the elements found in Group 7 of the Periodic Table 66

herbivore an animal that eats plants 29

hyphae the tiny threads that make up the body of a fungus 30

inert does not react 67

infra-red radiation thermal energy travelling through empty space or a material 170

inheritance the passing down of features from parents to offspring 46

in parallel describes two components in a circuit which are connected side by side 156

insulator an object or material which electric current cannot pass through 146

key a series of questions that leads you to the identification of an organism 42

magnesium (plant nutrition) a mineral salt that plants need to make chlorophyll 8

mass the amount of matter in an object, measured in kilogram (kg) 120–125

mass number the number of protons and neutrons in an atom added together 62, 65

micropyle a tiny hole in the covering of a seed, which allows the seed to absorb water when it germinates 17

mineral salts substances such as nitrate and magnesium, which plants absorb from the soil through their roots, and which they need for healthy growth 8

moment a measure of the turning effect of a force, calculated by moment = force × distance from pivot; measured in newton metres (N m) 134–137

natural selection the process in which individuals that are best able to survive in an environment are more likely to breed and pass on their characteristics to their offspring 52–57

nectar a sugary substance made by flowers, which attracts insects 12

negative charge one type of electric charge 60, 62, 142–145

neutral (electricity) describes an object with no overall electric charge 143

neutralisation a reaction in which an acid and an alkali react to produce a solution which is neither acid nor alkaline but neutral 100

neutrons particles found in the nucleus of an atom that have no electronic charge 60

nitrate a mineral salt that plants need to make protein and chlorophyll 8

noble gases the elements found in Group 8 of the Periodic Table 67

non-renewable energy resource any energy resource which, when used, will not renew itself 164

nuclear energy energy given out when nuclei of atoms split 165

nucleus (of an atom) the centre of an atom formed from protons and neutrons 60, 61

orbits electronic orbits are the paths followed by electrons around the nucleus of the atom 62

ore a rock or mineral that contains a metal compound 90

organic matter material that makes up, or has made up, part of a living organism's body 30

ovaries the parts of a flower that contain the ovules 12, 16

ovules the parts of a flower that contain the female gametes 12, 16, 17

oxidation reaction any reaction where a substance combines with oxygen 71

particle model the model of matter in which everything is composed of particles in motion 121

pascal the unit of pressure, symbol Pa 128

Periodic Table a table of all the elements placed in order of their atomic number 62

petals the colourful parts of a flower that help to attract insects 12

phytoplankton microscopic plant-like organisms that float in water 28

pivot the point about which an object is turned by a force 132

pollen tiny grains, produced in the anthers of a flower, which contain the male gametes 12, 14–16

pollination the transfer of a pollen from an anther to a stigma 14, 15

pollution the addition of substances to the environment that harm living organisms 34

positive charge one type of electric charge 60, 62, 142, 143

precipitate an insoluble solid formed when two soluble substances react 110

preliminary work some practical work you do before an investigation to find out how you will carry it out. For example you might find out the range or interval of the independent variable you will use 73

pressure the force acting per unit area on a surface 126–131

principle of moments an object is balanced when clockwise moments = anticlockwise moments 134, 135

protons positively charged particles found in the nucleus of an atom 60

quadrat a square area within which you can sample the organisms in a habitat 27

rate of reaction the speed of a reaction, measured by the time taken for the products to form or for reactants to be used up 104–117

reactivity how quickly or slowly a chemical reacts compared with another 85, 86

reactivity series a list of metals in order of how reactive they are. The most reactive are at the top of the list and the least reactive at the bottom 86

renewable energy resource any energy resource which will naturally renew itself 164

resistance the property of a component in a circuit which acts to reduce the current in the circuit 154

resistant not affected by a substance that kills or harms other organisms; for example, some bacteria are resistant to certain antibiotics 54

resistor a component in an electric circuit that reduces the current in the circuit 154, 155

salt a compound formed when a metal reacts with an acid e.g. magnesium chloride 84, 94, 96

sampling collecting data from a small part of a whole area, or from just a small number of a large number of individuals 26, 27

seed a structure that contains an embryo plant, and food stores to help it to begin to grow into a new plant 17

selective breeding a process of choosing individuals with desired characteristics to breed together; it is generally continued for many generations 50, 51

series circuit an electric circuit in which all components are connected end-to-end, one after another 149

shells electronic shells are layers around the nucleus of an atom where the electrons are arranged; the electrons move about within their shell 62

species a group of organisms that share the same features, and can breed together to produce fertile offspring 44

starch a type of carbohydrate that is stored inside plant cells 6

static electricity effects produced by electric charges when they are not moving 140–145

stigma the part of a flower that receives pollen grains during pollination 15, 16

surface area the total area of the surface of an object 108

testa the tough, protective outer covering of a seed 17

thermal conduction the transfer of heat energy through a material, without the material itself moving 166, 167

thermal conductor a material which will allow heat to conduct through it 167

thermal insulator a material which will not allow heat to conduct through it 167

thermite reaction a reaction where aluminium displaces iron from iron oxide. This reaction can be used to weld railway rails 90

trial run a test run of an investigation to check that you can carry out it out correctly 110

turning effect when a force causes an object to turn, it has a turning effect 132

variable resistor a resistor whose resistance can be changed 154

variation differences between the individuals in a species 44, 45

voltage a measure of the push of a cell in a circuit; symbol V 152

voltmeter a meter used to measure voltage 152

volume the amount of space occupied by an object 120

water vapour a gas of water molecules mixed into the air 10, 11, 172

zooplankton microscopic animals that float in water 28

zygote the cell that is formed when a male gamete fuses with a female gamete 16, 49

Acknowledgements

The authors and publisher are grateful for the permissions granted to reproduce copyright materials. While every effort has been made, it has not always been possible to identify the sources of all the materials used, or to trace all the copyright holders. If any omissions are brought to our notice, we will be happy to include the appropriate acknowledgements on reprinting.

The publisher would like to thank the language reviewer for reviewing the content:

Ángel Cubero, International School, Santo Tomás de Aquino, Madrid, Spain

Cover image: Steve Bloom/Alamy; pp. 9, 12, 13*m*, 19*tm*, 19*tr*, 21, 22*b*, 27*b*, 31, 36*bl*, 58, 99, 124*b*, 125, 132 Geoff Jones; p. 8*t* Art Directors & TRIP/Alamy; p. 8*b* Dennis Chang-Flora/Alamy; pp. 10, 24*t*, 51*b* Nigel Cattlin/Alamy; p. 11 Maximilian Weinzierl/Alamy; pp. 13*t*, 15 blickwinkel/Alamy; p. 14*t* Natural Visions/Alamy; p. 14*m* Medical-on-Line/Alamy; pp. 16, 35*tl*, 56*b* Dr Jeremy Burgess/SPL; p. 19*tr* José Julián Rico Cerdá/Alamy; p. 22*t* Kalle Pahajoki/Alamy; p. 23*t* Wayne Hutchinson/Alamy; p. 23*b* Michele Falzone/Alamy; p. 24*m* Michael Patrick O'neill/SPL; p. 24*b* Zuma Press, Inc./Alamy; p. 26*t* Phil Dunne/Alamy; pp. 26*b*, 27*t* Martin Shields/Alamy; p. 29 Jim West/Alamy; p. 30*t* Rob Walls/Alamy; p. 30*m* Biophoto Associates/SPL; p. 32 Mira/Alamy; p. 33*tm* Steve Bloom Images/Alamy; p. 33*tr* Robert Hernandez/SPL; p. 35*tr* NASA/GSFC/SPL; p. 36*ml* FLPA/Alamy; p. 36*mr* Images & Stories/Alamy; p. 36*br* Photoshot Holdings Ltd/Alamy; p. 37*t* Jeremy Sutton-Hibbert/Alamy; p. 37*m* Mark Conlin/Alamy; p. 39 Peter Barritt/Alamy; p. 40 David Davis Photoproductions RF/Alamy; p. 41 Geophoto/Alamy; p. 43*tl* Bubbles Photolibrary/Alamy; p. 43*tr* Ann Worthy/Alamy; pp. 43*bl*, 70 Peter Titmuss/Alamy; pp. 43*br*, 46*b* Blend Images/Alamy; p. 44 George Bernard/SPL; p. 46*tl* Tinap/Alamy; p. 46*tm* Martin Harvey/Alamy; p. 46*tr* Images of Africa Photobank/Alamy; p. 47 moodboard/Alamy; pp. 48, 53*r* Juniors Bildarchiv GmbH/Alamy; p. 49 Image Source/Alamy; p. 50*t* Tetra Images/Alamy; p. 50*mt* nobleIMAGES/Alamy; p. 50*m* blickwinkel/Alamy; p. 50*mb* NSP-RF/Alamy; p. 50*b* Francisco Javier Fernández Bordonada/Alamy; p. 51*tl* Wildlife GmbH/Alamy; p. 51*tr* Photocuisine/Alamy; p. 53*l* Naturfoto-Online/Alamy; p. 55*t* David Chapman/Alamy; p. 55*m* North Wind Picture Archives/Alamy; p. 55*b* Michael W. Tweedie/SPL; p. 56*t* Lebrecht Music and Arts Photo Library/Alamy; p. 56*m*, 86*t*, 116 SPL; p. 57 Lordprice Collection/Alamy; p. 61*t* Universal Images Group Limited/Alamy; p. 61*m* Archive Pics/Alamy; p. 61*b* VIEW Pictures Ltd/Alamy; pp. 71, 72, 82*m* Andrew Lambert Photography/SPL; p. 74 Cordelia Molloy/SPL; p. 77 Phil Degginger/Alamy; pp. 82*l*, 82*r*, 88*l*, 88*r*, 94*b*, 110 sciencephotos/Alamy; p. 86*m* Astrid & Hanns-Frieder Michler/SPL; p. 86*b* Jon Helgason/Alamy; p. 90 Vincent Lowe/Alamy; p. 94*tl* Adrian Arbib/Alamy; p. 94*tm* Action Plus Sports Images/Alamy; p. 94*tr* J Marshall-Tribaleye Images/Alamy; p. 94*ml* geogphotos/Alamy; p. 94*m* All Canada Photos/Alamy; p. 94*mr* studiomode/Alamy; pp. 96, 98 Charles D. Winters/SPL; p. 104 Leslie Garland Picture Library/Alamy; p. 108 Sergio Boccardo/Alamy; pp. 109, 133, 142*b* Martyn F. Chillmaid/SPL; p. 117 Mark Boulton/Alamy; p. 122 Alex Bartel/SPL; p. 124*t* Chris Brignell/Alamy; p. 126*t* Greg Amptman's Undersea Discoveries; p. 126*b* Accent Alaska.com/Alamy; p. 128 SDM Images/Alamy; p. 129 Wesley Roberts/Alamy; p. 130*t* Dinodia Photos/Alamy; pp. 130*b*, 146*b* GIPhotoStock/SPL; p. 134 Finnbarr Webster/Alamy; p. 140 Gary Dublanko/Alamy; pp. 142*t*, 146*t* Sheila Terry/SPL; pp. 148, 154, 156 Doug Martin/SPL; p. 152 Gustoimages/SPL; p. 160*t* Nathan Allred/Alamy; pp. 160*b*, 162*t* dbimages/Alamy; p. 162*b* Richard Folwell/SPL; p. 163 Iconotec/Alamy; p. 164*t* GFC Collection/Alamy; p. 164*b* Oleksiy Maksymenko Photography/Alamy; p. 165 epa european pressphoto agency b.v./Alamy; p. 168 Sergey Uryadnikov; p. 170 Premaphotos/Alamy; p. 171 Justin Kase zninez/Alamy; p. 172*t* Westend61 GmbH/Alamy; p. 172*m* graficart.net/Alamy; p. 172*b* Braam Collins; p. 178 David Parker/SPL.

SPL = Science Photo Library, *l* = left, *r* = right, *t* = top, *b* = bottom, *m* = middle

Typesetting and illustration by Greenhill Wood Studios www.greenhillwoodstudios.com